Captain James Cook, R.N.

One Hundred and Fifty Years After

Sir Joseph Carruthers

Anniversary Edition 2020

Edited & Annotated by

Dr. Zachary Gorman

Published by Connor Court Publishing Pty Ltd, 2020

CONNOR COURT PUBLISHING PTY LTD
PO Box 7257
Redland Bay QLD 4165
sales@connorcourt.com
www.connorcourtpublishing.com.au

First Published E.P. Dutton, New York, 1930.

ISBN: 978-1-925826-97-5 (pbk.)

Cover design by Renee Gorman

Photos in book taken from the E.P. Dutton edition, 1930.

Printed in Australia

Dedicated to the hopes and aspirations of ordinary Australians,
which Captain James Cook came to represent.

Contents

Part III: The Sesqui-centennial Celebrations in the Hawaiian Islands in 1928

Editor's Introduction

Why do Australians remember Captain James Cook? A "man on the street" might answer that Cook was a famed and talented explorer who discovered Australia, facilitating its establishment as a British settlement from which the current Commonwealth is descended. Nowadays they might add the stipulation that Cook was merely the first *European* to discover the southern continent, and that it had in fact been inhabited by Indigenous Australians for tens of thousands of years. If they were a bit more informed they might point out that "New Holland" was already on contemporary maps before 1770, hence even as a European Cook only discovered the east coast of Australia, though he did map what he saw thoroughly, collect numerous flora and fauna, and discover many other places as well. Crucially, where Cook landed in Australia happened to be the more fertile part, hence his "discovery" was acted upon unlike its predecessors and that is what mattered. Australia would not exist, at least not as the political and cultural unit that we know (and love), without James Cook, hence that is why we are now commemorating the 250th anniversary of his landing at Botany Bay.

This seems like a reasonably nuanced viewpoint that would not be out of place in contemporary Australian society, even with its delicate sensibilities when it comes to discussing our colonial past. However, there are some people who would argue that even this updated view is a harmful "myth". They point out that Cook's centrality to the story of Australian settlement is over-blown. It was men like Joseph Banks and James Matra, Cook's subordinates on the *Endeavour*, who made the case for colonisation when their Captain could see little merit in it. Meanwhile it was Arthur Phillip and the First Fleet who turned Cook's claim to the territory as a British possession, which he had dubbed

"New South Wales", into a tangible reality.[1] Before that it was little more than an empty boast.

Such criticisms can only go so far. In the teleology of fate we still would not be here without Cook and his considerable efforts, it is just that he should be more willing to share his podium with others. Why then has Cook been able to hog the spotlight or, more accurately, why has he had the spotlight shone almost exclusively on him? It is not necessarily a positive thing to have, for hagiography has a tendency of breeding reactionary attack pieces. Many who enjoy the prosperous democracy that has grown out of Australia's British roots can come to terms with our colonial past as a generally positive story, but one involving some genuine tragedies which should be acknowledged. This seems to be the only philosophically consistent view to take for those who appreciate living in Australia, for to enjoy the benefits while lamenting the entirety of the process which produced it is arguably hypocritical.[2] Despite this, others (who generally are less positive about Australia as it exists) have come to see an original sin for which we must eternally be held to account. Though his role as a participant in the actual process of colonisation is limited to making the initial claim on the territory of New South Wales, Cook is held to personify that sin, just like in an earlier era he was believed to personify our more positive characteristics.

And that is why Cook came to hold his exalted position, not simply for what he did, however tremendous that may be, but for who he was. He was a scientist pushing the boundaries of knowledge amidst the rising tide of the Enlightenment, he was an officer in the British Navy possessing all the qualities of a gentleman yet committed to peace over war, and he was a man of little education who rose by his own efforts to gain all the accolades of fame. Cook was no perfect person, he certainly had flaws like any man, but there is enough truth at the heart of these

---

[1] Cook only added the "south" as an afterthought, but it does give the name a sliver of uniqueness compared to other "new" places colonialism has dotted across the globe. People certainly grew attached to the name, as Henry Parkes' attempt to change it would show.

[2] Germaine Greer's self-imposed exile appears to follow this same logic, but from the more negative left-leaning perspective.

grandiose depictions to make them resonate. Cook was a magnificent canvas on which a young and tentative nation could paint a picture of what it wanted to be.

Those who do not like the picture that was painted can blame the canvas, but they must also blame the painter. According to Jillian Robertson, author of *The Captain Cook Myth*, and more recently Newcastle Academic Peter Hooker, one of the main painters of the Cook "myth" was the author of this book Sir Joseph Carruthers.[3] Robertson says that "If anything clinched the myth [of Cook as Australian founder], this did [Carruthers' Book]. It is written with all the energy and respect for the truth of the fanatic, and with it Cook arrived at the pinnacle that he still, falsely, holds in Australia."[4]

This "myth" is just one of a myriad of legacies that Carruthers has left his country. He was a "Father of Federation", one of the delegates elected to the National Australasian Conventions which wrote the constitution, and without his presence in the Reid Cabinet there is a strong argument to be made that federation would not have happened when it did.[5] Personal circumstances made Carruthers decline to join the Federal Parliament sitting in distant Melbourne, but he went on to become Premier of the largest Australian State and re-orientate nineteenth century liberalism to sit on the centre-right of Australian politics, a development that would then be copied at the Commonwealth level. Even once he had entered semi-retirement Carruthers continued to add to his achievements, helping to create an Australian icon by guiding the Sydney Harbour Bridge Bill through a somewhat hostile Legislative Council. After such a career, Carruthers was a man with a keen interest

---

[3]   Jillian Robertson, *The Captain Cook Myth* (Sydney: Angus and Robertson, 1981) & Peter Hooker, "Myths about James Cook", *Untold Lives Blog*, British Library, 2018.

[4]   *The Captain Cook Myth* p.139.

[5]   For background on Carruthers see Zachary Gorman, *Sir Joseph Carruthers: Founder of the New South Wales Liberal Party* (Brisbane: Connor Court, 2018). For how closely fought the federation issue was in New South Wales see Zachary Gorman, "Birthplace of a Nation?: Why Sydney voted 'no' to federation", *Agenda: A Journal of Policy Analysis and Reform*, due out 2020.

in building up a positive narrative for the country that he had directly helped to create.

For Carruthers' detractors that is where the problem starts and ends. How dare history be utilised for a purpose, surely it must be manipulated and distorted in the process. Without getting into an argument over historical relativism and how all history must be reflected through narrative lenses which inherently impact how it is seen, it is worth pointing out that Carruthers picked Cook because the facts of his life suited the positive story he was trying to tell. He was not trying to make the facts fit the story. It is clear that, despite having an agenda, Carruthers cared deeply for the truth. Facts have a shelf life and some of what he says has since been proven incorrect (as would be the case with any 90 year old history book), but he went to extensive efforts in a pre-digital age to acquire sources and took his task very seriously.[6] If anything, the clarity of his purpose is less distorting than with another historian, because we can see Carruthers' bias and account for it as we read.

More than this. Who Carruthers was, and the fact that he was ultimately successful (along with others) in shaping Australia's respect for Cook means that Carruthers' writings become history in their own right. What this Father of Federation and New South Wales Premier thought would be a good image for our nation to aspire towards is interesting to the historian and, hopefully, to the reader of this book.

Carruthers did not invent the idea of venerating Cook as an Australian founder. Indeed, his love for the man was allegedly kindled when he saw the unveiling of the Hyde Park Cook statue when he was just eleven years old.[7] But in the midst of a wave of national sentiment that accompanied both federation and the First World War, Carruthers helped to popularise the centricity of Cook. As Minister for Lands in the Reid Government he secured the site of Captain Cook's Landing

---

[6] Ironically, Carruthers is most prone to make mistakes when it comes to the details of his own life.

[7] This story is often repeated and comes from Carruthers himself, even if the dates do not seem to line up for him to have been quite so young.

at Kurnell as a public park where the "discovery" could be re-enacted, as a retired Premier he used his influence to get a statue of Cook erected in London as a roundabout acknowledgement of Australia in the heart of the Empire, and, as will be seen, in his greatest coup Carruthers even roped the United States Government into venerating Cook as a way of strengthening its Pacific alliances in the lead up to World War Two.

Why was Carruthers attracted to Cook, as opposed to other "founders" he could have focused attention on? Well part of it was the personal experience with the statue, another part was parochialism. Carruthers was the Member for St. George and Kurnell was virtually in his backyard.[8] To celebrate Cook allowed Carruthers to simultaneously celebrate the Empire and Australia's unique place within it, allowing an independent nationalism to evolve within the existing pervasive imperialist framework. As will be seen, there is an extent to which Carruthers viewed Cook as personifying Australia, hence allegations against Cook were taken as a slight on the country he helped to engender. Focusing on Cook rather than the First Fleet allowed people to side-step the convict issue, which was still considered to be a visceral stain on the Australian character at the time. Unbeknownst to him, Carruthers was actually the son of a convict, which brings us to the core attraction of Cook: the nineteenth century cult of the "self-made man".

Carruthers was the progeny of reasonably humble parents yet he had grown to take up some of the most prominent positions in the land. This was the Australian dream, a place where if you worked hard you would be rewarded for your effort, be able to save, and ultimately gain an independence unimaginable for a labourer back in Britain. Australia had the highest wages in the world from the mid-nineteenth century until around 1900.[9] Colonial Parliaments were full of self-assured success stories and classical liberalism was in its heyday. Cook was someone that Australian children, who were conscious of the British

---

[8]   One wonders if the current Member for Cook Scott Morrison, with his love for all things Cronulla and particularly the Sharks, takes a similar local pride in his elector-ate's namesake. Cook's face is even on the bins in what locals call "the Shire".

[9]   Ian McLean, *Why Australia Prospered: the shifting sources of economic growth* (Princeton: Princeton University Press, 2013).

aristocracy and its class limitations even though it was distant from them, could aspire to be. If you put in hard work and maintain a strong moral character you too can change the world; that was the message to be conveyed through Cook. Even the very name of his ship was a celebration of human endeavour.

Carruthers also had a deep sense of propriety which held that great men and women should be rewarded for their efforts (which in turn would inspire others to achieve similar fame, so this aspect also relates to Australians emulating Cook). The author's meritocratic ideals are perhaps best captured by an inspirational speech he gave as Minister for Public Instruction (Education) in the last government of Sir Henry Parkes. Drawing on his own experience, Carruthers told a group of disadvantaged youths that:

"Poverty arose from different sources, and much resulted from the vices of mankind; but its origin, no matter what it might be, should not stand in the way of alleviating suffering, and the people should never think of visiting on the heads of children any misfortunes brought about by the faults of parents. In spite of all difficulties, it was at the will of every boy and girl, no matter how poor, to achieve some meed of fame in the world, for the Almighty had designed it so that its good things could be shared by those who in early life had been deprived of their fair share of it. One in this country could combine words of hope with practical encouragement, for in our system of education, and under our form of government and social life, no great barriers were offered to any lad, no matter how humble, from going step by step from the lowest to the highest place in the community. In this country there were scores of instances of men who had risen by their own industry and perseverance to high, honourable, and dignified positions ... In conclusion he told them not to be ashamed of poverty – it was a noble sign they would bear in after successes – but to take advantage of the great educational facilities at their command, and never to forget the grand principles of self-respect, self-reliance and self-help."[10]

When later under the Reid Government Carruthers recovered the land at Kurnell, you can see how this line of thinking was attached to the image of Cook:[11]

"I desire to tender to his Excellency the Lieutenant-Governor the public thanks for his official act of dedicating this classic spot to the people of New South Wales for all time (Applause.) I also desire to express the warm appreciation we must all feel at the presence as a participator in the ceremony of the Commander-in-Chief of the Naval Force in these waters, his Excellency the Admiral.[12] (Applause.) It is extremely appropriate that the chief performer in this unique ceremony should be our most distinguished colonist, who for over 40 years has made his home amongst us, and who has largely devoted to the service of his adopted country the learning and experience of a master mind - (cheers) - and no less appropriate is the part which his Excellency the Admiral will take in these proceedings, for he is the worthy representative of that great sea Power to which we owe not only the discovery and the possession of these shores, but the continued security which for 129 years we have enjoyed in absolute peace in this far-distant quarter of the empire (Cheers.) It was England's great sailor, Cook, who in 1770 on this point first raised the British flag, it was an English admiral, Phillip, who pioneered the way of colonisation and again raised the flag in 1788; and to-day, after a lapse of over a century, it is again a sailor chief – our Admiral - who unfurls the flag which is to proclaim this spot sacred to the people in commemoration of the event which has been the germ of its great history and great destiny. (Applause.)

---

[10] *Sydney Morning Herald*, 22 April 1890, p.8. This message of hope and opportunity sold well in an immigrant society, and it helped greatly that Carruthers himself had successfully climbed the ladder from its lower rungs.

[11] *Sydney Morning Herald*, 8 May 1899, p.4. As recently as 2018 (notably when Morrison was Treasurer) the Australian and New South Wales Governments provided funding for the refurbishment of the site at Kurnell. A 250th celebration was planned before the coronavirus measures saw it cancelled.

[12] Admiral Sir Hugo Pearson, Commander in Chief of the Australian Station, the British naval command that looked after Australian waters from 1859 until our own navy took over in 1913.

"As the Plymouth Rock is the most sacred ground to the Americans, so may this historic place, rich in its traditions, be the one place in our island continent more consecrated than another to the great man who here first set foot upon our shores, and in his foresight secured for the empire and its people a territory unsurpassed in the whole universe. It is to no unworthy man that we give honour this day. Cook was no mere favourite of fortune. From the humble beginning of a lad in a village store, later on as a seaman on a collier, he rose, if rise it be, to the position of an A.B. seaman in H.M. Navy. In four years he gained the rank of master, and shortly afterwards that of captain, by his own sheer and indomitable energy and ability. (Applause.) When past the age of thirty he took up the study of mathematics, and in four years had so progressed as to be entrusted with work in surveying and in navigation which required the possession of no small amount of mathematical and scientific knowledge. As if it were an augury of the future of these great lands, our very founder was one who fought his way to success by unaided efforts, by industry and by patient but persevering labour. His life is a noble example to the people of Australia, who live under institutions which freely open the door of fame and power to all who display industry and ability. (Applause.)

"I have no desire to reflect upon the past; but it is a matter for congratulation that this land is at last rescued from the hands of any private individual or land corporation. What blind folly ever induced the Government of New South Wales to part with this area of land for a paltry quit rent of less than ½d per acre? It may be more sentiment on my part to rescue this as a national birthright; but after all *sentiment about great events and great men to whom the world owes much is but the spark which fires men to similar achievement.*[13] I was saying a moment or two ago that it was appropriate to have here to-day their Excellencies the Lieutenant-Governor and the Admiral. May I go a little further, and at the risk of a charge of egotism - a charge which I would like to avoid on this occasion, but which will be found excusable I trust - may I say

---

[13] My Italics. Carruthers truly believed that veneration would lead to inspiration, that was at the heart of this whole enterprise.

that there is a certain amount of coincidence at least in my participation in this function to-day, not merely because I am the Minister for Lands, but because I have the honour to represent a constituency which can lay claim to having been traversed almost throughout by the great captain. I have in my possession temporarily (thanks to the courtesy of Mr. Huntington) a facsimile of Cook's own chart of Botany Bay, and it shows that he proceeded in his boats up Cook's River as far as the dam and up George's River as far as Salt Pan Creek. He landed at the very point whence the steamers proceeded this morning, viz., at Sans Souci, for this chart has thereon marked his landing there at the site of an aboriginal well. His journals, too, record the fact that he made short exploring trips into what is now the municipal districts of Rockdale, Kogarah, and Hurstville, so that the Electorate of St. George can claim the singular distinction of having been visited along the whole length of its foreshores and across country by the great navigator.

"Your Excellencies and ladies and gentlemen can well appreciate the feelings of the people who live adjacent to this bay when I say, that to them particularly it will be a relief to know that in future they will not be trespassers when they visit this sacred ground. (Applause.) I need not dwell on the facts already so well known, that within this reserve there is the Commemorative Tablet or plate erected by the Philosophical Society, nor that yonder stands the tree planted by the present Duke of York - that planted by his brother, the Duke of Clarence, having, as of ill omen, died within a year or so of its being planted.[14] Forby Sutherland, who died of consumption, lies buried close by.[15] His burial place was pointed out years ago either by the blacks or by some member of Cook's own expedition, for it is tolerably certain that in Phillip's fleet there were some of Cook's fellow voyagers. At any rate, for years and years there was an enclosure, supposed to be Sutherland's burial place, and the old post stumps were found and identified quite recently. The site tallies with that given by Cook - namely, close by the stream from which he

---

[14]   Albert Victor, the Duke of Clarence and Avondale, died of influenza in 1892. In 1910 his brother the Duke of York succeeded to the throne as George V.

[15]   Forby Sutherland was a Scottish sailor on the *Endeavour*'s crew who became the first Briton buried on Australian soil.

took in his supply of water. There can be no reasonable doubt that this is the actual scene of Cook's landing, for we have the testimony of two old and respected colonists - Mr. Alexander Berry and Dr. Douglas - that in the early part of this century a blackfellow, hoary with age, who had actually witnessed the landing, identified to them this spot as the landing place. Cook's private log and his charts also leave no room to doubt that here on this silver beach he actually first trod Australian soil…

"…His Excellency the Admiral then pulled the halliards and released the union jack from the folds in which it had been arranged, and as the bunting fluttered in the breeze it was saluted by H.M.S. *Goldfinch* and also by the battery at Bare Island. The band of the Permanent Artillery played the National Anthem, and the people cheered. At the invitation of the Minister for Lands, cheers were then given for his Excellency the Lieutenant-Governor and for his Excellency the Admiral. Mr. Hawthorne called for cheers for the Minister for Lands, and there was a vigorous response. The ceremony being at an end, the people strayed over the site to note objects which have an especial historic interest mentioned in the speech of Mr. Carruthers. Afterwards the company embarked upon the several vessels by which they had reached the place."

This book is not exclusively about proving Cook's significance to Australia. Carruthers starts off by making an important historical point in arguing that Cook intentionally set out to find and claim the mythical "Great Southern Continent" for Britain, which for the author demonstrates that Cook is the legitimate "founder of Australia". After this however, Carruthers moves on from his homeland and embarks on an ambitious plan to convince a far more sceptical audience of Americans and native Hawaiians of the value of Cook. The book answers questions like why did Cook die and had any of his actions contributed to his demise? This involves unpicking a myriad of perspectives, from overzealous missionaries to disgruntled sailors, in an effort to appertain the truth. Carruthers is a very partial guide through all of this, but he provides the evidence firsthand and much like a Netflix true crime documentary, the reader has the ability to make up their own mind. I am hopeful that it sheds some valuable light on how to deal with contested colonial legacies.

Note on racial language

This book was written at a very specific time in history when discussions revolving around race were increasingly pervasive, before they were subsequently discredited by the rise of Nazism in Europe. As a man of his time Carruthers (born 1856) uses language and even holds some views which we would now find abhorrent. At the same time, Carruthers' track record shows that he was very sympathetic to the plight of native peoples. Carruthers had been virtually raised by Aborigines for a period on the north coast of New South Wales, and in that Colony's Parliament he had successfully defended the Indigenous right to vote. He had also been outspoken on issues relating to the administration of Western Samoa, going so far as to earn a public rebuke in the New Zealand Parliament over his comments. I think that it is very indicative and commendable that even those who have criticised Carruthers' praise of Cook have not used this dated language to try to discredit him. By the standards of the time he was significantly enlightened, even if he could have been more so. Hawaii itself became a lesson for him, teaching Carruthers that a multi-ethnic society could work long before the rest of the political class started to question the "Australian Settlement" and its white Australia policy.[16]

The text has been kept true to its original form as much as is practicable. The italics, punctuation and somewhat inconsistent capitalisations are the author's, as are the spellings of the various Hawaiian names. The author had made some limited use of footnotes, hence I have made sure to clearly indicate which notes are original and which are my own annotations.

---

[16]   *The Register*, Adelaide, 16 September 1924, p.11. *Founder of the New South Wales Liberal Party* p.349 lists a footnote with the right date but wrong newspaper ascribed for this important point, which I am glad to be able to rectify for the record.

There were a tiny handful of principled politicians who opposed the white Australia policy from its inception at the expense of their political success, notably Carruthers' Free Trader contemporary Bruce Smith.

Foreword

Admiral Dudley de Chair

Although much has been written on the subject of Captain Cook, I feel certain that a work such as this will be warmly welcomed by all those who hold honour in the memory of the great sailor.

It is only right that the unfounded and ignorant aspersions which have been cast upon his name by various writers should be finally and definitely disproved, and it is especially fitting that this work of vindication should have been undertaken by so brilliant and unquestioned an authority as Sir Joseph Carruthers.

Sir Joseph has devoted many years to the collection of material for this book from every possible source, and there is probably no man alive who has so thorough and intimate a knowledge of the subject. He has given us here a work which is not only full of fascination to all those who are interested in the growth of our Empire, but which henceforth sets the name and reputation of Captain Cook above calumny or reproach.

Sir Joseph served his country in various important public capacities, and for three years (1904-7) filled the high office of Premier of New South Wales. He deserves the gratitude and thanks of the community, and especially of the great British Navy, for educating the public mind in regards to Captain Cook's life and achievements.

It was Cook who put the east coast of Australia on the map; he discovered Hawaii, and he named the New Hebrides and New Caledonia. He played a considerable part in the founding of Australia, and was the cause of the settling of this great continent.

Australians must always honour the name of this great navigator, one of the finest the world has ever seen.

This book which is entitled "Captain Cook, R.N., One Hundred and Fifty Years After" will be of special value to the officers and men of the British Navy, as it will enable them to refute these slanders wherever they meet them, and clear Cook's memory of the slightest stain.

D.R.S. de Chair, Admiral.

Governor of New South Wales.

Government House, Sydney.

Foreword

William Morris Hughes

I am pleased to comply with Sir Joseph's request to write a short introduction to this book, which deals with certain incidents in the life and death of the greatest English navigator – Captain James Cook, R.N.

It is my good fortune to know Sir Joseph very well. For more than thirty-five years we have been associated in public life: at times in opposite political camps; our friendship has remained unbroken.[17] Sir Joseph has devoted his life to public service. He has not only done signal service to the State, but for the last decade and more has striven zealously to foster a truer appreciation of what Australia owes to Captain Cook.

Sir Joseph did a fine thing for the people when he rescued from private ownership that historic spot at Kurnell, Botany Bay, New South Wales, where Cook first landed and took possession of Australia on behalf of Great Britain. In 1908 he was instrumental in having erected the only statue in London to the great navigator, and of recent years he has been active in a movement for the dedication to the public of that portion of land in Hawaii where Cook was killed.

He has done many other things to keep green the memory of the real Founder of Australia, and this volume is the culmination of his work. Busy man as he is, Sir Joseph has found time during the past six or seven

---

[17] Carruthers' turbulent relationship with the Labor Party is discussed extensively in the *Founder of the New South Wales Liberal Party*. Hughes had also campaigned for 'no' at the federation referendums, and he had been one of the main instigators behind George Reid's downfall as Premier. However, the two men were bonded by a shared patriotism that came to the fore during WW1, particularly after Hughes became a "Nationalist" party member - *Editor.*

years to devote special attention to collecting information and data to enable him to present hitherto little-known facts in connection with the life and death of Cook. This has, of necessity, entailed a great amount of research work, both in Australia and abroad, but to him it has been a labour of love.

For many years the memory of Captain Cook has been besmirched by narrow-minded men, but the presentation of the facts as set out in these pages will put envious critics to confusion and give to the people of this and future generations a clearer understanding of one of the greatest navigators our race has produced.

I have the pleasure of commending this volume to the public.

W.M. Hughes.
Federal Parliament House,
Canberra.

Author's Preface

I feel justified in presenting this book to the English-speaking public. Too much has been said against Captain Cook by some writers, and too little has been done to refute mis-statements which have clouded his memory.

Moreover, Cook's claims as the real Founder of Australia as a British possession have been lightly treated by some, who rob him of his rightful place in order to accord honour to the lesser men who were spared to reap what he had sown.

The question of the Discovery of Australia has also been raised with unnecessary persistency to defeat claims which Cook himself never made. That is a matter of little moment in itself; but as a matter of controversy it is apt to make people lose sight of what Cook really did, when he so thoroughly charted the east coast of Australia and there raised the British flag. Such a controversy is unfair and mischievous.

Our young people nowadays have not a sufficient veneration for the men who laid the sure foundations on which is built British Dominion in the South Pacific. To permit the memory of Captain Cook to remain under a cloud is to contribute towards a slackness in that spirit of veneration which is an essential of the high character of our race. We cannot afford any such slackness.

I happen to have spent many years of my life in the district where Cook first landed in Australia, and represented that district in the Parliament of my native State for over twenty-one years. During my term of office in the Reid Government (1895-1901) as Minister for Lands, I rescued from private ownership a large area at Kurnell, the site of Cook's first landing in 1770.[18] It had been alienated with an utter disregard for the proper sentiment in the early days of colonisation in Australia. I caused that area to be dedicated for all time as a public park. I consider it to be sacred soil to the people of Australia and to the people of the race which produced such a man as Captain Cook.

In other ways I have acted with good effect: (i) As a result of my letter in 1908 to the London *Times*, steps were taken towards the erection of the only statue to Captain Cook in London;[19] (ii) As a consequence of my initiating the proposal, the Territorial Government of Hawaii is dedicating to the public the land in Kealakekua Bay, Hawaii, where Cook was killed in 1779.

Also, my suggestion publicly made in Honolulu in 1924 contributed to the movement which eventuated in the Sesqui-centennial celebrations in August, 1928, in the Hawaiian Isles under the auspices of the United States Government and that of the Hawaiian Territory.

Those celebrations were splendidly carried out and constituted a fine gesture of friendship from America to the people of Great Britain, Australia, and New Zealand, as well as a very proper act to honour Captain Cook's memory.

I was specially commissioned by the Prime Minister of Australia and the Commonwealth Government to attend these celebrations as the representative of Australia. I did so and, at the request of the American Commission, I delivered the principal address, at the spot where Captain

---

[18] Carruthers was a member of the Reid Government from its inception in 1894 until its fall in 1899. In his senior years Carruthers tended to place the events of his life at a later date than they occurred. Even his birth year is often recorded inconsistently as being either 1856 or 1857 – *Editor*.

[19] While veneration of Cook is now often thought of as an archaic legacy of our British past, Britain did not celebrate the Captain all that much. He was explicitly an Australian icon onto which Australian values were projected. Carruthers' meritocratic vision meshed well with the immigrant experience and its underlying hopes and dreams – *Editor*.

Cook died on 17th February, 1779.[20]

A full record of the proceedings will be found in this book and will serve to show how American sentiment has changed towards a more just conception of Cook and his work.

I have felt that there is a need to place Cook's achievements both in Australia and in Hawaii in a truer and better light than heretofore, so that the real worth and character of the greatest navigator of his own times or of any other age may be properly revered.

J.H. Carruthers.
Parliament House.
Sydney, *July*, 1929.

---

[20] On page 8 of the official public Report of the United States Commissioners they state: "Sir Joseph Carruthers was given a cordial reception by the Cook Commission and throughout his stay in Hawaii was a conspicuous figure. To him also had been delegated the post of honour, that of delivering the oration at Kealakekua Bay at the unveiling of the tablet set in the water to mark the spot where Captain Cook fell"- (*vide* official report of Commissioners for Sesqui-centennial Cook celebrations) - *Author*.

Part I

(i) Clouds gather round the memory of Cook and the need to clear them away as well as to do justice to others concerned in his death

(ii) The Discovery and Annexation of the east coast of Australia

The monument at Cook's landing-place, Kurnell, Botany Bay, NSW.
From left to right: Major L. Lloyd, Major-General J. H. Bruche, Captain J.F.
Robins, Sir Joseph Carruthers, Admiral Sir D. R. S. de Chair, and Mr W. Houston.

1

The clouds about the memory of Captain Cook and a call to clear them away

So much has been written concerning Captain James Cook, his voyages, his discoveries, and his death (in Hawaii), that the reader may say: "What new thing can now be written, 150 years after Cook's death?"

I venture, however, to assert that, with regard to three phases, viz.:

i.   Cook's discovery of Australia;

ii.   His death in Hawaii, in 1799; and

iii.   The character and point of view of the Hawaiians,

A light may be shed, which will reveal facts placing the memory of the great navigator on a sounder and better footing.

With regard to the first of these phases, the recent publication of the Secret Instructions of the First Voyage proves that the discovery and annexation of the east coast of Australia by Captain Cook in 1770 was not the result of a casual decision by a narrow majority in a council of the officers of H.M.S. *Endeavour*, held in New Zealand waters early in 1770, but was the consequence of very clear and definite instructions from the British Admiralty to Captain Cook, whereby he was enjoined to direct his ships' course to the east coast of what was then known as

New Holland[21], and then to survey and chart that coast from south to north, and, finally, to take possession of the territory, at two or more prominent points along the coast, in the name and on behalf of the King of Great Britain.

To Australians especially these outstanding facts, now fully revealed through the publication of the document I have referred to, place Captain Cook in an indisputable position as the real founder of British dominion in the Continent of Australia. Any question as to the first discovery of that Continent ceases to be of account when one is confronted with the fact, now made clear, that the annexation of Australia was of set design, and that, in carrying out that design, Captain Cook left nothing undone to render indefeasible the title whereby Australia has been held for 159 years by people of the Anglo-Saxon race as an integral part of the British Empire.

As to the second phase – the death of Captain Cook in Hawaii in February, 1779 – there is absolute need for a full statement of the facts associated with that event, in order to clear the memory of Captain Cook and his officers and men from many unfounded slanders which have gained currency, not only in the United States of America, but also in Great Britain and in some of the British Dominions.

We cannot afford to allow calumny to overcloud the reputation of so great a man as Captain Cook. In my humble judgement he stands

---

[21] Lest it be said that the Secret Instructions did not specifically mention New Holland, I answer that a plan of Tasman's chart, and also Dalrymple's plan (both showing New Holland), were supplied to Cook by the Admiralty. He was then directed to limit his search for the Southern Continent to 40°S. and thence above that latitude westerly.

Admiral Peircy Brett, who signed these instructions, had been with Anson in his previous voyage in these waters, and he designed the far-seeing policy of securing posts of vantage in the Southern Continent (*vide* Professor Holland Rose's address, p.109, *Geographical Journal*, February, 1929). Palpably he knew that the only value for colonisation lay north-west of 40°S. Tasman's chart showed a great coast-line marked as New Holland and was, in reality, the only southern continent worth searching for. No need to name it specifically in the instructions when the chart supplied to Cook so clearly indicated it – *Author*.

foremost among the men of the Anglo-Saxon race as an Empire Builder. No other man can be compared with him in this respect.

Not only Australia, but New Zealand, and many other important groups of Islands in the South Seas, discovered and annexed by Cook, now form important and prosperous British settlements, wherein to-day something approaching ten millions of men and women of British stock are securely established in their homes. The United States of America also ultimately gained its Pacific coast States (Oregon, Idaho and Washington) indirectly through Cook's discoveries in the N. Pacific.[22]

Yet there has grown up a most erroneous impression – to say the least – amongst a large body of English-speaking people, that Captain Cook, during the last few weeks of his life in Hawaii, totally belied his unbroken record for humane and honourable dealing with the native races.

It is alleged by some that Cook contributed to the cause which led to his own end, by the misconduct of himself and his men. I first heard this charge openly made in 1924, when I visited Honolulu to participate in an important conference held by the Pan-Pacific Union, and at which I represented the Government of New South Wales, of which I was then a member. I investigated this charge very carefully, and spent five years in thoroughly threshing it out, not only in the Hawaiian Islands (which I visited for that purpose in five successive years), but elsewhere from records, which I propose to cite in a later chapter.[23]

I satisfied myself that the charge was unfounded. I cannot claim to be wholly free from the natural bias which, I hope, every man has for the heroes of his own race. Recognising that bias, I have set out to overcome

---

[22] When divorced from the racial language surrounding it, this paragraph is the heart of the matter. Cook opened up the Pacific to the globe, including those non-British immigrants who have come to enjoy it more recently - *Editor.*

[23] This book is the product of an early political retirement caused by a heart attack which forced Carruthers to resign the Premiership in 1907. Though he was roped into serving in the Fuller Government (1922-1925) from the Upper House, this passion project dominated his final years at the expense of his own memoirs; much to my chagrin as his biographer – *Editor.*

it and to place myself in the position of a judge, bound to sum up impartially the evidence and the facts of the case.[24]

In so summing up, I hope to convince my readers that Captain Cook's actions in Hawaii were clean and pure, and that his death was due to an unfortunate misunderstanding, the responsibility for which lay more with the Hawaiians than with Cook.

I shall produce testimony from native Hawaiian sources, as well as from the authentic records of English eye-witnesses, to prove my case.

Let me say that the blame for the circulation of the calumnies on Cook's memory cannot be placed on any one set of men.

I have traced these calumnies to their sources, and find that Englishmen in England, Americans in the American Colonies, missionaries in Hawaii, and writers in various parts of the English-speaking world, all have their share in the publication. I am willing to believe that (with only a rare exception) there was not any malice on the part of these men. Whether that be so or not, the fact remains that, for over 150 years, the name of Captain James Cook has been unjustly tarnished.

A third matter which needs to be cleared up relates to the Hawaiian people. From time to time the Hawaiians have been described by Europeans (chiefly Englishmen) as "a race of cannibals." Only a year or so back, in an Australian Encyclopaedia, it was published that Cook was killed in Hawaii and his flesh eaten by the natives. The latter statement is quite untrue.

Many English writers have said that cannibalism was common in the Hawaiian Isles. In my school days, they were spoken of as the Cannibal Islands, and there was a popular music-hall ditty entitled "The King of the Cannibal Islands."

---

[24] This is a well-founded acknowledgement. The author clearly has a hagiographer's bent to him, and he does not always succeed at his efforts to maintain impartiality. However, his tendency to quote sources in extensive segments does allow significant scope for the reader to make up their own minds – *Editor.*

There is no foundation for this libel of cannibalism on a very fine race, whose culture goes back to a period when the inhabitants of the British Isles were in a state of semi-barbarism. The Hawaiians have keenly resented this dreadful imputation against them, which, unfortunately, is repeated by recent writers.[25]

When I have tried to impress Hawaiian audiences with facts which redeem the memory of Cook from the gross libels on him, I have been met with the reply: "You forget, Sir, that we too have suffered pain from the baseless charges made against our race. Whilst we are willing to have matters cleared up with regard to a man who you honour, we think you owe it to us to clear up also the good name of our race."

In all countries occasional cases of eating flesh occur. In my own experience, some fifty years ago, I was called upon to act as legal adviser for the member of the English crew of a yacht which sailed out to Australia. Undoubtedly, some of them maintained their lives by eating the flesh of another. It was alleged that he was killed. While I was satisfied that there was no killing of the victim, still it was true that the flesh of one who died a natural death was eaten by the survivors.

I have been informed by Hawaiians that, in the history of their race, occasionally an individual practised cannibalism, either through starvation or from degeneracy. Whenever such a rare case was discovered, the culprit was driven as an outcast from the society of his fellows and was treated as we would treat a ghoul.

---

25   On the matter of cannibalism of the Hawaiians: In Vol. VI of the *Three Voyages of Captain Cook*, there are two or three references made by Cook in his journal to the cannibalism of the natives of Atooi (Kauai), from which one may gather that Cook was led to believe, from their own statements, that these people were cannibals. As a matter of fact, his own story goes on to show that the propensity of the natives to answer "yes" to any question asked about which they were doubtful misled Cook. He questioned two or three natives whether they ate the flesh of their enemies whom they killed, and he records their answer as a "yes".

Dr. Samwell, in his published records, shows how Captain Cook and King were similarly misled in answers by natives on other matters through their habit of answering "yes" to all and every question asked, the real purport of which they did not comprehend. That habit remains even to-day a well-known characteristic of almost all the Islanders of Polynesia and Melanesia - *Author*.

The Hawaiians constitute a portion of the Polynesian race, studies of which I have made, extending over a period of years, in Tahiti, Tonga, Samoa, the Cook Group, and in the Hawaiian Islands; and it has been proved to me that cannibalism in all these parts was regarded with abhorrence similar to that felt by the English race. Writers who have spent long periods amongst these natives, speaking from personal knowledge, as well as from the information acquired, corroborate this view.

The Maoris of New Zealand constitute another branch of the Polynesian race. They, undoubtedly, once were cannibals.

Lying almost in the centre of Polynesia are the Fiji Islands, inhabited by a race of Melanesians. The Fijians were also cannibals. Cannibalism was a daily habit with them. It first began by following words of advice, handed down from generation to generation, namely – "Beware of the stranger cast upon your shores with salt and water in his eyes."

Bitter experience had taught the Fijians that new diseases were introduced by castaways, which decimated their population. To them, the only preventative method to save their race from further introduction of such diseases was to kill the stranger and burn his body. Then, hungry as they always were for flesh, in islands where there is very little animal food, they began the practice of eating the burnt flesh of their victims. The practice, once begun, became a habit.

The Fijians were much in contact with the Tongans – a neighbouring race – and, undoubtedly, to a slight extent, some of the Tongans indulged in the eating of human flesh during visits to the Fiji Islands. So the practice of cannibalism was introduced into the homeland of the Tongans; but only to a slight extent.

The Hawaiians also resent the imputations made against their womenfolk, that they were of easy virtue. One hundred and fifty years ago the Hawaiian idea of virtue differed somewhat from our idea. With the advent of the civilisation of the whites and with Christianity and its teachings, our idea of virtue has been accepted. Consequently, the

Hawaiians of to-day resent the fact that their womenfolk of early days are spoken of in the way mentioned. In their rites of hospitality 150 years ago, and earlier, what is considered blameable to-day was not then regarded as a moral offence. There was no evil in the Hawaiian mind in the practice of their rite of hospitality.

At any rate, the conditions of the days when Cook visited the Islands and those of to-day are fundamentally different. There is a different sense of right and wrong in the Hawaiians now from what there was then. They now resent any emphasis being placed upon habits and customs which implied no moral wrong-doing under the conditions of older times, but which, to-day, would be regarded as reprehensible and immoral. We have to view this matter from the standpoint of Hawaiians of earlier days.[26]

Another matter to be similarly viewed is with regard to the law of *meum* and *tuum*. One hundred and fifty years ago, theft as we know it, and theft as Hawaiians knew it, were totally different things. There was a different sense of the value and rights of property current then amongst these native people.

At the time of Cook's visit (1778-79) the feudal system was operating amongst the Hawaiians. That system had been in existence during many centuries preceding. The ruling class constituted an aristocracy which owned the land and had practically all property rights. From that class the King and Chiefs inherited not only their titles, but the land. They were the rulers and the priests, and they defined the *tabus* and punished the violation of them. We had something similar for centuries in English history, when the common people were in the same state of serfdom as had existed in the Hawaiian Islands. There was a common basis for the language used by both classes of Hawaiians – namely, the Polynesian language. But the ruling class spoke what is known as the Court language, just as, after the Norman Conquest, Norman French

---

[26] Carruthers has an understanding that when judging the past, allowance needs to be made for the standards of the time. The same goes for judging this text, which at 90 years of age is an artefact in its own right – *Editor*.

was spoken in England as the Court language. The common people in Hawaii spoke a vernacular of their own Polynesian basis.

The point I wish to make is that we may visualise the customs of the Hawaiians if we consider those of England in the period just preceding the Norman Conquest and afterwards, until the feudal system was abolished. The rights of property in each case varied according to the class. The common folk, to a large extent, shared what they had, one with the other, and did not magnify into a charge of theft the taking or using of what one had a surplus of and the other was in need of.

The Hawaiians were no more thievish than the common English people. In our English code, not until comparatively recent years were the severe laws against interfering with personal property enacted and enforced. The period was never reached in Hawaiian history when similar laws were made and enforced, except in regard to the property of the ruling class.[27]

Hence, one can understand how the Hawaiians of to-day resent the broad accusation against their ancestors by Europeans, that they were all prone to thieving and to a disregard of the rights of property.

This matter may be thought to be of little importance; but when one considers that the trouble, which ended in Cook's death in 1779, began in acts of pilfering and thieving committed by a few natives, it is worthwhile to pay regard to the native view of such acts.

Cook, himself, oft-times in his log, refers to this practice of thieving which was rampant in all the other Islands that he visited. He was only severe when matters reached a serious stage, as, for instance, when some article of considerable value to the ship, or to the work of the ship, was stolen. In this particular case in Hawaii to which I am referring, the

---

[27] The theory that civilisations advanced in a set pattern was pervasive at this time. Many now view this as condescending, which in many ways it was, but in the early days of cultural interaction it was a way of making sense of the unknown by comparing it to the known of your own history. In this sense there was an empathetic aspect to it. Books like *Guns, Germs, and Steel* by Jared Diamond have modernised a similar idea - *Editor.*

Resolution had put back to port at Kealakekua Bay, where Cook had spent some weeks in peace and amity with the native king, chiefs and people. The *Resolution* had sprung her main mast, and repairs had to be effected. Hence, the ship returned to her old moorings in the Bay unexpectedly. On this occasion the natives on shore were without king and high chiefs to maintain discipline and good order amongst them, as had been the case when Cook was there before.

One of the results of the absence of the people in authority was the stealing, which was openly and fragrantly carried on. Cook and his officers viewed this conduct in a serious light when it impeded them in the important work which had to be carried out in a period of dire emergency. Some of the natives, with only a minor chief or two to control them, looked upon it as the chance of a lifetime to take and keep whatever they could lay their hands on, more especially as their sense of value differed from that of the English. For instance, when they stole the cutter of the *Discovery* it was to obtain the nail in the fasteners – the only party that they valued.

That began the trouble, which ended in Cook's death. The Hawaiians did not appreciate the gravity of the offence which they had committed. But, when Cook sought to obtain restitution through the King, who had returned, the natives began to sense that what to them was little more than a practical joke might end in a tragedy to many of them.

It is very hard to understand the mental attitude of the natives in regard to the thieving which so disconcerted Captain Cook and his officers. One can hardly excuse the Hawaiians for what they did, yet the actions of a section that were "out of hand" during the absence of their High Chiefs and their King hardly warrant any wholesale imputations against the whole of the race. Petty larceny is fairly common in civilised countries. Yet no one would found a charge against a whole community because thieving occurred.

2

The secret orders or additional secret instructions to Lieutenant James Cook of H.M.S. Endeavour, issued by the Admiralty, 30ᵗʰ July, 1768, and not officially published until September, 1928

I now propose to deal with the Additional Secret Instructions to Cook, issued to him just as he was sailing on the first voyage.[28]

It is worth noting that one of the three signatories to these instructions is Admiral Percy Brett, who had been an officer under Commodore Anson in his voyage to the Pacific (1740-44). Brett and Anson were both strong advocates of a far-seeing Pacific policy for securing posts of vantage in the Southern Continent.

They and other British officers, who had knowledge of the Southern Sea and the Pacific, were convinced that somewhere in the position indicated in the Instructions and on Tasman's map (a copy of which was supplied to Cook) the only habitable Southern Continent existed.

Their influence and the need of the times were factors in the issuing of the explicit orders contained in this important document. Without such orders Cook (only just appointed to the rank of lieutenant) would

---

[28] The original said third voyage. Such basic errors were far more common in publishing at the time as editing was more arduous and consequently sub-par.

These secret instructions were a major historical discovery that Carruthers was one of the first people to write about. They fundamentally changed our understanding of how and why the east coast of Australia was first annexed – *Editor.*

hardly have dared to annex great territories in the way that he did.

The full text of the instructions is as follows:

"Secret Orders." P.R.O. Admiralty 211332.

Additional Secret Instructions to Lieut. James Cook, Commander of His Majesty's Bark *The Endeavour.*

Published by the Navy Records Society (*Naval Miscellanies*, Vol. 3, 1928, pp.343-50).

"Whereas the making discoveries of countries hitherto unknown, and the attaining a knowledge of distant parts which though formerly discovered have yet been but imperfectly explored, will redound greatly to the honour of this nation as a Maritime Power, as well as to the dignity of the Crown of Great Britain, and may tend greatly to the advancement of the trade and navigation thereof; and whereas there is reason to imagine that a continent, or land of great extent, may be found to the southward of the tract lately made by Captain Wallis in His Majesty's ship the *Dolphin* (of which you will herewith receive a copy) or of the tract of any former navigators in pursuits of the like kind; you are therefore in pursuance of His Majesty's pleasure hereby required and directed to put to sea with the bark at your command, so soon as the observation of the transit of the planet Venus shall be finished, and observe the following instructions.

"You are to proceed to the southward in order to make discovery of the continent above mentioned until you arrive in the latitude of 40 deg., unless you sooner fall in with it: but not having discovered it, or any evident signs of it, in that run, you are to proceed in search of it to the westward, between the latitude before mentioned and the latitude of 35 deg. Until you discover it or fall in with the Eastern side of the land discovered by Tasman and now called New Zealand.[29]

"If you discover the continent above mentioned, either in your run to the southward, or to the westward, as above directed, you are to employ yourself diligently in exploring as great an extent of the coast as you can; carefully observing the true situation thereof both in latitude and longitude, the variation of the needle, bearings of headlands, height, direction, and course of the tides and currents, depths and soundings of the sea, shoal, rocks, etc…

"You are also carefully to observe the nature of the soil and the products thereof, the beasts and fowls that inhabit or frequent it, the fishes that are to be found in the rivers or upon the coast and in what plenty; and in case you find any mines, minerals or valuable stones, you are to bring home specimens of each, and also such specimens of the seeds of the trees, fruits and grains as you may be able to collect, and transmit them to our Secretary, that we may cause proper examination and experiments to be made from them.

"You are likewise to observe the genius, temper, disposition and number of the natives, if there be any, and endeavour by all proper means to cultivate a friendship and alliance with them, making them presents of such trifles as they may value, inviting them to traffic…

"You are also with the consent of the natives to take possession of convenient situations in the country, in the name of the King of Great Britain; or, if you find the country uninhabited, take possession for His Majesty by setting up proper marks and inscriptions, as first discoverers and possessors.[30]

---

[29] Newcastle Academic Peter Hooker has argued that this piece of information undermines Carruthers' claim that Cook deliberately set out to find the Great Southern Continent around New Holland, for it was expected to be located east of New Zealand. The fact remains that Cook went searching for a southern continent and found one; surely acting outside of the instructions means that if anything he should take greater credit than otherwise – *Editor.*

[30] "Convenient situations" suggests that the intent may have been to set up trading posts rather than to take full possession, in a similar manner to how western colonialism developed in China. In the event Australia was not wealthy enough for this to be worthwhile - *Editor.*

"But if you should fail of discovering the continent before mentioned, you will, upon falling in with New Zealand, carefully observe the latitude and longitude in which that land is situated, and explore as much of the coast as the condition of the bark, the health of her crew, and the state of your provisions will admit of, having always great attention to reserve as much of the latter as will enable you to reach some known Port where you may procure a sufficiency to carry you to England, either round the Cape of Good Hope, or Cape Horn, as from circumstances you may judge the most eligible way of returning home.

"You will also observe with accuracy the situation of such islands as you may discover in the course of your voyage that have not hitherto been discovered by any Europeans, and take possession for His Majesty and make surveys and draughts of such of them as may appear to be of consequence, without suffering yourself however to be thereby diverted from the object which you are always to have in view, the discovery of the Southern Continent so often mentioned.

"But for as much as in an undertaking of this nature, several emergencies may arise not to be foreseen, and therefore not particularly to be provided for by instructions beforehand, you are, in all such cases, to proceed, as upon advice with your officers, you shall judge most advantageous to the service on which you are employed.

"You are to send by all proper conveyances to the Secretary of the Royal Society, copies of the observations you shall have made of the transit of Venus, and you are at the same time to send to our Secretary, for our information, accounts of your proceedings, and copies of the surveys and drawings you shall have made. And upon your arrival in England you are immediately to repair to this office in order to lay before us a full account of your proceedings in the whole course of your voyage, taking care before you leave the vessel to demand from the officers and Petty Officers the log books and journals they may have kept, and to seal them up for our inspection, and enjoining them, and the whole crew not to divulge where they have been until they shall have permission so to do.

"Given &c. the 30^(th) of July 1768.

"Ed. Hawke.

"Py. Brett.

"C. Spencer.

"To Lieut. James Cook,

"Comr. Of His Majesty's Bark

"the Endeavour."

Why were these orders or instructions issued with such secrecy? Why also was that secrecy so closely observed from 1768 until they were released for publication by the Admiralty late in 1928 – a period of 160 years?

These are the reasons that one may assume:

About the time of Cook's Voyages (from 1768 to 1779) Great Britain was in an almost constant state of war with France and with the revolutionary American Colonies which, in that period, became the Independent United States of America.

France had lost her great colony of Canada; and she felt that loss very greatly. Great Britain had lost her American colonies, and this loss also deprived her of an outlet for convicts formerly sent to work on the plantations.

Both countries, - Britain and France – therefore, were seized with a desire to acquire new colonies so situated as to afford not only an outlet for their surplus population, but also for convict settlements.

The great Southern Continent loomed largely in the view of not only these countries, but also in that of other European maritime countries, such as Spain and Holland. Very exaggerated ideas were current as to the wealth, population, and undeveloped resources of this continent.

Dalrymple, the hydrographer of the British Navy, openly gave out his opinion, that the great Southern Continent contained over 50,000,000 people, and must be far wealthier than the American Colonies. He was Cook's bitter enemy, owing largely to the fact that he had been a rival candidate for positions that the Admiralty had conferred upon Cook – including the command of the *Endeavour* on the first voyage of discovery in the South Seas.

Spain had openly questioned our right to the Falkland Islands, annexed for Great Britain in 1765 by Captain Byron (grandfather of the poet). War was imminent with Charles III of Spain, who ineffectually sought an alliance with Louis XV of France in pursuance of what was known as the "Family Compact."

Spain eventually gave way to our threatening naval preparations in the far North Pacific and elsewhere. Thus the air was electrical and bid fair for storms, involving Great Britain with two European powers and with the American Colonies.

Hence, there was a necessity for secrecy in the dispatch of the *Endeavour*: and the purpose of the First Voyage had to be cloaked.

Astronomers were keen on the coming transit of Venus, which would be fully visible only in the Southern Hemisphere. Otaheite (Tahiti) had been discovered and visited by both English and French ships, and its waters were charted and the friendly character of the natives was assured.

So the purpose of the voyage was publicly given out as for the observation of the Transit of Venus in Tahiti. This was a scientific purpose, pregnant with beneficial results to the science of astronomy in all civilised countries.

It was customary for nations at war to afford immunity and protection to scientific expeditions and to ships engaged therein even in time of war.

As a matter of fact, France and, later on, the United States issued orders for that purpose to their naval commanders and to their shipmasters in regard to Cook's first and subsequent voyages.[31]

It is very doubtful indeed whether such orders would ever have been issued if the Secret Instructions to Cook had been made public.

After the voyage was completed, and its main objects achieved, it was obvious that these Secret Instructions should not be revealed. A hue and cry would have been set up and, again, good relations between Great Britain and other Powers would have been imperilled.

Only two copies of these Instructions existed – one that was retained by the Admiralty, and the other that was Cook's copy. It seems strange that Cook was permitted to retain his copy: but he was a man to be trusted.

Cook's copy came to light only in 1923, when the Bolckow Collection of Captain Cook manuscripts was sold in London and purchased by the Government of the Commonwealth of Australia.[32] Even then the buyer did not realise the nature of the document which came into its possession.

In order to indicate the alertness of the mind of the French to any new discoveries in the South Seas I will refer to a paper read before the Royal Geographical Society at its meeting of 17th December, 1928, when Admiral Sir Herbert Purey-Cust, whom I now quote, said, in part:

"One aspect of Cook has not been touched upon, and that is the very great appreciation of him and his works that was shown in France at the time from the King downwards. Louis XVI was a keen student of literature, he especially liked books of travel and geography, and one

---

[31]   Later in the book Carruthers lauds the fact that Benjamin Franklin instructed American ships to give free passage to Cook for his journeys of scientific discovery as an early example of American and British cooperation, without ever quite realising the irony that he admits at the start that these scientific purposes, while never neglected, had previously been used as a ruse for something far more political – *Editor.*

[32]   Henry Bolckow was a wealthy Prussian industrialist who built a mansion on top of Cook's birthplace and began collecting any and all Cook artefacts he could acquire – *Editor.*

of his favourite works was the 'Voyages of Captain Cook.' The study of Cook made a deep impression on the King's mind. Why, he asked himself, should not France as a maritime nation and a naval Power share in the glory of discovering new lands and penetrating untravelled seas? He sends for the Comte de Fleurieu, the principal geographer in France, whom on account of his knowledge of geography the King had chosen to be tutor to his son the Dauphin, and whom a few years later he makes Minister of Marine. They thoroughly talk the subject over together, and the King decides (1785) that a voyage shall be undertaken; two ships of the Navy, *La Boussole* and *L'Astrolabe* are selected; and on the recommendation of the Marquis de Castries, the then Minister of Marine, that fine fellow La Perouse, described as the ablest seaman in the French Navy, is chosen for command.[33] Born in 1741, he had joined the Marine Service in 1756, and by this time become a very distinguished officer. Ever since his boyhood he had longed to follow in the footsteps of discoverers such as Byron, Carteret, Wallis, Louis de Bougainville, and over and above all, Cook. To the end of his life, down to the final days of his very last voyage, La Perouse revered the name of Cook.

"Over and over again in the instructions now prepared for the voyage – several times on a page in some places – appear references to what Cook had done and to what Cook had left to be done, showing that both King Louis and Fleurieu knew his voyages and his charts, not merely as casual readers, but intimately. The King in a special audience given to La Perouse, a little vain of his own geographical knowledge, explains to him the instructions verbally before handing them to him in writing. In the picture gallery at the Palace of Versailles is an oil painting by Mansiau called 'Louis XVI giving instructions to M. de La Perouse for his voyage around the world,' a copy of which may also be seen in the Mitchell Library, Sydney. In May 1786 La Perouse arrives at Owhyhee, the island where Cook had been killed a few years before, and writes in

---

[33] It is an interesting thought that the French King's envy of what the British had in Cook made him pay for this expensive expedition, contributing in some small way to the financial hardships that begat the French Revolution and ultimately cost him his head – *Editor.*

his journal, 'Full of admiration and respect as I am for the memory of that great man, he will always be in my eyes the first of the navigators… Chance might enable the most ignorant man to discover islands, but it belongs only to great men like him to leave nothing more to be done regarding the coast they have found.[34] Navigators, philosophers, physicians, all find in his Voyages interesting and useful things which were the object of his concern. All men, especially all navigators, owe a tribute of praise to his memory."

La Perouse told Lieutenant King, R.N., in Botany Bay, on 25th January, 1788 (the day before the settlement in New South Wales was founded): "Mr. Cook has done so much that he has left me nothing to do but to admire his works."

I may be pardoned for interpolating that, during a visit made by me to Versailles in 1908 (when I was Executive Commissioner for Australia to the Franco-British Exhibition that year), I saw Mansiau's oil painting above referred to. Seized with the value of it from a historical standpoint, I asked the New South Wales Government to approach the Government of France for permission to have it copied by a good artist. The request was made, and President Fallieres and his Ministers went further and caused a fine copy to be made and to be presented to my Government.

---

[34]   Cook's thorough and methodological approach to his "discovering" is what most impressed his competitors. His maps were remarkably accurate and stood the test of time – *Editor.*

Captain Cook memorial, Papeetee, Tahiti, where Cook's expedition observed the transit of Venus in 1768

3

The discovery and annexation of Australia not an accident but according to instructions

Captain Cook's greatest achievement, undoubtedly, was his discovery of the east coast of New Holland, his charting of that coast from end to end, and his taking possession of Australia (as New Holland was afterwards called) on behalf of His Majesty the King of Great Britain.

Frequently one hears of cavilling against Cook as the discoverer of Australia. Cannot those who cavil on this point perceive that this world of ours is very old, and it stands to reason that hundreds of years ago Malays and Arabs, Venetians, Spaniards, Dutch, and Portuguese, as well as Englishmen and others, perhaps saw and landed in Australia? Australia is too big a place to have been "undiscovered" for countless centuries. The only claim made by any reasonable man is that Captain Cook is the real discoverer of Australia in the sense that he stands alone as the one man who made good his discovery, and founded an indisputable title to possession for the British race.[35]

No new fact was needed to prove that. The point left in doubt until now has been whether Cook deliberately set sail to find Australia, and to take possession (as he did in 1770), or whether an accidental stroke of luck intervened when he was sailing home on his first voyage after

---

[35] Newcastle Academic Peter Hooker has recently critiqued this viewpoint for "downplaying" Cook's predecessors and denying the prior existence of the indigenous population. Arguably, it is a comparatively nuanced perspective that dismisses the very idea of a debate about "discovery", in the traditional sense, as irrelevant – *Editor.*

completing his task of observing the transit of Venus at Otaheite.

Most authorised accounts, including those of his associates on the *Endeavour*, seem to indicate that, in 1770, after Cook had sailed around New Zealand and charted those islands, he called his officers into consultation as to the course he should take to return from New Zealand to England. So far as one can gather, the impression is conveyed that, if the majority at that council had decided for an eastern route, via Cape Horn, that majority would have prevailed and Australia would have remained undiscovered during the return voyage of the *Endeavour* in 1770.

The records, however, seem to show that there was a close division in the council and it was left to Captain Cook to give a sort of casting vote. He decided on sailing westward, and in view of the Secret Instructions this was the only decision open to him.[36]

It must be remembered that the *Endeavour* sailed on the First Voyage on the 26th of August, 1768. When the council of officers was held, about 1st April, 1770, nineteen months of voyaging had been completed. The condition of the ship had naturally suffered during that long period. The sails and rigging, according to Sir Joseph Banks, had been rendered so bad by the gales off New Zealand that it was doubtful to many of the men who met in council whether the ship was in a condition to face hard gales and wintry weather in the passage home, especially by way of Cape Horn. A six months' supply of provisions, at two-thirds allowance, was all that remained on the ship and, in Cook's view, that was only enough for the shorter voyage westward which he favoured taking.

That view is given by Professor G. Arnold Wood in his *Voyage of the Endeavour*, published in 1926. This fine work deals only with the First Voyage. It analyses all previous publications on that subject, summarising the views of the writers, and presents an account in which

---

[36] If, as Hooker suggests, the instructions related to searching for the southern continent only to the east of New Zealand then Cook's personal intervention here is far more decisive than Carruthers realises. Whether Cook's decision was based on a desire to explore the westward ocean in pursuit of the elusive continent or more practical reasons can only be speculated at. As Carruthers will discuss, Tasman's map may well have given him good incentive to keep looking – *Editor*.

the deductions of the author are made with the authority of a skilled historian who had given intense study to the subject.

Wood, in his work, refers to Cook's instructions, and it is assumed by some in Australia that he had access to the additional instructions issued by the Admiralty on the 30th of July, 1768.

There were at least three sets of instructions issued to Cook after he received his appointment as commander of the expedition. They included:

i.   The Sailing Instructions – which are not of a secret character, at any rate amongst his officers and, after the voyage, were open to anyone;

ii. The first set of Secret Instructions – which were published with the original accounts of the voyage – and,

iii. The Secret Orders, P.R.O. Admiralty 2/1332, entitled, "Additional Secret Instructions to Lieut. James Cook, Commander of His Majesty's Bark *The Endeavour*" (as cited in chapter two herein).

I doubt the accuracy of the statement made by one or two in Australia, that Professor Wood had seen and studied this last-mentioned document. If he did study it he certainly missed the most important point of it. As I have pointed out in the preceding chapter, Cook's own copy of the Secret Instructions, including his *log*, were offered for sale in London in 1923 and were purchased on behalf of the Government of the Commonwealth of Australia. They reached Australia in the following year, and were kept by the Librarian of the Mitchell Library at Sydney for several years before they were handed over to the Library at the Federal Capital City of Canberra.[37]

Certainly, these documents were never published in Australia, even up

---

[37] Carruthers had played a central role in the choice of Canberra as national capital, for as New South Wales Premier he refused to hand over the land initially requested at Dalgety. Ironically, the electorates surrounding what became the A.C.T. had voted "no" at the federation referendums (Queanbeyan, Yass, Goulburn, Braidwood, Argyle) – *Editor*.

to the time of my writing, but were kept in a sealed case at the Mitchell Library. No one who saw or read them ever called public attention to the contents of the Secret Instructions.

The Admiralty possessed the original copy and, for the good reasons cited by me in chapter two, had never made public the contents until in 1928 they finally released this document.

It was not, however, until a meeting of the Royal Geographical Society was held on the evening of 17th December, 1928, that the full text of the Secret Instructions, together with the great import of that text, was made manifest to the public, through a paper by Professor J. Holland Rose, Professor of Naval History at Cambridge University. At that meeting the President of the Society, Colonel Sir Charles Close, said that most of the members of the Society did not before know the valuable information contained in those Secret Instructions for the First Voyage, which Professor Holland Rose had read to them that evening, and for which he certainly, for one, had never heard of. He said that he thought the appearance of them was due to Professor Rose's pertinacity in persuading the Admiralty to hunt for the records.

What leads me to believe that Professor Wood had never seen or, at any rate, never closely studied the Secret Instructions, is from reading the third chapter of his work (p. 82). Therein he states that "there was no suggestion that Cook might return by way of the east coast of New Holland, but that he was allowed to think things out for himself and was free to return to England by such route as he might think proper."

My readers may study the text of the Secret Instructions and then see for themselves how incorrect is Professor Wood's view. I refer again to passages in these Instructions to support my statement above.

They begin by reciting

"that the making discoveries of countries hitherto unknown, and the attaining a knowledge of distant parts which though formerly discovered have yet been but imperfectly explored, will redound greatly to the honour of this nation as a maritime power... and whereas there is reason to imagine that a continent, or land of great extent, may be found to the southward of the tract lately made by Captain Wallis in His Majesty's ship the *Dolphin* (of which you will receive a copy) or of any tract of any former navigators in pursuit of the like kind: You are therefore in pursuance of His Majesty's pleasure hereby required and directed to put to sea with the bark at your command, so soon as the observation of the transit of the planet Venus shall be finished, and observe the following instructions."

May I interpolate here and say that Captain Wallis in 1766-7 reached and discovered Tahiti, and after that effected nothing, and sailed home.

The Instructions the proceed, directing Cook:

"You are to proceed to the southward (from Tahiti) in order to make discovery of the continent above mentioned until you arrive in the latitude of 40°, unless you sooner fall in with it: but not having discovered it, or any evident signs of it, in that run, you are to proceed in search of it to the westward, between the latitude before mentioned and the latitude of 35° until you discover it or fall in with the Eastern side of the land discovered by Tasman and now called N. Zealand."

(Note: Tasmania, Victoria and N.S. Wales on the east coast of Australia lie between 30° and 42° S.)

Possession to be taken

Then the Instructions proceed to elaborate in detail what Cook was to do if he discovered the continent either in his run to the southward or to the westward. He was to "explore as great an extent of the coast as you can; carefully observing the true situation thereof both in latitude and longitude, the variation of the needle, bearings of headlands, height, direction, and course of the tides and currents, depths and soundings of the sea..."

Finally he was directed "to take possession of convenient situations in the country in the name of the King of Great Britain."

The document provides directions in case Cook should fail in finding the new continent before falling in with New Zealand. He was directed to observe the latitude and longitude of that land and explore its coast. He was to preserve sufficient stores and provisions for continuing his voyage homeward. He was specially directed that, in making surveys of islands and lands discovered in the course of his voyage (*Note:* This includes N. Zealand as islands), he was only to do so *"without suffering yourself to be thereby diverted from the object which you are always to have in view, the discovery of the southern continent so often mentioned."* Finally he was told: "In case of any emergency arising and not foreseen by the Admiralty, you are in all cases to proceed as, upon advice with your officers, *you shall judge most advantageous to the service on which you are employed."*

It is true that the Secret Instructions do not expressly mention New Holland, but the maps and charts accompanying them do so.

In order to understand matters accurately it must be realised that, in the eighteenth century and for centuries before that, the minds of men had been haunted by the idea that there was a great world to the southward, spoken of as *Terra australis incognita*, or the *Great Southern Continent*.[38]

Spain, in the Middle Ages, under a Papal Bull, was given dominion over all the unexplored oceans and the undiscovered islands or continent of such oceans. At that period, and for some time after, Spain was a great maritime nation, and the world owes a great deal to her navigating explorers like Columbus, Magellan, de Quiros, and Torres. They, in reality, were the discoverers of the southern ocean; but the English followed closely on the tracks of the Spaniards. Drake proved that, to the south of Cape Horn and the group of islands close by, there

[38] It is a little-remembered fact that both the word and the concept of Australia long predate its European discovery. The idea of the antipodes, continents on the far side of the world necessary to help to balance the globe, goes all the way back to the Ancient Greeks. Australia when it was actually discovered was something of a disappointment, possessing hardly any of the wealth or population of the Americas. That countless efforts of individual exertion have subsequently turned Australia into one of the most prosperous places in the world is thus all the more remarkable – *Editor.*

stretched open seas – the Antarctic and the South Pacific, including what we now know as the South Seas.

After the Spaniards came the Dutch, in the early part of the seventeenth century.[39] Tasman was the greatest explorer in the southern waters, and he nearly came to a solution of the problem of the southern continent when in 1642 he sighted Tasmania, and on a later voyage New Guinea. He left a map upon which he charted his discovery of Van Diemen's land and showed, north of it, what he described as New Holland. As a matter of fact, Torres in 1606 had also sailed along the south to New Guinea, so that Tasman had a knowledge of Tasmania on the south, and of New Guinea on the north. He was right when marking the intervening space as occupied by the east coast of what he termed New Holland. It was mere conjecture on the part of Tasman according to all evidence procurable or left by him or others. He had to fill in the gap, and he filled it in and made the map accordingly. It happens that it was a correct conjecture.

Cook had with him on the *Endeavour* a copy of this map of Tasman, and also of Dalrymple's chart and booklet. Therefore, when he was told in the Instructions

"You are to proceed to the southward in order to make discovery of the continent above mentioned until you arrive in the latitude of 40°, unless you sooner fall in with it: but not having discovered it, or any evident signs of it, in that run, you are to proceed in search of it to the westward, between the latitude before mentioned and the latitude of 35° *until you discover it* or fall in with the Eastern side of the land discovered by Tasman and now called New Zealand.

"If you discover the continent above mentioned, either in your run to

---

[39]   Some observers see our limited reverence for Tasman in comparison to Cook as a kind of negative British parochialism, but during the seventeenth century the Netherlands and England were intimately linked by both Protestantism and steady flows of people, goods, and ideas. John Locke wrote many of his famous and influential writings in exile in Amsterdam, hence much of what was valued about "Britishness" in the 19th and early 20th centuries owed something to the Dutch – *Editor.*

the southward, or to the westward, as above directed, you are to employ yourself diligently in exploring as great an extent of the coast as you can; carefully observing the true situation thereof both in latitude and longitude, the variation of the needle, bearings of headlands, height, direction, and course of the tides and currents, depths and soundings of the sea, shoal, rocks, etc…"

New Zealand was not known to be an island, but was thought to be a part of the mysterious southern continent. Cook properly assumed that he was not to consider his mission fulfilled when he had sailed around New Zealand and charted its coast, but that he still had the job before him of finding the southern continent in a region not further south than latitude 40° and between that and latitude 35°. That was the main purpose of his voyage: - not to find New Zealand, but to find the great southern continent: - and it was indicated to him that it would be north of 40°, not south of it, and, according to Tasman's map, somewhere to the westward of New Zealand, which Cook now proved to be two or three islands and in no way connected to New Holland or the supposed southern continent.

If he failed to discover the continent that he was to search for, he was given the option of returning home either around the Cape of Good Hope or Cape Horn, according as the condition of the bark and the state of provisions would admit. Also, he was instructed to observe, with accuracy, the situation of any islands that he might discover and take possession for His Majesty – and then come the very important words – *"without suffering yourself however to be thereby diverted from the object which you are always to have in view, the discovery of the Southern Continent so often mentioned."*

I think there was thus a deliberate suggestion in the directions that Cook should return by way of the east coast of New Holland, as shown on Tasman's map. In point of fact, when he sailed westward from New Zealand, it would be very hard for him to miss the east coast of New Holland, and Cook must have known this from Tasman's map.

Anyhow, after he had charted the position of New Zealand, following the words in his instructions – "without suffering yourself to be thereby diverted from the object which you are always to have in view" – Cook set out to find the east coast of New Holland (Australia). This he found and, carrying out the instructions of the Admiralty, charted from south to north. He took possession for the Government of Great Britain at two points – at Botany Bay and at Cook Town (the Endeavour River). Two things have been rendered very clear by the publication of this very important document; viz., that the observation of the transit of Venus at Tahiti was merely, to quote Professor Rose:

"a preliminary incident in the voyage, the real importance of which lay in the discovery and annexation of valuable posts in the southern continent. Here is the clue to all Cook's proceedings. He did not annex Tahiti because Captain Wallis may have previously annexed it (1767); but after surveying the coasts of New Zealand with a care which still makes his charts valuable, he annexed those islands, though he had himself proved that they were separated from the great southern continent. Very similar were his proceedings on the east coast of New Holland, re-named by him as New South Wales. After surveying it carefully from Cape Howe to Cape York he annexed the whole of this immense and valuable coast-line. He was careful to explain that this coast had not been discovered by Europeans – a statement which was correct; for Tasman in 1642 had touched only at the south part of the land, which he called Van Diemen's Land, and then stood away east towards New Zealand. Cook therefore was within his instructions when he annexed the whole of the east of New Holland."

I think it is clear from the foregoing facts in this chapter and in chapter two that the discovery and annexation of the east coast of New Holland was no mere accident on Cook's part, but was the result of his faithful adherence to the definite instructions which he was enjoined "not to suffer himself to be diverted from."

It only remains to be added that Cook was dispatched on his Second Voyage to clear up all doubt as to the existence of a southern continent inhabited or fit for habitation south of 40° S.[40] He explored deep down into the Antarctic Ocean; he and his crew enduring terrible privation and suffering, and succeeded in proving that the mysterious southern continent with its wealth and teeming population only existed in the imagination. That Second Voyage definitely confirmed the discovery by Cook in 1770 of the real southern continent of Australia.[41]

[40] There was still some hope of finding a *Terra Australis* that might live up to the grand expectations that had been concocted in European imaginations. When Cook landed at Botany Bay it had not been a "eureka" type moment, but that does not undermine the achievement in the way that *The Captain Cook Myth* appears to suggest – *Editor.*

[41] It was Matthew Flinders who applied the pre-existing name to the continent, after his circumnavigation proved its vastness – *Editor.*

4

French efforts to get a footing in Australia

When the copy of the painting in the Royal Palace at Versailles, referred to in a previous chapter, was received in Australia in 1911, I published some notes on the same, for the information of visitors to the National Art Gallery in Sydney (N.S. Wales), of which I was a trustee.

These notes recount how for a time the French Government made persistent efforts, not only to search for La Perouse, but to carry out the instructions of Louis XVI given when La Perouse sailed with his ships in 1785.

As these notes summarise the efforts of France to gain a foothold in Australia during the period from 1785 to 1802, and also show how these efforts were frustrated by the action of Governor King of New South Wales, I include them in this chapter just to show how the missing link in our title to Tasmania as part of the Australian Commonwealth was forged to complete our title by possession.

Captain Cook was not aware in 1770 of the fact that Van Diemen's Land (now Tasmania) was an island.

These notes are reproduced as follows:

"The historical value of the picture in the Versailles Gallery, especially to Australians, deserves to be fully explained now that the National Art Gallery of New South Wales possesses a copy made under the authority of the French Government.

"The rivalry between England and France in the eighteenth century was intense. In India, Wellesley had annihilated French influence and had consolidated British dominion. France had also lost to England her finest possessions in America, although she had retaliated with some success in helping the North American colonies to gain independence. The loss of these colonies led Englishmen to establish a new field for work in Australia, which had been visited by navigators from England, Spain, and Holland[42] prior to Cook's memorable and eventful visit of annexation in 1770.

"Eighteen years elapsed between Cook's first visit and Phillip's arrival with the earliest colonists in 1788. At the time of the despatch of Phillip's fleet the French King in 1785 despatched La Perouse on his voyage to circumnavigate and to specially explore the coasts of New Holland. His instructions were particularly clear as to exploring and surveying Terre de Diemen and the Baie des Tempetes, on the south of what is now called Tasmania. The records all go to show that France contemplated the formation of a settlement in this locality which Cook had not taken possession of, and to which England could lay no claim.

"The picture shows the King, Louis XVI, in the act of pointing out to La Perouse the course of the voyage, at the same time giving him his instructions. One can well imagine that the King is impressing on La Perouse his desire to establish the settlement on Van Diemen's Land, in order to check the English claim to undisputed possession of the new continent.

"On the 26th of January, 1788, La Perouse with his ships, the *Boussole* and the *Astrolabe*, arrived at Botany Bay, just five days after Phillip had anchored there, and *on that very day* the City of Sydney was founded; so that, to Australians, the interest attaching to this picture is intense, when one realises that on the very day from which we date the foundation of the City of Sydney and the Dominion of Australia, La Perouse arrived

---

[42] Dampier (England), de Quiros (Spain), Torres (Spain), The *Duyfken* (Dutch), Tasman (Dutch), amongst others - *Author.*

close by the site of the city in the course of carrying out his King's instructions.[43]

"On the 10th March, 1788, La Perouse left Botany Bay and sailed away to vanish as in the darkness of space. But in 1809, Captain Bunker of the ship *Venus* found buried on the coast of Tasmania, a bottle containing letters from La Perouse, dated one month after his leaving Botany Bay. The last letter, written by him (7th February, 1788) whilst in Botany Bay, noted his intention to proceed to the south coast of Van Diemen's Land.

"There can, therefore, be little doubt that La Perouse carried out his master's instructions, perhaps even to the extent of taking formal possession, as well as of surveying and exploring the coast of Tasmania.

"In 1792, Admiral Bruny D'Entrecasteaux was sent by the French National Assembly to search for La Perouse, and it is remarkable that he concentrated his endeavours on the south coast of Tasmania, as evidenced by the fact that that region is studded with names given by him to prominent parts, viz., Bruny Island, D'Entrecasteaux Channel, Recherche Bay, Port Esperance, Huon River, Cape Raoul, &c.

"On the 19th of October, 1800, Napoleon, as First Consul, sent Commodore Baudin in the *Georgraphe* and Captain Hamelin in the *Naturaliste* thoroughly and carefully to survey and explore the southern and eastern coast of Tasmania.[44] There is every ground for a strong suspicion that Napoleon's designs were to carry out the purpose of La Perouse's voyage, and to have the French standard raised in Van Diemen's

---

[43]   The claim that the Dominion of Australia was founded on January 26th could be seen as creating a teleology in which federation is viewed as inevitable. As a "Father of Federation" Carruthers had a vested interest in pushing this narrative, but it is worth noting that at the time this book was originally published a debate was raging as to whether "New South Wales Anniversary Day" should be appropriated as the national "Australia Day" or kept as an exclusive N.S.W. holiday in the manner in which it had long been celebrated – *Editor.*

[44]   At sixteen years of age Napoleon Bonaparte had applied to join La Perouse's expedition. Had he not been rejected, history would have been sent down a very different path – *Editor.*

Land, so that a French colony might be established there.[45] Confirmation of this belief is to be found from a reading of Peron's account of the voyage of this French Expedition, and from the 'Edinburgh Review,' August, 1810, and Rusden's 'Discovery of Port Phillip,' p.3.

"The early records of New South Wales give full details of how the French ships visited Port Jackson in 1802, and subsequently sailed for Tasmania on 18th November, 1802. Governor King, however, had been thoroughly aroused to the danger of allowing any act of annexation by the French officers, and he despatched the *Cumberland* to follow after the French frigates and to forestall any action on their part by formally hoisting the English flag on Tasmanian soil in their presence and notifying them that the territory belonged to England.

"On the 14th December, 1802, Lieut. Robbins, in command of the *Cumberland*, made a formal landing on King Island in full view of the French fleet and hoisted the English colours on a large tree, posted at the foot of the tree a guard of three marines with loaded muskets, fired three volleys, gave three cheers, and took formal possession of the island for King George.

"On 23rd December, 1802, or nine days after this event, Commodore Baudin wrote to Governor King, protesting against Lieut. Robbin's action and using these words, 'several days before Lieut. Robbins thought proper to hoist his flag above our tents, we had taken care to place in four prominent parts of this islands proof sufficient to show the priority of our visit.'

"I think that the pertinacity of the French in sending these two well-equipped expeditions under Admiral D'Entrecasteaux and Commodore

---

[45] The likelihood that Australia would have been colonised by another European power if the British had failed to do so is a point often brought up in the discussion of the morality of colonisation. Britain arguably had a significantly better record of treating its subject peoples humanely than other European powers, however this grants no immunity from scrutiny when it comes to her failures. If one wants to make the case that Britain was the "best of" or "least worst" of the colonisers, the stronger evidence is to be found in the political and economic success of her former dependencies – *Editor.*

Baudin within the space of ten years, and the concentration of the efforts of these expeditions on the south and eastern coasts of Tasmania, afford strong evidence that La Perouse's instructions directed him to lay the foundation of a French possession in what is now known as Tasmania.

"In light of these facts, with what interest must Australians regard the vivid portrayal in the painting, of the eventful moment when the French King confided to La Perouse those instructions which, if carried out and enforced, would have established a claim for the French upon Australian soil!"

I may add to these notes that in the Electorate of St. George, which I represented in the New South Wales Legislative Assembly from 1887 to 1908,[46] there resided a family, the children of Captain Dillon who, in 1827, at the Island of Vanikoro (later on called Mallicolo) in the New Hebrides group, discovered many relics of La Perouse's expedition. Captain Dillon obtained from the natives the story of the fate of La Perouse.[47]

His two vessels were wrecked on this island, and from the natives' story to Dillon, it appears that La Perouse built a two-masted vessel out of the remains of his ships and some months later sailed away in this craft down towards the Barrier Reef on the eastern shore of Queensland, probably on his way to Botany Bay or Sydney.

Again he met with disaster, as he encountered a hurricane and was wrecked on or near Temple Island on the Barrier Reef off Cape Palmerston, south of Mackay in Queensland. That was the end of this

---

[46]   Technically Carruthers had represented the multi-member electorate of Canterbury from 1887 until 1894, but this covered the territory that would then become the electorate of St. George – *Editor*.

[47]   Peter Dillon was a merchant seaman of Irish descent for whom the fate of La Perouse would become a lifetime obsession. He died in Paris in 1847 while still receiving a state-pension from the French Government; he even named one of his sons Napoleon - *Editor*.

ill-fated expedition and of its brave leader.[48]

The relics from Vanikoro and also from Temple Islands are now in the Musee de la Marine, Paris, and were identified as part of the original ships of the expedition.

Captain Dillon was rewarded for his efforts in clearing up the mystery of La Perouse's disappearance by being created a Chevalier of the Legion of Honour by the French Government. Many of his descendants are still alive in New South Wales and West Australia, and his son in 1908 informed me that his records and papers relating to La Perouse were then in his possession.

---

[48] Reports of the discovery of La Perouse's wreck have proven illusionary over the years. In 2017 Dr Garrick Hitchcock reasoned that it must be near Murray Island in the Torres Strait. This was based on an article, first recorded in an Indian newspaper, which documented that in 1818 two ships travelling from Sydney to Calcutta were wrecked there. The survivors found muskets and swords which were clearly European but not British.

Before La Perouse made his way to Botany Bay he had been in Samoa where twelve of his crew had been killed. The ill-fated voyage illustrates that Cook's success, as both a navigator and an ambassador dealing with native peoples, took a considerable amount of skill and luck - *Editor.*

Part II

Vindicating the good name and reputation of Captain Cook

5

Local opinion in the Hawaiian Islands somewhat unfavourable to Captain Cook. His last days and his death in Hawaii

I have visited the Hawaiian Islands five times, viz., in 1924, 1925, 1926, 1928 and 1929.

On my first visit, in 1924, I addressed a large gathering of the Pan-Pacific Club in Honolulu.[49] I made a passing reference to Captain James Cook, R.N., as a link associating Australia with the Hawaiian Islands, because he was the discoverer of both places during his voyages from 1769 to 1779. I also said that "all good Australians cherished the most grateful reverence for the memory of the great navigator to whom they owed their homeland, and I hoped that feeling was shared in by the people of the Hawaiian Territory."

To my great surprise I was told, next day, by a prominent citizen of Honolulu, that Australian sentiment regarding Captain Cook was not sympathised with by the local folk. "As a matter of fact," he said, "Cook and his crews behaved badly, committed great excesses contributing to his death and left behind a trail of evils which have afflicted the Hawaiian race ever since. There is no reason why Cook's memory should be venerated here."

---

[49] Carruthers' first visit to Hawaii was for a Food Conservation Conference, the islands even then being famous for exporting pineapples. Carruthers had become a hobby farmer in his semi-retirement and had a personal interest in this, but he also acted to promote Australian trade. He managed to lift an embargo on Australian fruits entering the islands and fell in love with the place – *Editor*.

That is the substance of what was said to me, though not the exact words.

Inasmuch as this statement was not the mere word of a "man in the street", but the expressed opinion of a prominent citizen of high repute and of great influence, I deemed it an obligation upon me to make the fullest inquiry into all available facts, so that I could satisfy myself whether this strong condemnation of one of the greatest heroes of English history was justified or not by actual facts.

I found, through inquiries amongst scores of most reputable men and women in Honolulu and in other parts of the Islands, that there was a considerable diversity of opinions. Most people told me that the views of my first informant were too strong and bitter, but that there was a substantial substratum of fact to warrant a somewhat milder condemnation of Cook. A considerable minority, however, differed from this, and expressed their opinion that only one side of the case had ever been put before either the Hawaiian or the American public; and that there was an absolute need for someone to put forward the other side from the narratives of Captain Cook and his officers, who had recorded, at the time, the actual occurrences of 1778 and 1779.

The most helpful man to whom I appealed was the late Professor Baillou, in charge of the Carter Library (a fine but little used historical library) in Honolulu. The only view he expressed was terse and to the point when he said:

"The people here do not know the facts and do not trouble to learn them. This library contains the facts from every available source. The conclusion one must arrive at on the facts shows Cook as a just and honourable man throughout all his voyages. His tragic death at Hawaii was due to misunderstandings on both sides, and was deeply regretted by the natives. Cook cannot be held responsible personally for consequences following on the breach of his orders by his men, nor can the Hawaiian people be blamed as a whole for the actions of those who broke their rules and created trouble.[50] Cook's death was a sad mishap, and those chiefly responsible for it were not Cook or his trusted officers or the Hawaiian rulers (King and Chiefs), but were those who disregarded authority and misbehaved themselves."

This view, from such a thorough student of all the available history of the events of 1778 and 1779 appertaining to Cook's visits to these Islands, I was compelled to adopt from the results of days of study in the Carter Library and from my investigations on the Islands and elsewhere.

Briefly stated, the admitted facts from all sources (English and Hawaiian) prove as follows:

Captain Cook made two stays at Kealakekua Bay, Hawaii, extending over some weeks in 1778 and 1779. He was made very welcome there by the King, the chiefs and the High Priest. Food and other necessaries were abundantly supplied to his ships, and Cook reciprocated with presents which were of no great value in our eyes, but were extremely valuable to the natives. Iron, for instance, was esteemed as priceless by these primitive people who had absolutely no local supply, but who needed it for their weapons and tools and for fishing hooks – these last being of constant use in obtaining their main supply of fish food. Some historians belittle the value of these gifts by Cook, forgetting that he had little else to offer, and that the value consisted in the scarcity of the supply to a people who sadly needed such gifts.

Cook's orders to his officers and crews rigorously forbade intercourse with the native women and excluded them from the ships. Dr. Samwell, the chief surgeon of the fleet, has left his written statement on this point, and has shown how he insisted on their being carried out and observed. Any sick person in the crews was strictly confined to the ships

---

[50] It is worth noting that throughout the book Carruthers is keen to exonerate the Hawaiian people from wrongdoing, as well as Cook. The central message of this section is that sometimes things are not anybody's fault, misunderstandings abound when new cultures come into contact with each other and communication is key. This underlying compassion grounds the piece and keeps it from descending into the outright hagiography it might otherwise have been – *Editor*.

so that no disease might be communicated to the natives.

But Dr. Samwell, as well as Captain Cook and Captain King, left on record a confession that, despite all their efforts, their well-laid plans miscarried, and some of the native women, as well as some of the members of the crew, contrived to set the regulations at naught. Human nature once more proved its frailty, and broke all commandments.

Cook and his officers did their utmost to quarantine disease, whilst some of their subordinates did their worst, and these found Hawaiian confederates in wrongdoing – and the wrong-doers prevailed as opportunity favoured.

To blame Cook for this is a cruel misjudgement of the man.

I am reminded of an inscription on an American tombstone:

He did his best: an angel could do no more.

Early in 1779, Cook sailed away from Hawaii with his two ships, and if the voyage had then ended, history would have no blame for Cook. But, unfortunately, a heavy storm occurred off the Hawaiian coast, and the main-mast of the *Resolution* was sprung so badly that the ships were compelled to return to Kealakekua Bay for repairs. Thus, in a few days, Cook and his fleet were unexpectedly back again, to the surprise of the natives.

Undoubtedly, the natives were none too pleased at this return, because it meant to them a further depletion of their food and supplies, already too low for their worst season – the island winter. Moreover, the King had left the locality just as Cook sailed. And so also had the principle chiefs. Authority was largely absent; and the natives were inclined to murmur at new exactions to help strangers. Hence strained relations soon manifested themselves, and "nerves" began to give way on both sides.

The High Priest exercised his authority, pending the arrival of the King and of the higher chiefs, who were notified of Cook's return. Some minor chiefs started pilfering and stealing, and their example led to more and more laxity from the common people. Quarrels ensued, and the strain intensified. Then a band of the more daring, under the lead of a minor chief, stole, at night, the ship's cutter, riding at the stern of the *Discovery*. Subsequently, it was admitted that this valuable boat was stolen and burnt for the sake of the iron and copper nails used in her structure. These nails were much coveted because of their value in making "fish-hooks." When the theft was reported to Captain Cook he was very angry, and, as the King arrived back about this time, Captain Cook saw him and requested him to use his authority to find and punish the culprits, and to secure the return of the stolen boat. The King did his best, but failed to secure any satisfactory result. Then Cook called a council of his officers and proposed to get the King on to his ship by a "ruse', and once there hold him as a hostage until the stolen boat was returned. He asked his second in charge, Captain Clerke, to go ashore the next day and invite the King to come aboard. From this moment things began to miscarry as if Destiny took a hand. Captain Clerke demurred to his undertaking the task because of his state of health. As a matter of fact, Clerke was then dying of consumption (he died at sea a few weeks later).[51] Clerke said to Cook: "There is no one else but yourself to carry out the task, and as I confess myself unequal to it I pray you to see the King and get him to accompany you aboard."

So it was agreed as Clerke suggested; and again things miscarried, since next day Clerke, who remained on the ship, gave an order to fire on a canoe which was evading a temporary blockade of the port, and the shot killed a friendly chief on the canoe just as Captain Cook was escorting the King to one of the ship's boats lying close to the southern shore of the bay.

Cook did not know that this killing had occurred, but the news was

---

[51] Consumption was the name then given to tuberculosis. This was a tragic end for a man who had joined the Royal Navy at just thirteen, fought in the Seven Years War, explored the Pacific on the crew of the H.M.S. *Dolphin*, and accompanied Cook on all three voyages. At age 38, decades of cramped ships, unhealthy living conditions and inadequately nutritious naval rations must have taken their toll – *Editor.*

carried by a swift native runner to an excited crowd of about 2,000 natives, who were suspiciously watching Cook and the King on their way to the boat. Immediately, the natives sized up the situation, and concluded that the killing of one of their chiefs, and the action of Cook in taking their King aboard one of his boats, were all parts of definite hostilities. Their state of mind at this moment can easily be imagined. They realised that the theft of the cutter was an unpardonable offence that needed some punishment. But the vast majority of the natives were innocent of any complicity in the theft. The killed chief was certainly innocent, and was known to be most friendly to Cook. The King was also innocent, and had striven to find the guilty parties. So they reasoned that they had to save their King from danger.

Quickly, Captain Cook realised the temper of the natives and said to Lieut. Phillips, who was walking by his side: "I won't take the King to the boat. There is too much angry excitement, and blood may be shed whilst this mood continues. I will tell the King to go back, and we will come for him when matters have quietened down."

So the King was told; and Cook and Phillips walked towards the boat, which was a score or so yards further on.

I have walked twice over the same path that Cook and the King traversed on that fatal day, and I have pictured in my mind exactly what took place. The path is rough, though on level ground – but, rough as it is now, so it was then, because of the broken lava which lies just as it remained when the flow cooled off hundreds of years ago. One has to pick one's steps in lava beds like this, and no doubt Cook and his companion had to look where they were walking instead of using their eyes to observe what the crowd of natives around them were doing.

Very few of the natives showed signs of attacking either of the two English officers. But, after a few paces towards the boat, an attack was made by a minor chief – probably the same one responsible for the theft. (On this point native historians are definite.)

Lieut. Phillips called Cook's attention to the contemplated attack on him, and Cook turned and fired at his assailant from one of his two pistols – loaded with small shot. The shot took no effect owing to a thick war mat worn by his assailant which was shot proof. Then the two officers walked on a few more paces, and again Cook's assailant advanced to attack him. This time Cook turned and fired a pistol loaded with ball, but he missed the attacker and hit instead another native who was peering over the other fellow's shoulder. Cook then told Phillips to hasten down to the boats and tell the marines not to continue firing their muskets into the crowd, as they had started to do. Cook emphasised his order by facing towards the boats – then about fifteen or twenty yards away from where he stood – and as he held up his hands with a gesture of "desist," he was both stabbed and bludgeoned to death from the rear.[52]

That is how Captain Cook died. Brave as a lion to the last, but withal prompted by his humane instincts to prevent bloodshed. His fault on that day was that he overrated his own personal influence with the natives, and trusted too much in his own ability to carry out his plans. Of course, he did not foresee the killing of the friendly chief who had violated the blockade from probable ignorance. In point of fact, Cook died without a knowledge of this occurrence. Military and naval men may find fault with Captain Cook's actions, because he was carrying out what was technically "an act of war" without taking steps for adequate

---

[52]   Vancouver, in the account of his Voyages (Vol. III), speaking of meetings with the King (at that time King Kamehameha) and with other chiefs at Hawaii, was asked by one of them if he would care to see Pareea, the chief (as they said) who killed Captain Cook. They told him that after the death of Cook Pareea was ostracised by all the other chiefs and made an outcast. They said that the man was suffering a great remorse for his deed. Vancouver thought he was acting the better part to show forgiveness towards the man, and he therefore agreed to meet him.

(I can find no account of the actual meeting or of what took place. Pareea was the Chief concerned in both the stealing of oars and later on the stealing of the cutter of the *Discovery*. He, of all men, had most to fear if due punishment was meted out for these thefts. Hence he stirred up the angry passions of the crowd on the day of Cook's death.) – *Author*.

support in case anything went wrong with his design.[53]

But once before in Tahiti, when somewhat similar offences had been committed by the natives, Cook induced the ruling chief to come aboard his ship, and then – having got him there – he sent word to the natives that he would keep him as a hostage until they made restitution. In that case everything went through according to plan, and the natives "came to heel" without any further trouble.

But in Hawaii "the pitcher was taken once too often to the fountain" and was broken.

With these facts established as they are and amply so, by every authentic account, one may acquit Captain Cook absolutely of any wrongdoing, and may regard the tragedy of that day as the result of over-confidence on the part of Cook, and of regrettable misunderstandings on the part of the mass of the Hawaiians. Of course, there were some villains in this case – to wit, those who stole the ship's cutter and who feared punishment for their offence, and who were, in the end, Cook's actual murderers.

In my summing up of the facts in the foregoing narrative, I have striven to be fair and impartial. At any rate, I have accepted the narratives of eye-witnesses, both English and native, and have only excluded the few exaggerated stories palpably invented or concocted, long after the event, by writers with no first-hand knowledge of what actually occurred.

---

[53] Cook's actions may well have been more misguided than Carruthers admits, however trying to peacefully rectify the situation given the language barrier and other limitations did pose an intractable problem. Cook's real genius was that he had so far gotten away with such shows of confidence and bluff. There must have been a powerful charisma to the man who could communicate so much without speaking directly, though he was said to have some knowledge of what were generally related native languages - *Editor.*

6

The moulding of unfavourable opinion regarding Captain Cook largely attributable to the publication in America and in London in 1781 of the accounts of John Ledyard (an American, who was corporal of marines on the Resolution), which forestalled the official account

Now to deal briefly with some of the stories referred to in the previous chapter:

In the first place it must always be remembered that at the time of Cook's voyages the American Revolution was in operation. Very strained relations existed between England and the American Colonies, or States, then and for long after. A fratricidal strife is always more bitter than one between races with no blood ties. To-day, we of the British race cannot correctly appreciate the American feeling in 1779 and following years. In America it does not take a British visitor long to perceive the vast difference between the American and British points of view on the War of Independence, over 150 years ago. It is still an article of faith in the American creed to teach their school children the American view of the Revolution and War of Independence. Societies such as "The Sons and Daughters of the Revolution" are very strong institutions, and they keep green the memories of those days long ago:

and, of course, there is more or less of a bias towards the rights of the case apportioned liberally to the American and the wrongs of the case apportioned with similar liberality to the British.[54]

Naturally, however, the strong feeling of bitterness has died down like a fire whose embers still glow. But when Captain Cook was pursuing his peaceful mission of exploration from 1768 to 1779, the passions of the American people were at their height – bitterly hostile to Britain and all her naval and military officers. France was at war with England at the same time, but she was chivalrous enough to issue directions to her naval commanders that they should not treat Cook or his ships as enemies, but as neutrals engaged on humane and scientific work. Benjamin Franklin was the Minister for the American State at the French Court, and he proposed to his Government to issue a similar letter exempting Captain Cook's expedition from hostile treatment. At first the American Congress delayed in ratifying Franklin's proposal, explainable because his letters of advice were belated in reaching them, and the Constitutional Congress had not been called into existence; but ultimately that body did ratify. On this point I refer readers to the published statement of Edmond S. Meany of the University of Washington appearing in the Washington *Historical Quarterly* of April, 1929, extracts from which are to be found in chapter twenty herein.

On Cook's vessels was an American – a corporal of the marines – named Ledyard. He was with Cook's fleet during the events at Hawaii, and claimed later on to be one of the party which landed with Captain Cook on the fatal day when he died.

Soon after Cook's death, Ledyard deserted from the British Navy, and, of course, was liable to severe penalties if captured. He spent some years

---

[54] This organisation still exists and boasts George W. Bush as one of its members. It only emerged in the late nineteenth century however, hence it reflects a tide of nationalism similar and simultaneous to that which Carruthers himself was a part of in Australia – *Editor.*

abroad in Russia and elsewhere but eventually reached America again.[55] Then two or more years after the events of 1779 he told his story of Cook's last days and death to some of his fellow townsmen. Probably this was the first news of the particulars associated with Cook's death to reach American ears. The news was worth recording; so a committee was formed, and funds raised to publish Ledyard's story. In justice to this committee, it must be said that they exhibited some sense of justice to the dead. The editor they appointed to supervise the publication has left it on record that a revision of Ledyard's statements was necessary because, after the lapse of some years, from February, 1779, to the date of Ledyard's statements in America, his memory seemed to be at fault, especially as he had no writings or notes of his own to refresh his memory. (Note: He had, however, access to and procured the brief interim account issued by the Admiralty, and he copied several pages of this.)[56] "A proneness to exaggeration on his part," was also noted by the editor, and had to be corrected.

On the whole, Ledyard's statements contained a considerable amount of detail more or less in accord with the brief Admiralty version

---

[55] Ledyard arrived in Huntington Bay, Long Island Sound, U.S.A., in December, 1782, on a British man-o'-war. He obtained seven days' leave to visit his mother, "evidently intending to return no more" (*Life and Travels of John Ledyard*, by Jared Sparks, p. 168). He saw his mother and on the expiry of his leave he deserted from the British Navy and went to Hartford (p.170). Here he remained from the 1st January to about the 1st May, 1783, "in which period he wrote the *Journal of Cook's Voyage*" (p.171). This, therefore, was compiled two years after the termination of the voyage.

Yet it is stated that in 1781 he had published in London anonymously his account of Cook's voyage. As a matter of fact, after his arrival in England, in 1780, his papers (together with those of other officers and men) were taken away. Notwithstanding this he contrived to get into touch with a publisher and published his account of 1781.

Later, Ledyard went to Russia and stayed there for some time. He was arrested there by order of the Empress and expelled from the country. He was then taken across the border to Poland, and was told he would never be permitted to return to Russia. The reason given was that he was regarded as a French spy – *Author.*

[56] The 1781 anonymous published account that Carruthers ascribes to Ledyard has also been ascribed to John Rickman, second lieutenant on the *Discovery.* Their overlap may well be due to the fact that Ledyard used the anonymous account to fill in the gaps in his memory. If Rickman was the source then the charges against Cook (agreeing to be worshipped and belligerently tearing down the temple fence) may have a more substantial basis than Carruthers allows, see Howard Palmer, 'Captain James Cook', *The Geographical Journal*, Vol. 77, No. 5 (May, 1931), pp. 491-496 – *Editor.*

aforementioned, a document which would hardly be available except to a few Americans during the disturbed period of and following the war. But Ledyard, in his story, gave a twist to minor events occurring, or alleged by him to have occurred, in the last few days prior to Cook's death. He claimed that excesses occurred at the hands of the English such as vandalism and the desecration of holy places; also that violence was used to a chief and to several Hawaiians. He urged that this conduct led up to hostile feelings against Cook and his crews – ending finally in Cook's death, when he sought, with force, to make a hostage of the King.

There is just a scintilla of fact – no more - in these statements, and a great amount of bias in the way Ledyard twists and magnifies the least things against Cook and his associates.

The alleged vandalism consisted in the using of an old fence round the temple at Kealakekua Bay for firewood on the ships. Captain King, in his published narrative, written day by day as the events occurred (and not years after, as in Ledyard's case), fully explains this. The next chapter gives King's statement from his journal and also deals further with this matter.

An educated native historian, Kamakau, in a publication wrote that – "the outer fence of a temple was not regarded as sacred, nor the idols that were fixed thereon. As they became old and decayed, they were used as firewood." (See also letter of I.G. Thrum in next chapter.)

Of course, Ledyard would not know anything about Captain King and the High Chief and their talk, so that possibly when he saw the fence and an odd effigy being carried to the ships, he would gossip with others as ill-informed as himself, and conclude that Captain King had forcibly commandeered the stuff. In point of fact, Ledyard, in his account, states that Captain Cook himself took the wood and the idols, and nearly caused a "fracas" thereby. Yet it is clear from Captain King's account that Cook was not on shore at this time, but had left the matter to King. Ledyard also refers to the priest Kirikiki as being present, whereas King makes it clear that the priest was Kooa. Knowing little or nothing of the facts of the matter, Ledyard came to unwarranted conclusions. Of course, allegations of this kind by Ledyard would be accepted by an American audience, and a construction be put upon them to the injury of Cook's reputation. Mark that the audience was in a fit state of feeling against the British to accept any such story. Atrocity-mongering is good propaganda in war time. But the Americans were to be excused because that was practically the only detailed version of Cook's last days available to them. The Admiralty was to blame for this because they allowed several years to elapse before publishing the *full* account from Captain King's *log* and from other accounts of eye-witnesses. A brief summary was published earlier which gave little or no details and certainly did no justice to Cook. See also extracts from the letters of the Poet, William Cowper, published with his poems and cited in chapter eight herein.

The other so-called "excesses" were not open to such a term. When Cook and his officers found that oars, ironwork, small boats, etc., etc., were being forcibly taken by a chief and a few of his retainers, they naturally took steps to recover their property. No one was killed or maimed or wounded in the course of recovering the stolen property; but in one case an irate bluejacket used the broad blade of an oar to teach sense to a thief; and in another case an officer smote the mischievous chief (Pareea) on his back with either the scabbard or the flat side of his sword. That is about the sum total of the alleged excesses and outrages.

The trouble with the native women and the crew was always there; and a man like Ledyard, who held no commissioned rank, would probably see and know more about that than Cook or his officers, from whom the misbehaviour would be concealed through fear of punishment. Ledyard's story being, for years, practically the only source of information in the hands of the Americans, contributed very largely to the creation of a very wrong impression in their minds of Captain Cook and his officers and men.

There is, however, a valuable piece of evidence in the British records made at the time concerning Ledyard's own reputation, and it is this:

Captain Burney (a lieutenant under Cook on his last two voyages) left on record some salient facts regarding him. He states that Ledyard had been a candidate for the office of lexicographer to the expedition, and presented a specimen of his power of descriptive writing to help forward his application to Captain Cook. Captain Clerke dealt with the applicants for the post of lexicographer, and rejected Ledyard's application. Burney, who apparently was associated with Captain Clerke in dealing with the applications, says that one of the reasons for rejecting Ledyard was that "his ideas were thought to be too sentimental, and his language too florid. He was considered to be a man of ardent disposition, with a passion for lofty sentiment and description."

Thus we obtain the testimony of one of Ledyard's superior officers written at the time when the Third Voyage was being undertaken – and written with no motive except to record the reasons for refusing Ledyard's application for the post of lexicographer. That testimony should convince any impartial person that Ledyard was rejected as a possible writer of the records of the voyage because of his tendency to colour highly his writings with florid language and with sentimental description. That is a mild way of suggesting that he was prone to exaggerate, and was unreliable in describing ordinary occurrences. Even the Americans who edited and published his biography (on p.49 of that work), refer to his defective memory of the events of 1779 and his efforts "to revive his memory by reading a brief sketch of Cook's Voyages published in London by the Admiralty, from which he made extracts and copied several pages." The biographers then candidly admit: "A narrative thus drawn up must be in many respects imperfect." They also refer to his "proneness of exaggeration."

Yet it is on this narrative of Corporal Ledyard that American opinion of Captain Cook and his last days has been based for the last 140 years. What that American opinion is, can be gathered from this extract from the most authoritative work of reference published in America – *The New International Encyclopaedia*, 1903, Vol. IX, p.173, which reads as follows:

"In 1567 Mendena located scientifically the position of Kauai, in the Hawaiian Islands, as has been shown by Spanish scholars; but it was reserved for Captain James Cook, while on his third voyage in the Pacific, to find this group in 1778. After returning from the Bering Strait, to pass the winter in Hawaii, *he abused the hospitality of the natives, and in a squabble lost his life.*"

That false statement is a relic of Ledyard's story, and is not based on authentic history.

Hawaiian out-rigger canoes of the type which Captain Cook saw in 1779.

7

The alleged worship of Captain Cook as the god Lono at Kealakekua Bay, Hawaii, early in 1799; how the story began from native sources; the facts as recorded by Captain King

When Cook arrived in the Islands in 1778 at Kauai, and in 1779 at Hawaii, he was received with ceremony by the priests and natives. The common people prostrated themselves before him at both places, and at Hawaii the High Priest conducted him and Captain King into the temple alongside the landing-place.

As to the charge against Captain Cook "that he permitted the Hawaiians to worship him as a god," – it appears to me that there is a very simple and conclusive answer to this.[57]

The evidence on this matter comes from two very distinct sources, each of which has a different view-point. Undoubtedly, the native versions were founded on *their understanding* of the ceremonies and rites

---

[57] It reveals much about how perspectives change over time that this charge against Cook is so vital to the author. In our secular age Cook's involvement in the religious ceremonies might be thought a necessary way to engage with and befriend his hosts, which would have been offensive if it did cross the line into outright worship, but which was otherwise shrewd. But to a more Christian era the sacrilege that might thus be committed was dire, to the extent that it might be believed that it had even have directed "fate" against Cook – *Editor.*

with which Captain Cook was welcomed at the *heiau* (or temple) at Kealakekua Bay. This temple is close to the present village of Napoopoo (Kakooa in King's Journal) and very near the well where Cook's vessels took in water. I visited this place in 1924, 1925, 1926 and 1928, and studied the lay-out of the temple carefully.

Naturally, the priests, whose influence was great with the natives and was exerted favourably on behalf of Captain Cook and his crew, would seize the opportunity readily available to them when Cook landed at the small beach about fifty yards away from the temple, so that any ceremony of welcome could be proceeded with *instanter*. It suited the purposes of the priests to play up to the natives' belief that Cook was their old super-man *Lono*.

Lono, in actual life, long prior to Cook's coming, had been a popular chief in Hawaii. In a fit of anger he had killed his wife; and suffered great remorse for this deed. He became a changed man in his mode of life, and devoted himself to kindly deeds amongst the natives. He led them in their games and taught them new ones. His kindness and sport-loving habits endeared him to the people. For some reason he wished to leave the island. So he caused a large canoe to be built and arranged to go away. The natives tried to dissuade him from that purpose. He persisted, however, and told them that some day he would return in a large ship with a small forest of trees in her and he would come back to the Bay of Rainbows (Kealakekua Bay).

So he sailed away; and the natives held to the belief that he would fulfil his promise. After he had gone they raise him to the rank of a god, just as in some Christian Churches, men and women, conspicuous in good works, after their deaths, are canonised as Saints. As Christians do, the Hawaiians fixed a day or period of veneration for their saint or god. *Lono*'s days were those following the opening of the New Year.

The gods of the Hawaiian differ from our conception of a God. There was no god whom they loved. They feared them, and propitiated them by either human or other sacrifices, by gifts to their temples and priests, and by rigid *tabus* or periods of penance or abstention. *Lono*, of all their gods, was the only one for whom they cherished a feeling of affection, and in the *Lono* Saint Days (a term that most nearly indicated the fact) they offered no human sacrifices to him, but only those of dumb animals.

Thus the legend of *Lono* had led to his ultimate worship as a god, and his return was looked forward to. So when Cook and his ships arrived, the opportunity of playing upon the credulity of the people and of thereby improving the occasion was too great for the priests to let pass by; more especially as they possibly believed in the old superstition, which in its fulfilment would add to their influence and power. Thus it came about that Cook was hurried into the temple for ceremonies and rites which needed little or no rehearsal or preparation, because the scene was ready, and lay close to where Cook had landed on the neighbouring beach.

Events might have happened otherwise, if the necessity had arisen for the chief participator – Cook – to be taken to some other place at a distance. Then, explanations would have become necessary, and perhaps a real understanding of the nature of the ceremonies and of the need to visit another place would have been a condition precedent.[58] In such an event Cook's consent would have had to be sought and assuredly he would have had to be satisfied as to what it all meant before such consent would have been forthcoming.

But it is quite clear from the narratives of both sides – those of the natives and of the British officers – that the whole business was of an extempore and unrehearsed character. It was carried through without the least consultation with Cook or any of his officers, and without any explanation of the nature or need of the ceremony. It was conceived solely in the minds of the native priests, who hurried the proceedings through, without the least reference to Cook's wishes.

It appears to have been quite clear in the native mind that the ceremony represented a welcome to their old god *Lono*, who was coming back to them, reincarnated in the flesh. Especially would this be so, when their

---

[58] It is worth noting that Carruthers was a solicitor and his legalistic training often comes to the fore as he examines the evidence gathered herein – *Editor.*

priests gave the lead and fostered the idea.

This view of the natives was handed down as an historical fact, by them, to the missionaries who came some few years later on. In the natives' mind there would be not the least doubt as to the facts as they understood them. The missionaries in their turn would accept this oft-reiterated version until they too adopted it – and would judge Captain Cook accordingly. There was no one at hand to question this version or to put the story in the way that Cook and King regarded it; and, in fact, had recorded it on the very day of the occurrence.

Thus, it happened that as the missionaries became the early historians of Hawaiian discovery by the white people, they gave prominence to the native version. Moreover, these worthy men in the prosecution of their labours in bringing the Christian faith and its teachings into the life of an idolatrous people would naturally emphasise the wrong done by any human being who assumed a title to be venerated and worshipped as a god – heathen or otherwise. Their mission was to destroy and condemn idolatry and not to condone it. They were rigid Puritans and Calvinists, of a type unknown to-day.

Unfortunately for the reputation of Captain Cook, this native or missionary view became stereotyped as a correct interpretation of the actions and motives of *all* who participated in the ceremony of those fateful days.

But, on the other hand, there is, and always has been in existence from those days, the published narrative of Cook's own officers who were present on this memorable occasion.

Captain King in his Journal describes with completeness the facts of the matter according to the understanding of the white man. The account is to be found at considerable length in Book V, Vol. VII, of *Cook's Voyages* (pp.4 *et seq.*).

He (King) refers to the fact that Cook's ships moored at the northern side of Kealakekua Bay (Karakakooa in King's Journal) about a quarter mile from Napoopoo (or Kakooa in King's version). He speaks of the fine sandy beach with a *morai* (temple) at one end and a small well of fresh water at the other end.

Thus he lays the scene exactly as one finds it to-day, except the *morai*, or *heiau*, as it is now called, is in the process of demolition by age and neglect, after being several times reconstructed or reconditioned.

Then King proceeds to speak of the respect that was paid to Cook and the peculiar ceremony with which he was received. He describes fully the ceremony within the *morai* or temple, and Captain Cook's repugnance, first of all at being presented with a dead pig, placed in his arms, and next his discomfort in keeping his hold on the rotten pieces of scaffolding on which he was led. He goes on to describe how Cook suffered himself to be directed by Priest Kooa throughout the whole of the ceremony, and also his manifest objection to being fed with the chewed-up flesh of a hog.[59]

King says that the ceremony was ended as soon as possible, after which Cook went outside and distributed some pieces of iron and other trifles amongst the people, with which they seemed highly gratified.

Cook and his men then went on board and Captain King states:

"We immediately went on board, our minds full of what we had seen, and extremely well satisfied with the good disposition of our new friends. *The meaning of the various ceremonies with which we had been received, and which, on account of their novelty and singularity, have been related at length, can only be the subject of conjectures, and these uncertain and partial: they were, however, without doubt, expressive of a high respect on the part of the natives; and, as far as related to the person of Captain Cook, they seemed approaching to adoration...*"

It should be remembered that when Cook arrived at this Bay the whole place was under a *tabu* imposed by those in authority. It was the New

---

[59] Being thought of as a god was evidently not as enjoyable as one might assume, but considering this was the third of his voyages, Cook must have had ample practice at feigning politeness during unfamiliar cultural practices – *Editor*.

Year and that period was dedicated to the memory of *Lono*, and the *tabu* was associated with the veneration of *Lono*. This *tabu* meant that ordinary daily life was under strict restraint, and the priests were left in charge. The commonfolk were, therefore, under a tribal and religious restraint which involved prostrations when they walked abroad or approached their priests or chiefs or certain places. It meant possibly death for a common man if he violated the *tabu*. Hence the unusual demeanour of the people as Cook first met them.

As he was regarded as a visitor of high rank and protected by the priests, the natives had to prostrate themselves as he passed, not necessarily as an act of worship but in accordance with their laws and customs. It is obvious that to them Cook was of the Chiefly rank.

Throughout the whole of the narrative of Captain King, it is made manifest that neither he nor Captain Cook understood the ceremony in which they had participated to be more than the custom of the country when the natives desired to honour a guest of rank. He makes it clear, too, as I have emphasised, that no explanation was vouchsafed as to what the ceremony meant. No interpreter was there to enlighten Cook as to the real nature of the ceremony and of the words used in it by the High Priest. One cannot ignore the material fact that the actual participants in the ceremony were mutually ignorant of the language of each other. That fact is overlooked in the local narratives.

8

Continuing *re* the alleged worship of Captain Cook; Corporal Ledyard's version analysed; William Cowper's (the poet's) hasty conclusion; the early American missionary view; the Rev. W. Ellis's account; and Dr. Fornander's criticism

It is hardly necessary to labour the case by citing all of Cook's officers and men as witnesses on his behalf. Suffice it to say that, with little if any exception, no support is given to the story that Cook was worshipped as a god at Hawaii.

The exception is Ledyard, Corporal of Marines on the *Resolution*. If he had any bias it was certainly not towards Cook or the English – rather the contrary. Anyhow, his Memoirs (published about three years after Cook's Third Voyage ended) contain reference to the ceremony at the temple when Cook landed at Kealakekua Bay.[60]

It is not clear that Ledyard claims to have seen and heard all that he describes of the proceedings on shore on this occasion. It is very probable that he writes more from hearsay than as an observer.

Ledyard professes to describe what took place within the temple, but the accuracy of his account is at once open to question, because as he himself says: "Cook was then conducted to the *morai*, a sacred enclosure which none but the Chiefs and their attendants were allowed to enter." How then, could Ledyard claim to a knowledge of what transpired there? King, we *do* know, accompanied Cook within the enclosure. King was regarded as a chief of high rank, and the natives deemed him to be the son of Captain Cook. These three persons – the Hawaiian Priest and Captains Cook and King – alone were present within the temple, except when a few attendants entered on necessary duties.

---

[60] Author's note: It is difficult to quote Ledyard definitely in a single passage relating to any one event, for the reason that from 1781 to 1824 there appeared about six editions of his story and also his memoirs (compiled by Jared Sparks), and in each of these there is a variance in his statements, amounting in some cases to absolute contradictory accounts.

For instance, in one edition there appears the statement quoted by me, that Cook sought to buy the temple fence from a priest, whom Ledyard calls Kirikiri, and that eventually Cook ordered it to be seized with the idols and carried to the boats, with an angry crowd of protesting natives around. In the 1781 edition he says that the natives offered this fence to Cook for firewood.

Two or more varying accounts also occur in different editions relating to the ceremonies in the temple, when High Priest Kooa and captains King and Cook were present. In some of these the only implication against Cook is that he permitted a *tabu* to be placed on the site given to him for a house or hut near the temple; in others worship as god is implied. Whether Cook consented is definitely not asserted in the edition before me.

With so many confusing accounts it is difficult to quote Ledyard without the risk of being called to account, and confronted with a totally different version by Ledyard.

Sometimes, also, Jared Sparks, or some other editor or compiler, records *his* impressions of what Ledyard said; and thus gives rise to further confusion.

In the 1781 edition the editor says in his "advertisement" (*sic*): "The Editor does not take upon him to say that the Journalist has not upon some occasions exaggerated circumstances, or that his prejudices have not sometimes prevailed over his candour in representing characters…" He adds that some errors of the Editor himself "have arisen from haste and some from misunderstanding of the Journalist's orthography, who, being at a great distance, could not be consulted without retarding the press."

There is not much need to dispose of Ledyard's account of the proceedings within the temple enclosure and its 10 feet stone walls. His conclusions are second-hand and not those of a privileged eye-witness like Captain King.

What he did see, and is entitled to relate, is the behaviour of the common people (the natives) outside, as Cook passed through their lines. There were abject prostrations on all sides by these natives, and Ledyard himself provides the reason, when he says:

"The people were under the restriction of a *tabu* which no native dare violate, being restrained by the superstitious fear of offending the *Atuas* or invisible spirits of the Island. This caution surprised Cook a little, as he had not witnessed it among the natives of the other South Sea Islands. It appeared reasonable and Cook consented to it, not foreseeing the mischiefs to which it would ultimately lead."

Ledyard (so his biographer says) considered it to be the origin of all the disasters that followed. One of these "mischiefs" was contributed to – if not originated by – Ledyard's method of presenting his story.

What Cook "consented to" in Ledyard's version is none too clear from his various stories in his writings. He states no facts to support any charges that Cook was a consenting party to his supposed deification. Apparently Ledyard understood even less about the real nature of the ritual and ceremony than did Captains Cook or King, who were within the temple, from which Ledyard and others were excluded. Yet neither Cook nor King understood them, and in their Journals they recorded that fact.

Ledyard is correct in his interpretation of the *tabu* and its observance as an inviolable custom of the country on which they had landed. But, to say that "the proceedings of this day were the origin of all the disasters that followed," is merely in keeping with his disposition as described by Captain Burney.

It is clear that Ledyard's intention was to convey the impression that

Cook *was* a consenting party to all that took place on this day, viz., the temple ceremony, the superstitious attitude of the natives and the religious *tabu* which no native dared violate, and the *tabu* placed over ground assigned to the expedition for a shore house.

Ledyard was the first white man to set this story going.

It would be charitable perhaps to excuse Ledyard because of "his passion for ardent sentiment and florid description" which lost him the appointment as lexicographer to the Fleet. Possibly he did not mean to charge Cook with actually consenting to being worshipped as the god *Lono*. However that may be, the story with all its implications got its start from Ledyard's writings.

Thus we have the natives' story of their view that they believed Cook to be their god *Lono* and worshipped him as such; and we have one white man's (Ledyard's) story, implying that Cook lent himself to the deception.

It does not matter much who and what Ledyard was. He started this story – just as one old woman started the story of the "Three Black Crows" by an unwarranted exaggeration.[61] And Ledyard's story grew in the telling and was made to fit with the natives' stories – *even though they had acquitted Cook of any understanding of the matter.*

Now we come to happenings in London, England, that helped the lie along without anyone intending it.

After the return of the *Resolution* and *Discovery*, in 1780, the Admiralty called in all the diaries, journals, and papers of the officers and crew, in order to prevent imperfect accounts of the voyage being presented to the public. The Admiralty, however, published an abbreviated and interim account of the voyage, before 1781, but did not issue the official account until 1784, or five years after Cook's death.

---

[61] This was a famous fable about information being passed on incorrectly, teaching a similar lesson to the children's game "whispers". It is now used in finance to describe markets trending downwards over several days – *Editor.*

Ledyard secured one of the abbreviated accounts when published. He published his memoirs at Hartford, U.S.A., in 1783. But in 1781 there was published in London, *John Ledyard's Journal of Captain Cook's last voyage, faithfully narrated from the original MSS*. It is described as "anonymous."[62]

It was a surreptitious publication anticipating the authorised Admiralty account by more than two or three years. It is certain that it was written by Ledyard, Corporal of Marines of the *Resolution*. A Dublin edition was published of the Ledyard book in 1781; a new edition in London in 1785, and a French version in Paris in 1782.

Certainly while the Admiralty slumbered on its records, Ledyard and his friends were busy and had the field to themselves for three years.

The British public was eager for all and any news about Captain Cook and his last voyage, and when Ledyard brought his information a ready and credulous audience awaited him.

Among the most interested was William Cowper, the poet.[63] He had closely followed the news of Cook's first and second voyages and had commented, in his poems – as in Book I of "the Task"- and letters, on incidents in these.

On 8th October, 1784, Lord Dartmouth lent to Cowper some volumes giving an account of Cook's last voyage. That night he started to read the volumes and the next day wrote to his friend the Rev. John Newton a letter, from which I quote. It is palpable that Cowper had read Ledyard's account by the references in his letter.

"...The reading of those volumes afforded me much amusement and, I hope, some instruction. No observation however forced itself upon me with more violence than one, that I could not help making on the

---

[62] Again, this may not have been Ledyard. Though Carruthers' arguments about the validity of "consent" when there were so many barriers to understanding remains valid regardless of the originator of the account– *Editor.*

[63] William Cowper is now perhaps best remembered for the support he gave to the abolitionist movement. Martin Luther King Jr. was known to quote him extensively – *Editor.*

death of Captain Cook. God is a jealous God, and at Owhyhee the poor man was content to be worshipped.[64] From that moment the remarkable interposition of Providence in his favour was converted into an opposition that thwarted all his purposes. He left the scene of his deification, but was driven back to it by a most violent storm, in which he suffered more than in any that had preceded it. When he departed he left his worshippers still infatuated with an idea of godship, consequently well disposed to serve him. At his return he found them sullen, distrustful, and mysterious. A trifling theft was committed, which, by a blunder of his own in pursuing the thief after the property had been restored,[65] was magnified to an affair of the last importance. One of their favourite chiefs was killed too, by a blunder. Nothing, in short, but blunder and mistake attended him, till he fell breathless into the water, and then all was smooth again. The world indeed will not take notice, or see, that the dispensation bore evident marks of Divine displeasure; but a mind I think in any degree spiritual cannot overlook them. We know from truth itself, that the death of Herod was for a similar offence…"

All this was a re-hash of Ledyard's fanciful story.

Cowper afterwards published his Letters in an edition of his poems, and so spread abroad his view. I have the clearest evidence that Cowper's published letters reached the missionaries in Hawaii. That evidence is, that copious extracts from them are printed in a newspaper, The Friend, published in Honolulu. My photostat copy from the Archives, Honolulu, is dated 1 October, 1862, and is Vol. 19, thus pointing to a continued publication from 1840 or earlier. This paper was issued under the auspices of the missionaries.

Probably Cowper's unconsciously mischievous misrepresentation did not long deceive the English public when they read Captain King's

---

[64] Cowper was famously wracked by existential dread and a fear of damnation, so much so that he was once locked up on the grounds of "insanity" as he grappled with his religious beliefs. His judgement of Cook was thus hardly one of a level-headed observer – *Editor*.

[65] The property (the *Discovery*'s boat) was never restored. – *Author*.

Journal in the official reports published a little later.

In 1819 the American Board of Missions sent a number of missionaries to Hawaii, where they heard the natives, - forty years after the event – and some at least of them accepted these as corroboration of the story that Ledyard had started in his biography.

These missionaries were fine men, whose memory is deservedly held in high esteem in the Islands. But they were Puritans of the Puritans, and held to the old Calvinism of the original Pilgrim Fathers. None the worse for that perhaps; but as interpreters of the events of 1779 they were not liberal minded or generous to the memory of the dead. I venture to assert that five minutes of talk with either Captain Cook or Captain King in their lifetime, and these missionaries would have relegated this mischievous and one-sided fable to its deserved oblivion, and would have done justice to the part Cook played in the temple ceremony of 1779. But, unfortunately, the missionaries accepted the idolatry story and used it for propaganda purposes to convince the natives of the Divine wrath that followed "idolatry."[66] So they helped to stereotype into local and American history this unjust stain on the memory of Captain Cook.

The Rev. William Ellis, of the London Missionary Society, joined up with the American missionaries in Hawaii in 1819 and spent three years travelling through the island. He has left a fine book of his travels, as his record of what he saw and heard in that period. And his testimony, derived from natives then living who had been participants in the events of 1778 and 1779, in no way implicates Captain Cook as a consenting party to any idolatrous worship of himself as a god.

The natives told Ellis that they thought that Cook was their old god *Lono*, returning to the islands in fulfillment of a prophecy, and were confirmed in that belief because his ship with its mast and rig was similar to the accepted insignia associated with the memory of *Lono*. But the natives never once alleged that Cook himself attempted to pose as other

---

[66] A shrewd insight into the myriad of vested interests that determine the presentation and dissemination of "history" – *Editor.*

than he really was, namely, the captain of his expedition. In effect, they admitted that neither by word nor deed did Captain Cook play up to the natives' view that he was a super-man or god. Nor did Ellis find any support to the charges of excesses on the part of Cook. They all said that they deeply regretted his death when it occurred, and they treated his bones and his body with the highest respect. Unfortunately, their method of "respect" happens to be quite at variance with European notions, but all the same it was according with their customs.

Let me cite another authority to rebut this charge of idolatry.

The best writer on the Polynesian race is universally conceded to be Dr. A. Fornander, an educated and highly respected Swedish gentleman who married an Hawaiian Princess and lived very many years in the Hawaiian Islands.[67] He spent most of that time in a thorough investigation of the race to which his wife belonged, and published his conclusions in a masterly treatise of three volumes.

In Vol. II, p.181, he deals with this charge of idolatrous worship of Captain Cook at Hawaii in 1778. The conclusion he arrives at is in his own words:

"I think that a candid posterity judging him as his contemporaries would have judged him, will acquit him of a wilful assumption of divine honours, or of a conscious participation in his own deification."

Dr. Fornander then proceeds to clear up the matter further by showing that, when Cook arrived at Kealakekua, the bay was under a *tabu* owing to the festival days of the New Year not having expired. The *tabu* was of a most rigid character prohibiting, under a penalty of death, any work being done either on land or on water. This would have meant that no one could have launched a canoe or have procured or carried supplies to Cook's ships. To obviate this consequence of the rigid *tabu*, the High Priest (in the absence of the King) proclaimed an exception

---

[67] Abraham Fornander swore allegiance to the King and became a prominent Hawaiian citizen, serving on the Privy Council and advocating for thorough and non-sectarian public education. His theory that the Polynesians were actually Aryans has aged far worse than his philanthropic efforts – *Editor.*

in favour of Cook and his ships, and invested Cook himself with the *caste* of an *Akua*, or superman,[68] thus "by a lucky thought providing a well-timed compromise to gratify the natives' curiosity and soothe their consciences, for most assuredly without such an arrangement not a single canoe would have dared to ripple the quiet waters of the bay."[69]

Fornander characterises the missionary literature on the subject as "a lamentable defect in critics, the more so when the object of their criticism is dead and cannot reply to the charge, and has left no material for his friends from which to argue what his own construction of the affair might have been" (Vol. II, p.180).

Note: The *Resolution* and *Discovery* arrived at Stromness in the British Isles on 22nd August, 1780, and at the Nore on 4th October, 1780.

The Admiralty then called in all the journals, diaries, and other records from all officers and men. Until 1784 there was no complete official publication of the events of the Third Voyage. Captain Cook being dead it was left to Captain King to compile this record. A second edition was issued in 1785. A very brief account of the Voyage was issued by the Admiralty some time earlier than 1784.[70]

Ledyard's publications of his Journal and Life are dated respectively 1781 (London), 1781 (Dublin edition), 1783 (Hartford, U.S.A., edition), 1782 (French edition, Paris), and further editions 1783, and Jared Sparks's *Life and Journals of Ledyard*, 1828 (Hartford, U.S.A.), and as well several other editions of which copies have not been seen by the Author.

Jared Sparks, in the 1828 publication, states that in 1782 Ledyard sold his notes for twenty guineas to Nathaniel Pallen a publisher in Hartford,

---

[68] The red cloak worn by a Hawaiian High Chief or *Akua* denoted his rank, and the temple priest placed a red coat on Cook as he was leaving his *heiau* or temple. – *Author's Note.*

[69] Vol. II, p.182, Fornander, *Polynesian Race.*

[70] The Admiralty's secrecy and delay is easier to understand in light of the Secret Instructions for the First Voyage which reveal how Cook's voyages were seen as having direct political consequences – *Editor.*

and this probably accounts for the earliest London edition published anonymously.

Thus it seems clear that five or six editions of Ledyard's journal were available to English, Irish, and French readers before the full authorised account was published by the Admiralty in 1784.

A perusal of the Admiralty account, compiled by Captain King from the ships' logs and from journals by Cook, King and others, discloses no statement to warrant a charge against Cook either of consenting to his being worshipped by the natives or of sacrilegious seizure of the temple fence. Let any curious reader peruse Chapters I and II of the Admiralty publication, and they will be abundantly satisfied on that point. But on the other hand, Ledyard's accounts in the 1781, 1783, and later editions – confused and contradictory as they are – will prove that Ledyard set going the stories against Captain Cook's good name in regard to both matters, viz., the alleged idolatrous worship of Cook and the alleged sacrilegious seizure of the temple fence. In the Hartford edition, printed in America in 1783, it is stated that: *"The third day after our acquaintance, Captain Cook was invited on shore by a number of the chiefs, among whom was a priest, to a kind of entertainment, or rather a ceremony, that he could not understand; as they either could not or would not explain it to him, he was obliged to comply at a hazard with their requests to come at the knowledge of a circumstance they were more anxious to communicate than he was to receive."*

In other editions (1781-1783) this explanation is omitted, and the readers is left to his own conclusions as to whether Cook was a consenting party or not.

But on the matter of sacrilege all except one edition blame Cook unmercifully as the wrong-doer. In the exceptional case, Ledyard says that the natives offered the temple fence to Captain Cook for firewood and the offer was accepted and the fence removed without objection.

It will be seen from this brief summary that a reader of Ledyard's Journal from 1781 to 1828 would draw his conclusion according to the copy or edition in his hands. It is obvious, however, that the majority of readers would only see those editions in which Cook was blamed both in regard to the temple ceremonies and the taking of the fence.

9

Continuing *re* the alleged worship of Captain Cook; the London missionary, William Ellis, spends three years among the Hawaiian natives (1823-6) and publishes in 1827 a full narrative of what he learnt from them

The testimony of the Rev. William Ellis, referred to in the preceding chapter, deserves fuller notice.[71]

In company with the American Missionaries – Asa Thurston, Artemas Bishop, and Joseph Goodrich – Ellis made a three years' tour through the Islands of Hawaii, beginning early in the summer of 1823. In 1827 he published his Journal of the tour through Hawaii, which is generally accepted as the most complete statement of affairs in that island, and its traditions and history of his times, of any which have been published. The information he gives was gathered from the narratives of natives with whom he conversed in 1823, forty-four years after Captain Cook's death.

Speaking of his visit to Kaawaloa (called by him Kaavaroa), where Cook was killed, Ellis says:

---

[71] Born to poor London parents in 1794, Ellis had a religious calling. He was or-dained a minister at 21 and became a lifetime missionary who was later involved in the partial conversion of Madagascar – *Editor.*

"There are a number of persons at Kaavaroa, and other places in the Islands, who either were present themselves at the unhappy dispute, which in this vicinity terminated the valuable life of the celebrated Captain Cook, or who, from their connection with those who were on the spot, are well acquainted with the particulars of that melancholy event. With many of them we have frequently conversed, and though their narratives differ in a few smaller points, they all agree in the main facts with the account published by Captain King, his successor.

"'The foreigner,' they say, 'was not to blame; for, in the first instance, our people stole his boat, and he, in order to recover it, designed to take our King on board his ship, and detain him there till it should be restored.

"'Kapena Kuke'" (Captain Cook's name is thus pronounced by the natives) "'and Taraiopu'" (Kalaniopuu was his Hawaiian name) "'our King, were walking together towards the shore, when our people, conscious of what had been done, thronged around the King, and objected to his going any further. His wife also joined her entreaties that he would not go on board the ships.

"'While he was hesitating, a man came running from the other side of the bay, entered the crowd almost breathless, and exclaimed: *It is war! The foreigners have commenced hostilities, have fired on a canoe from one of their boats, and killed a chief.*

"'This enraged some of our people, and alarmed the chiefs, as they feared Captain Cook would kill the King. The people armed themselves with stones, clubs, and spears. Kanowna entreated her husband not to go. All the chiefs did the same. The king sat down.

"'The captain seemed agitated, and was walking towards his boat, when one of our men attacked him with a spear; he turned, and with his double-barrelled gun shot the man who struck him. Some of our people then threw stones at him, which being seen by his men they fired on us.

"'Captain Cook then endeavoured to stop his men from firing, but could not, on account of the noise. He was turning again to speak to us, when he was stabbed in the back with a pahoa; *a spear was* at the same time *driven through his body*; he fell into the water, and spoke no more.

"'After he was dead, we all wailed. His bones were separated – the flesh was scraped off and burnt, as was the practice in regard to our own chiefs when they died. We thought that he was the god *Lono*, worshipped him as such, and after his death reverenced his bones'" (pp.98-99, Ellis's Journal).

Ellis then says:

"We" (he and his companions, [the Revs.] Thurston, Bishop and Goodrich) "have several times inquired, particularly of the natives acquainted with the circumstances, whether Captain Cook was facing them, or had his back towards them, when he received the fatal thrust; and their answer, in general, has been as here stated, which accords very nearly with Captain King's account, who says: 'Our unfortunate commander, the last time he was seen distinctly, was standing at the water's edge, and calling out to the boats to cease firing, and pull in.'

"If it be true, as some of those present have imagined, that the marines and boatmen fired without his orders, and that he was desirous of preventing any further bloodshed, it is not improbable, that his humanity on this occasion proved fatal to him; for it was remarked, that whilst he faced the natives none of them had offered him any violence, but that having turned about, to give his orders to the boats, he was stabbed in the back, and fell with his face into the water."

Ellis then proceeds with the natives' statements to his party:

"Many of the chiefs frequently express the sorrow they feel whenever they think of the Captain; and even the common people usually speak of these facts with apparent regret. Yet they exonerate the King Taraiopu from all blame, as nothing was done by his orders...

"More than once, when conversing with us on the length of time the missionaries had been in the Society Islands, they have said: 'Why did you not come here sooner? Was it because we killed Captain Cook?'[72]

---

[72]   The Society Islands are an archipelago centred around Tahiti – *Editor.*

"We have sometimes asked them what inducement they had to steal the boat, when they possessed so many canoes of their own. They have generally answered, that they did not take it to transport themselves from one island to another, for their own canoes were more than convenient, and they knew better how to manage them; but because they saw it was not sewed together, but fastened with nails. These they wanted, - therefore they stole the boat, and broke it into pieces the next day, in order to obtain the nails to make fish-hooks with.

"We have every reason to believe that this was the principal, if not the only, motive by which they were actuated in committing the depredation which ultimately led to such unhappy consequences.

"They prize nails very highly; and though we do not know that they even went so far in their endeavours to obtain a more abundant supply, as the Society Islanders did, who actually planted them in the ground hoping they would grow like potatoes or any other vegetable, yet such is the value they still set on them, that the fishermen would rather receive a wrought nail to make of it a fish-hook according to their own taste, than the best English-made fish-hook we could give them" (p.100).

Continuing Ellis says:

"It has been supposed that the circumstances of Captain Cook's bones being separated, and the flesh taken from them, was evidence of a savage and unrelenting barbarity; but so far from this, it was the result of the highest respect they could show him.

"We may also mention here, the reason for which the remains of Captain Cook received, as was the case, the worship of a god.

"Among the kings who have governed Hawaii during what may in its chronology be called the fabulous age, was *Lono*, or *Orono*; who, on some account, became offended with his wife, and murdered her; but afterwards lamented the act so much, as to induce a state of mental derangement. In this state he travelled through all the islands, boxing and wrestling with everyone he met.

"He subsequently set sail in a singularly shaped canoe for Tahiti, or a foreign country. After his departure he was deified by his country-men, and annual games of boxing and wrestling were instituted in his honour.

"As soon as Captain Cook arrived, it was supposed, and reported, that the god *Lono* was returned; the priests clothed him with the sacred cloth worn only by the god,[73] conducted him to their temples, sacrificed animals to propitiate his favour, and hence the people prostrated themselves before him as he walked through the villages.

"But when, in the attack made upon him, they saw his blood running, and heard his groans, they said: 'No, this is not *Lono*.' Some, however, after his death, still supposed him to be *Lono*, and expected he would appear again" (pp.100-1).

"From the above account," continues Ellis, "as well as every other statement given by the natives, it is evident that the death of Captain Cook was unpremeditated, and resulted from their dread of his anger; a sense of danger, or the momentary impulse of passion, exciting them to revenge the death of the chief who had been shot.

"Few intelligent visitors leave Hawaii without making a pilgrimage to the spot where he fell... We have never walked over these rocks without emotions of melancholy interest. The mind invariably reverts to the circumstances of their discovery; the satisfaction of the visitors; the surprise of the natives; the worship they paid to their discoverer; and the fatal catastrophe which here terminated his days; and, although in every event we acknowledge an overruling Providence, we cannot but lament the untimely end of a man whose discoveries contributed so much to the advancement of science, introduced us to an acquaintance with our antipodes, and led the way for the philosopher in his extended researches, the merchant in his distant commerce, and the missionary in his errand of mercy, to the unenlightened heathen at the ends of the earth..."

This account by Ellis, derived first-hand from Hawaiians, is probably

---

[73]   Again, the red cloak of a High Chief. – *Author's Note.*

the earliest and most complete ever compiled and published by a man of European descent. His companions were American missionaries of high standing, and they never questioned Ellis's account. The Hawaiians whom Ellis received his information from were eye-witnesses or participators in the events at Kaawaloa in 1779.

With regard to the alleged worship of Cook as *Lono* the god, Ellis clearly indicated that this was solely on the part of the Hawaiians and that Cook and King did not know its real import in the native mind.

10

The Moolelo Hawaii of 1838 and Cook and Lono compiled by the American missionaries from the native sources and published in 1838

I am indebted to Victor S. Houston (retired Commander, U.S. Navy), now Delegate for the Territory of Hawaii to the United States Congress, who is a leading Hawaiian, for the following literal translation of that part of Jules Remy's text of the *Moolelo Hawaii* that refers to the stay of Captain Cook at Kealakekua Bay, and of his death there.[74]

This work – the *Moolelo Hawaii* (i.e. Hawaiian history) – was compiled at Lahainaluna, Maui, from material largely furnished by the scholars of the Lahainaluna Seminary in the Island of Maui.[75] It was published in two editions. The first constituted a small book and appears to have been revised only by the Rev. Sheldon Dibble (missionary in charge of the Seminary) and issued in 1838 in the Hawaiian language only. It was translated into English in 1839 and M. Jules Remy published a French translation in Paris in 1862. A second edition was published in 1858 and included extensive extracts from the fine work of David Malo (*Hawaiian Antiquities*). This second edition was also compiled by

---

[74] Neither I, nor apparently Mr. Houston, could procure or see a copy of the original *Moolelo Hawaii* 1838 edition in Hawaiian language. Hence the use of the translation of Jules Remy's French version – *Author's Note.*

[75] *Moolelo* means story, myth, or history, and the book is still treasured as an invaluable source on Hawaiian custom and traditions prior to European contact – *Editor.*

a missionary (Rev. J.F. Pogue), and bears the trace of the hand of David Malo in the literary style and in the identity of the language in many passages of the two books (the *Moolelo Hawaii* and Malo's *Antiquities*).

Some points relating to the former work need emphasising. The first is, that the book was practically made to the order of the missionaries who conducted the Lahainaluna Seminary for the education of young Hawaiians. As I have stated before theses missionaries were good men to whom great praise must be accorded for their unselfish labours. They represent the Calvinistic frame of mind to the strictest Puritans – none too liberal or charitable to others outside their narrow creed.[76] The students were asked to collect the material from the elders in their families or villages. Prior to doing so, these students had received, unconsciously, from their mentors a clear bias against or mental suggestion of the alleged wrongdoing of Cook in permitting himself to be treated as *Lono* returned as a god to Hawaii.

Most of the Polynesian race are notoriously "cute" in this way – that if they are asked a question on some moot point, they try to sense what answer would be most pleasing: and so frame their answer to please the questioner.

Consequently one must bear in mind not only the point of view of the Puritan clergy, but also the mental suggestion which influenced the students in collecting the material for compilation.

The 1838 edition was compiled and published fifty-nine years after Cook's death, when many old Hawaiians were still living who could have known some of those events of 1779. Some of these old people also must have conversed with the missionaries.

Hence it is a better document to refer to than the edition of twenty years later, which had been expanded by another set of compilers who

---

[76] Carruthers' distaste for Calvinism may have been influenced by his brother, the Reverend James Edward Carruthers, a prominent leader of the more positive Methodist movement in Australia at the time. The rise of Methodism has been linked to the rise of humanism and many of the core transformations of the nineteenth century, of which Australia was both a beneficiary and a pioneer – *Editor.*

were out of touch with the actors on the stage in 1779.

I now give the translation of Jules Remy's edition of the *Moolelo Hawaii*, noting that *Lono* is the name given to Cook by the native authors and editor:

"*Lono* having left Maui approached the coast of Kohala. He arrived there on the 2nd December. The mountains of Hawaii were covered with snow. The place where he anchored was near Kukuipatu.

"The natives ran down to see the vessel, and they saw strangers eating raw food from a container, (water melons). Then the natives exclaimed: 'In truth they are gods, here they are eating human flesh and the fire burns their mouths.'

"*Lono* bought pigs at this place, one pig for an iron ring, which was used to make hatchets and fish-hooks.

"*Lono* sailed thence, passed to seaward of Hamakua, Hilo, Puna and Kau, and after having made nearly the whole circuit of Hawaii, he anchored at Kealakekua, in Kona.

"It was on the 17th of January that the vessel arrived at the anchorage in the year 1779. At the time of *Lono*'s arrival in Hawaii, Kalaniopuu was the King of Hawaii. However, Kalaniopuu was on Maui making war against Kahekili.

"The arrival of *Lono* happened on one of the days when canoes were not allowed to navigate, because of the *tabu* relating to the commencement of the New Year. But, owing to the presence of *Lono*, the natives thought that it would be proper to launch their canoes, inasmuch as the god *Lono* himself had arrived on his vessel.

"*The thought was well established amongst the natives that Lono (Captain Cook) was a real god, and that his vessel was a temple.*[77]

"And the natives saw the strangers putting oakum in the sides of their

---

[77]   This amply proves that the natives came to a conclusion without Cook's knowledge or consent – *Author's Note.*

vessel; they gave to these strangers the name of the race of *Moku Halii*, or God's constructors of canoes.

"And the natives saw other strangers with fire in their mouths, and they gave them the name of *Lonopele* (Fire God).

"As *they thought*[78] they were gods, the natives ran in crowds, to worship *Lono*. The women in great numbers went on board to prostitute themselves with the strangers. The strangers gave them iron and mirrors. As they examined the mirrors they saw their reflection in the glass; they were frightened at the size of the reflections which they saw in the mirrors. They washed the silvering off the glass and the reflection from the mirrors was gone, and they regretted much, no longer seeing anything.

"Owing to the fact that the natives thought *Lono* to be a god, *they paid him a large tribute of worship and adoration.*[79] They made him offerings of pigs, food, native cloth, and all sorts of things, like the offerings made to the gods, without requiring a price for anything.

"The priests approached him, prostrating themselves, threw a red cape over his shoulders,[80] withdrew a little, gave him pigs and this and that thing, whilst pronouncing long speeches, which they recited with many words constituting prayer and worship. When *Lono* went ashore, most of the natives ran away full of fear, and those which remained prostrated themselves in adoration. He was conducted into the House of the Gods, as well as to the temple, and there he was worshipped.

"*Lono* accepted this worship like Herod, without making any objection. The thought might occur to us, that for this sin, as well as for having introduced amongst us the disease of the fornicators and adulterers, that God struck him dead.

"The 24th day of January, Kalaniopuu returned from Maui; he put the *tabu* on the canoes to prevent the women going out to sea, and the

---

78   The italics are mine – *Author.*
79   The italics are mine – *Author.*
80   Such capes were worn by chiefs - *Author.*

strangers flocked ashore to behave indecently.

"Kalaniopuu showed himself generous and good towards *Lono*; he gave him feather cloaks and kahilis." (*Note: These were ceremonial poles or wands ornamented with feathers and beautiful to look on.)*

"Kalaniopuu truly worshipped him.

"The fourth of February *Lono* left, and off Kawaihae he discovered that one of the masts of his vessel was rotten; he turned back to Kealakekua for repairs. When the vessel was back at the anchorage, the natives continued their intercourse which, however, was not as frequent or intimate as before.

"The amorous relations of the strangers with the women had lasted a long time, and some of the women were really in love with the strangers, as a result of which the natives arose against *Lono* and his men.[81]

"When the natives began to show opposition, the strangers lost no time firing their guns.

"The strangers in addition confiscated the canoe of a Chief – named Palea; he resists and is struck down by the strangers with the blow of an oar. Then his followers offered more resistance and pelted them with stones.

"Palea picking himself up, and fearing to be killed by *Lono*, stopped the fight.

"A little later Palea stole one of the ship's boats; this theft was probably occasioned by resentment, and perhaps by covetousness of the iron.

"That was the cause of the war.

"*Lono* ordered the Chief to find and return the ship's boat to the vessel. It was impossible for the Chief to do this because it had already been broken up by the natives for its iron.

---

[81] Carruthers covers the topic of venereal disease later on, but he is perhaps a bit un-der-appreciative of the role that this fraternisation, which went against the orders Cook had given his men, may have played in the rise of resentment and ill-feeling – *Editor.*

"*Lono* and his men, armed with guns, went ashore to seize the Chief and bring him on board, where he was to remain until the small boat was returned.

"Whilst *Lono* was going for Kalaniopuu to conduct himself on board, Kekuhaupio rushed from Keei to Kaawaloa and at the same time another Chief arrived by another canoe. And the strangers who remained on board ship fired on this Chief, whose name was Kalimu, and he was killed on the spot.

"Kekuhaupio also having witnessed the death of Kalimu hastened to land at Kaawaloa. It was he who urged Kalaniopuu not to go on board, and when the natives had learned that a Chief had been killed, they gave vent to shouts of war.

"A man approached *Lono* with a wooden dagger in his hand. *Lono* fearing this action fired; this started the fight. *Lono* unsheathed his sword and struck the Chief, whose name was Kalaimano-Kahoowaha.

"This Chief took hold of Lono with a firm grip, merely to hold him not to kill him. He thought, as a matter of fact, that *Lono* being a god could not die. But as *Lono* uttered a cry of pain in his falling, Kalaimano-Kahoowaha thought that he was a man.

"No longer thinking *Lono* was a god, he struck *Lono* until he died on the spot.

"Then the strangers who remained in the boat fired their guns; many men were killed by this fire.

"Having no guns the natives tried in vain to protect themselves with matting against the bullets.

"Then the guns of the vessel opened fire and several natives were killed.

"After that Kalaniopuu fled towards the hills, with the natives and the Chiefs, and they carried with them the body of *Lono*, as well as the bodies of four strangers who had died at his side, and they reached the top of the pali of Kaawaloa.

"There Kalaniopuu offered *Lono* as a sacrifice and when the ceremony was finished they stripped the flesh from the bones of *Lono*, and the bones were preserved as well as the palms of his hands and his inwards (heart).

"And they burnt the flesh. The inwards of *Lono* were eaten by some children; they had mistaken them for the inwards of a dog. That was their reason for eating them.

"Kupa is the one who with Mohoole and Kaiaikokoole ate them.

"Some of the bones were returned on board of the vessel; the others were kept by the priests and worshipped.

"The 23rd of February the vessel left Kaawaloa and on the 29th of the same month it stopped off Kauai; from Kauai the vessel went to Nihau and on the 15th day of March it disappeared all together."

Some manifest errors and omissions are evident in this document, which does not accord in some material facts with the accounts published by Ellis eleven years earlier. No mention is made of Cook's acknowledged appeal to the King for restitution of the stolen boat. Moreover the account very fairly shows that the natives thought the visitors were gods and that Cook was *Lono*. No suggestion is made that Captain Cook knew what their thoughts were or in any way accepted their views.

Waimea, Island of Kauai, where Captain Cook landed in January, 1778

11

Analysing the Rev. Sheldon Dibble's statement; comparing that with Ellis's and Bloxham's impressions from the native accounts; Mr. Cook and his reception in Kauai; Mr. Stokes's views

I propose to add a little more before concluding the consideration of the alleged worship of Captain Cook.

I think it is clear that Cowper's hysterical outburst of 1783 in his Letters had been read by the Rev. Sheldon Dibble, Head of the Lahainaluna Seminary, when he edited and published, in 1838, the student's compilation of *Moolelo Hawaii*.

Dibble in 1845 published his history of the Sandwich Islands and adopted the view set out in the *Moolelo Hawaii*. On page 21 of his work, Dibble says: "Cook (*Lono*) accepted the worship. Like Herod he did not forbid it."[82]

Is it a mere coincidence that William Cowper in 1783, and the Rev.

---

[82]   Acts 12: 21-23 "On an appointed day Herod put on his royal robes, took his seat upon the throne, and made an oration to them. And the people shouted, "The voice of a god, and not of man!" Immediately an angel of the Lord smote him, because he did not give God the glory; and he was eaten by worms and died".

The Sandwich Islands was the old European name for the Hawaiian Islands – *Editor*.

Sheldon Dibble in 1845, both compare Cook with Herod? There is some excuse for Cowper's outburst, because he had not time or opportunity to learn the facts fully. Dibble, however, had the opportunity of his whole lifetime to have become acquainted with the actual story of events written at the time of their occurrence by Captain King, a high-minded and honourable man universally held in the highest esteem by everyone who met him, Europeans and Hawaiians alike.

Evidently Dibble did not trouble to read the other side of the case. In all crime or wrongdoing the essence of guilt lies in the "intent" associated with the act. In this alleged act of worship the "intent" was entirely on the side of the natives. Even that is challenged by some students of the race who hold that the ceremony in the temple or *morai* was merely an investiture of Cook with the rank of high chief evidenced by the placing of the red cloak on his shoulders. This was done, so it is claimed, to give Cook and his followers the benefit of the laws protecting the chiefs under the native *tabus*. Ellis, in his *Journal of Travel*, says that the natives informed him and his other three missionary companions:

"The foreigner (Cook) was not to blame. After he was dead we all wailed.

"Many of the chiefs frequently express the sorrow they feel whenever they think of the Captain, and even the common people usually speak with apparent regret."

Is this voluntary testimony of Hawaiians – eye-witnesses of or participators in the events of 1779 – consistent with the view that Cook wilfully and intentionally countenanced or practised some deception so as to delude them into an idea that he was one of their gods?

Would there not be resentment exhibited instead of the kindly sentiments manifested in the words of the natives to Ellis? To say the least, there was an entire lack of Christian charity in the attitude of Dibble and other missionaries of a similar extreme type.

Dr. Fornander – their contemporary in Hawaii – chastises them for their biased attitude (see chapter eight herein).

The Rev. Dr. W.B. Westervelt, a fine type of the missionary (still living), in articles published in the magazine, *Paradise of the Pacific*, September, 1912, wrote: "In 1824 Mr. Andrew Bloxham, Naturalist of H.M.S. *Blonde*, states in his diary that he and his brother, the Chaplain of the *Blonde*, were permitted to take away two great wooden images which stood in the temple where Cook stood when the ceremony was performed in 1779, *unconscious as he* (Cook) *was at the time of the honour thus disposed [sic] on him*."[83]

This narrative of Bloxham's shows that in 1824 at the very scene of Cook's last days and death, the impression conveyed to him by the natives who gave the images to Bloxham was that "Cook was unconscious of the honour thus disposed on him."

Mr. Westervelt in all his writings – and he has written much of great value about Hawaiians – is most careful to express the view that if Captain Cook was conscious of accepting worship he did a wrong, but that probably he did not realise the intent of the natives. No one can take exception to that view: and the pity is that any other ever gained currency.

The occurrences at Kealakekua Bay, when Cook landed there, are not of an isolated character. In many other islands of the Pacific, Cook was greeted by the natives with the greatest respect, as if he were of the Chiefly rank.

Cook specially refers to this, in Volume VI of his Voyages. On pages 160 and 161 thereof he says, regarding his landing at Kauai (the northernmost of the Hawaiian Islands), on 19th January, 1778:

"The very instant I leaped ashore the collected body of the natives fell flat upon their faces, and remained in that very humble posture till, by express signs, *I prevailed upon them to rise*. They then brought a great

---

[83] The H.M.S. *Blonde* was then engaged on a sombre mission to return the bodies of King Kamehameha II and Queen Kamamalu to their homeland. They had died whilst on a historic visit to England; the Queen of measles, the King of both the disease and a broken heart. This occurred in 1824, so the ship was not actually in Hawaii until the following year – *Editor*.

many small pigs, which they presented to me, with plantain trees, using much the same ceremonies that we had seen practised on such occasions at the Society and other Islands; and a long prayer being spoken by a single person, in which others of the assembly sometimes joined, I expressed my acceptance of their proffered friendship by giving them in return such presents as I had brought with me for that purpose..."

Again, on pp.185 and 201, speaking of a long walk that he took on the same island, he says:

"A numerous train of natives followed us; and one of them, whom I had distinguished for his activity in keeping the rest in order, I made a choice of as a guide. This man, from time to time, proclaimed our approach; and everyone whom we met fell prostrate upon the ground, and remained in that position till we had passed. *This, as I afterward understood, is the mode of paying their respect to their own great chiefs.*[84]

"As soon as we got upon a rising ground, I stopped to look round me, and observed a woman, on the other side of the valley, where I landed, calling upon her country-man who attended me. Upon this, the chief began to mutter something which I supposed was a prayer; and the two men, who carried pigs, continued to walk round me all the time, making at least a dozen circuits before the other had finished his oration. This ceremony being performed, we proceeded; and, presently, met people coming from all parts, who, on being called to by the attendants, threw themselves prostrate on their faces, till I was out of sight..."

Yet no one has presumed to say or write that Cook was worshipped as a god at Kauai.

There is ample evidence from native sources that after Cook left Kauai, the news of his visit spread to the other islands of the group and he was spoken of as *Lono*.

I am indebted for what immediately follows to a brother Australian, Mr. John F.G. Stokes, who for many years has been on the staff of

---

[84] The italics are mine – *Author.*

the Bishop Museum at Honolulu, engaged there in ethnological and historical research.[85] He has been a close student of Hawaiian customs, lore and history.

Mr. Stokes kindly submitted to me some notes on my first draft manuscript of this book and I quote him as follows:

"In my opinion the priests sincerely believed that Cook was a god (*Lono*).

"We must differentiate between the ideas of divinity as variously conceived by a highly developed civilisation like the Caucasian and a more primitive one like the Polynesian. The gaps between the human and the divine were not as great in the Polynesian. In addition, there was no love of the Polynesian for his god – a being only to be feared and propitiated. The being represented as *Lono* was the mildest of the Hawaiian Trinity.

"Observe the vindictiveness with which the natives destroyed the temples and images in 1819 once they felt safe from divine vengeance, the fear of which had kept them in subjection.

"A point which has always puzzled me is that according to the native definitions the temple of Hikiau at Napoopoo should have been, and probably was originally, dedicated to *Ku* the war god, whose 'ritual was arduous', while the ritual of *Lono* was mild. Human sacrifices were made to *Ku*, but not to *Lono*, and had Cook been mistaken for *Ku*, any deification would have been accompanied by an immolation of a human corpse!

"There were many concepts of the individuals in the Hawaiian Trinity. *Lono* was also the god of the New Year, and since Cook arrived on the Island of Hawaii at about the local New Year festivities which lasted for some time, the impression of the natives previously formed on Kauai that he was *Lono* might well be strengthened. The effigies of the New

---

[85]   Stokes was a pioneering archaeologist whose work focused on excavating the heiau
       of Hawaii – *Editor*.

Year's gods were deposited in the temples of *Ku* – which being the governmental temple controlled the New Year's services.

"The prostration was demanded in the Chief's presence from almost the entire population and on all occasions. *The Chief or King was regarded as divine.*

"The *tabu* was undoubtedly present on account of the New Year services when Cook arrived. That *Lono* should break the *tabu* would have been a matter for him to decide in the people's mind if they thought Cook was *Lono*.

"Whatever *Lono* wanted – no matter how unreasonable – would have been immediately furnished without question.

"…In the unfortunate events leading up to Cook's death there are, I believe, a number of factors to be considered, amongst others:

"The native reaction: It must be remembered that under the religious system which maintained, the chiefs as well as the commoners were greatly oppressed. They were all compelled to make heavy contributions in property and in labour and, in frequent instances, in lives. Cook's (or *Lono*'s) presence in Kealakekua and the over generous contributions to him from the King did not meant that the King offered them from his personal resources, but that he secured them by levy on the people.[86] Lieut. King's narrative, I believe, referred to the people stroking the well-fed sailors towards the end of the visit and urging them to depart and come again when there was more food in the country. From the native view-point, of course, the sailors were *Lono*'s retainers…"

I deduce from these statements of Mr. Stokes that as Cook's arrival, both in Kauai and in Hawaii, occurred in the month of the New Year when the idea of *Lono* was active in their minds on account of the festival associated with that god – the mental suggestion pressed strongly on the natives that Cook was *Lono* returned. This auto-suggestion influenced them.

---

[86] This adds weight to Carruthers' emphasis on the importance of the temporary absence of high-ranking Hawaiians when Cook initially turned back for repairs – *Editor.*

Cook and his officers knew nothing of this motive influencing the Hawaiians. They assumed that great respect was being paid to them: and in accepting it they acted quite innocently of any evil intent such as was later construed into the matter by rather narrow-minded men.

12
Further dealing with the alleged act of sacrilege in regard to taking the old fence around the temple for firewood, as stated by Ledyard

In chapter six I made some brief reference to the statements by Ledyard asserting that, during the second visit to Kealakekua Bay by Cook's ships, "excesses occurred" at the hands of the English, such as vandalism and the desecration of holy places, violence to a chief and to other Hawaiians. He also alleged that these things created hostile feeling to Cook and his crews, ending finally in Cook's death.

I purpose now to deal with this libel, and to disprove it. Ledyard started it in 1781, and it has been repeated over and over again by some who have never troubled to read other accounts from more trustworthy sources.

My knowledge of this false story first came when I made a journey in 1926 from Honolulu to the Island of Hawaii. I had primed myself with a tourist guide-book. The best procurable – a rather fine work – was called *The Island of Hawaii*, issued in 1913 by the Hilo Board of Trade. (Hilo is the chief city of that Island.) It was a revised edition of 1916 and the revision was made, of all men, by an Englishman, some of whose family have rendered splendid service as admirals and officers in the British Navy. In this document I read what was practically Ledyard's account of Cook's alleged worship – highly embellished by a more gifted writer. Then follows:

"After the first ten days the natives began to tire of their guests, who committed many excesses. One of the seamen died and was buried in the *heiau* with both Christian and pagan rites. This was enough to show the natives that the strangers were mortal like themselves, but no violence was offered them until a few days later, when Cook, being in need of firewood, broke down the sacred wooden fence surrounding the *heiau* and even burned some of the idols surmounting it. This flagrant abuse of the *tabu* roused the natives to a pitch of fury and a violent quarrel ensued, which, however, had no serious result at the time."

I read this whilst I was at Kona (Hawaii) in very comfortable quarters at Host Wall's ranch house. I repeated what I had read to Mr. Wall, who was an old resident of the part and whose parents were very early settlers in the locality. He told me that most, if not all, of the accounts published about Cook in Hawaii were very unreliable except that of Rev. William Ellis, who had collected from the natives very faithful accounts of the days of 1779.

I had read Captain King's story in his Journal, included in *Cook's Voyages*, Book V, Vol. VII. I knew that King's account absolutely varied from the lurid statements in the tourist guide and so I informed Mr. Wall. This is what Captain King says on pages 24 and 25 of his Journal:

"… The ships being in great want of fuel the Captain desired me, on the 2nd of February, to treat with the Priests, for the purchase of the rail that surrounded the top of the *morai*. I must confess I had, at first, some doubt about the decency of the proposal, and was apprehensive that even the bare mention of it might be considered by them as a shocking impiety. In this, however, I found myself mistaken. Not the smallest surprise was expressed at the application, and the wood was readily given, even without stipulating anything in return. Whilst the sailors were taking it away, I observed one of them carrying off a carved image; and, on further inquiry, I found that they had conveyed to the boats the whole of the semi-circle. *Though this was done in the presence of the natives, who had not shown any mark of resentment at it, but had even assisted them in the removal*, I thought it proper to speak to Kooa (the Priest) on the subject; who appeared very indifferent about the matter, and only desired that we would restore the centre image I have mentioned before, which he carried into one of the priest's houses."

From this clear statement by Captain King, the only man actually concerned in obtaining the firewood from the High Priest of the temple, there appears to be no ground whatever for the story of Ledyard.

I am at liberty to quote a letter received by me from Mr. Thos. G. Thrum of Honolulu, Compiler and Publisher for many years of the *Hawaiian Annual*, and a man exceptionally well informed on all matters appertaining to the natives – their customs, religion, and their views. He volunteered the following statement to me, after a meeting at which I had addressed an audience, and offered to put it in writing with the actual quotations from the author and historian, Kamakau. The letter is dated 24th July, 1925, and reads as follows:

"…In refutation of the assertion that Captain Cook's death at Kaawaloa, Kealakekua Bay, Hawaii, was the resentment by the natives for his desecrating their *heiau* (temple), in his taking the *paehumu* (surrounding fence) images for firewood, I am pleased to furnish the following translation of the Hawaiian historian, S.M. Kamakau, as an authority for my views, long held, that the *paehumu* images were not sacred objects of the temple, as the idols. Furthermore: This alleged cause is nowhere to be found in any Hawaiian account in palliation (of their killing of Captain Cook); it is an unwarranted introduction by foreign writers not familiar with the facts Kamakau presents.

"'The outstanding images of the *paehumu* were for ornamentation only outside of the temple; they were not idols of worship for any man to bend the knee.

"'These images erected outside of the temples were not sacred, and restricted (*sic*) as oven firewood. At certain times those who kept the houses of the gods used these images for that purpose. Note in the history of Kawelo on his sailing for Kauai to make war: at Kawelo's consecration of the temple of *Puehu*, at Waianae, at the close of the sacrificial offering ceremonies, he ordered that the woodwork on the *paehumu*, the wooden fence, and the images of the temple be taken for firewood, to prepare food for the war on Kauai' (S.M. Kamakau). (Signed) "Thos. G. Thrum."

In Captain King's Journal he very fully records day by day the events occurring at Kealakekua Bay. He makes it absolutely clear that not one word was said by any native, high or low, in regard to this matter of the old wooden fence. Not the slightest notice was taken of that event by anyone. And, as the native historian, S.M. Kamakau, is quoted in Mr. Thrum's letter, no native account mentions it.

Captain King goes on in his Journal to speak of the goodwill and kindness of the Hawaiians during the period immediately following. He records the fact (proved also from many other sources – Hawaiian and English) that natives, chiefs, and common people entreated him to remain with them and become one of the chiefs or leaders. He had to argue with them and show that loyalty and his duty bound him to his leader Captain Cook. They offered to conceal him if he remained until the ships had sailed.

Does this affection towards him support the story that his action outraged the feelings of the natives? Sane minds will regard it as absolutely disproving that story.[87]

Captain Lord Byron of H.M.S. *Blonde* in 1826 visited this bay with his ship and met many who were present in 1779 during Cook's visit. No one mentioned to him anything of the alleged vandalism, though they referred to the worship of Captain Cook, who, they said, was unconscious of the fact. Captain Byron says that Cook regarded the

---

[87] It is quite remarkable the lengths to which Carruthers goes to exonerate his subject from what is essentially an act of cultural misunderstanding (admittedly a belligerent one). In the previous chapter the extract from Stokes dismissed the Hawaiian religion as "primitive", yet here the author is keen to demonstrate that Cook did nothing to belittle or abuse it. There is a fundamental empathy and respect here that cuts through, despite the dated language and teleological understanding of "civilisation" – *Editor.*

temple ceremony as prompted either by great respect for him or fear of his ships. He (Captain Byron) gathered this impression while mingling with natives and others during his stay in the Islands. Amongst others whom he met in Kealakekua and Kaawaloa were the local chief and his wife, both well acquainted with the facts relating to Cook's visit, and the son of the High Priest Kooa, who was the chief figure in the temple ceremonies with Captains Cook and King and who also dealt with King when the old fence was taken away with his consent.

Submerged memorial tablet at the actual spot where Captain Cook died

13

Other statements by members of the Third Expedition or Voyage; Zimmermann's narrative; and testimony of Henry Roberts (mate of the *Resolution*)

When the Third Voyage ended and the *Resolution* and *Discovery* arrived in England, the Admiralty ordered that all journals, diaries, and other manuscripts relating to the voyage, made by officers or men, should be handed to the Commander, who would transmit them to the Admiralty.

This step was taken in order to prevent the publication of unauthorised or incorrect accounts of the Voyage, as well as to prevent any forestalling of the official publication of a trustworthy story from the ships' *logs* and journals of the officers. This publication, as already mentioned, was unduly held back for about five years owing to delay in engraving the plates of illustrations. Evidently some of the notes of officers and men were not handed in as ordered. From time to time these have been published wholly or in part. Also some accounts alleged to have been written by members of the crew have been circulated, although never yet published because of doubts as to their authenticity.

I myself had a copy of the Journal of Midshipman Alexander Hume, or Home, who was on the *Resolution*. He rose to the rank of Admiral, so it is stated. This account is most interesting and is well written. It enlarges on many matters that are only lightly referred to in the official and other accepted stories of the Voyage. It corroborates in the main the English accounts of the events leading up to the death of Cook, and the writer expresses the highest opinion of his Captain's character as a man and officer.

I hesitate to quote from Hume's diary because it is open to doubt as to its genuineness until the experts have come to a judgement on that point.

But there is no question about the narrative of Seaman Henry Zimmermann of the *Discovery*, published first in Mannheim in 1781. This man was a German who in 1776 signed on as a common sailor.[88]

At the outset of the Third Voyage Zimmermann decided "to write down in a little notebook all the discoveries and events of the Voyage" – to use his own words. He kept this book when the voyage ended – thus disobeying the order of the Admiralty. He justifies this by saying: "I was under no contract to sell my memory. Why should I not have the right to tell my own story in my own way, or to write it down and have it printed?"

Anyhow, he is candid; and though he did forestall the official publication, his narrative substantially accords with it in those things which are of real importance.

Naturally in many events of which he was not an eye-witness or in which he was not a participator, he diverges from the authorised account because he did not have full opportunity to obtain a correct knowledge.

Many copies of this German edition of Zimmermann's book long ago reached England, America, Australia, and New Zealand. I am not aware of any English translation published until that done by Miss U. Tewsley of the Library Staff of the Alexander Turnbull Library, Wellington, New Zealand, under the direction of the Librarian. This translation was published by the Library under the authority of the New Zealand

---

[88] Heinrich Zimmermann is emblematic of the diversity of the crews during this age of exploration. After his voyage on the *Discovery*, Zimmermann tried unsuccessfully to get both the Austrian then the Russian governments to sponsor further expeditions. Cook's discoveries were a British achievement, not because his men were British, but because the British actually fronted up the cash to drive the Enlightenment's pursuit of scientific knowledge forward – *Editor*.

Government.

Zimmermann corroborates Cook's story of the visit of the ships when Kauai (in the Hawaiian group) was discovered in January 1778. He says:

"As soon as Cook set foot on shore all the people fell on their faces; Cook looked round him and laughed heartily; then he lifted up some of the eldest, embraced them, and gave them presents."

Zimmermann wrongly assumes that some of the natives went away and brought the King to Cook. The natives' records and all others show that Cook did not meet the King or any of the chiefs. As a matter of fact, by the native account, the King was not on the island.

Speaking of the women, Zimmermann says:

"The women here, besides being beautiful, were very obliging, outdoing in both these respects the women in any of the other islands in the South Seas. Captain Cook had, however, forbidden us to have any dealings with them on pain of a heavy punishment; indeed, the whole crew had to submit to an examination, and any men who were found to be diseased were refused permission to go ashore."

Again showing the handicap that Zimmermann was under in framing his story, he calls the island Nihau. In reality it was Kauai, and he calls Nihau, the smaller of the two islands, by the name of Kauai. I am using the correct names.

Zimmermann writes also of the events which happened at Hawaii, which Cook visited in January, 1779. He says:

"The inhabitants of the island raised Captain Cook to the dignity of a god, and set up an idol in his honour which they called after him *O-runa no te tuti*, *O-runa* meaning god, and *tuti* Cook[89]..."

There is no similar statement *re* the idol from any other writer, native or European!

---

[89] *Orono* does not mean god. It was the title of *Lono* – in other words his Hawaiian name. – *Author*.

He then describes what he calls "one of these heathen ceremonies," but the account has no bearing on matters in controversy to which I am referring in this book. He speaks of other ceremonies which were carried out on the other side of the *island*, evidently meaning on the other side of the *bay*. "But", he says, "what was the nature of these ceremonies, what sacrifices were offered, I cannot say, as my duties did not permit me to attend." He points out that on these occasions the King or the chiefs wore their red cloaks or capes. This point corroborates the view which I have expressed before in the preceding pages, that when the priest Kooa invested Cook with a red cape it was in order to put him on a similar footing with the chiefs and the King.

Zimmermann gives an account of the loss of the boat which was cut from the moorings of the *Discovery*. He says:

"It was the best boat we had, and when I, being one of the deck watch, perceived at daybreak what had happened, and reported it to Captain Cook, he at once sent out six boats, well manned with men with muskets and side-arms. Four of the boats were ordered to barricade the harbour, and not to allow any of the canoes of the natives to pass out. With two of the boats he himself went ashore, landed with Lieutenant Philipps, of the Marines, and about twelve men, and gave Naval Lieutenant Williamson orders to remain in the boats with the rest of the men, who numbered about fourteen."

He states that "it was Captain Cook's intention to arrest the King, bring him aboard the ship, and keep him as a hostage until the boat should have been returned." He says "he might have succeeded in this purpose if he had left the armed men behind and had inveigled the King aboard with kindness and friendship. But unfortunately *he was too angry to do this*, and this it was which brought about his most regrettable death."

Here again Zimmermann speaks without a full knowledge of the motives of Captain Cook. He attributes Cook's actions to sudden anger. I think it is clear that many hours were allowed to elapse before Cook took the measures which Zimmermann relates in this passage. Cook did not act hastily inasmuch as he had tried to get the King to make search for and return the boat, and had waited a day, or the best part of it, until the King had proved to him that he could not find the boat. Then he called a council of his officers and deputed the task of going onshore to Captain Clerke. Clerke, in his ill state of health, said he was unfit for the task; and he urged Cook that he himself was the best man to undertake the work. Naturally Cook was distressed. It was a serious thing for him to go back to England and report that he had lost one of his principal boats, and it was also a very embarrassing thing that his second in command (Clerke) was unfit for duty. Cook had too much work thrown on his shoulders. It was enough to make any man angry under the circumstances, but to say that Cook was *too angry* was only the expression of a man who did not understand all the circumstances. As a matter of fact to be deduced from all accounts Cook was "very worried"

Zimmermann gives an account of what happened on shore. It mainly coincides with the authorised version, but he did not have the advantage which Lieutenant Philipps and others had who were on shore and were actual participators or observers at very close quarters of events, which he saw at a long distance while he was carrying on his work on the *Discovery*.

He speaks of the death of the old Quartermaster, William Whatman, who was interred in the native burial-ground within the temple walls by permission of the High Priest. He says that "the death of our quartermaster destroyed the people's previous belief in our immortality, and this belief being lost, their reverence for us was gone."[90]

Zimmermann also refers to the removal of the poles, or fence, around the temple or burying place. He says this "was done with the permission of their King, who received six axes in exchange." As a matter of fact, permission was not given by the King, but by the Chief Priest who was in charge of the temple, and he got nothing in payment for it. A reference

---

[90] Zimmermann's earlier description of the "obliging" nature of the women he encountered and the social power that the belief that one was "immortal" and in some way connected to the divine would give a man "wooing" a potential partner, again suggest that, despite Cook's orders to the contrary, the fraternisation of the crew may have bred ill-will, particularly when that immortality subsequently proved false – *Editor.*

to Lieutenant King's account, appearing in chapter seven, will fully explain this. In point of fact the King was away at this time or not in evidence.

I mention these matters to show the danger of accepting the account, even of a friendly member of the crew, upon details of which he was ill-informed.

After speaking of the death of Captain Cook, Zimmermann states:[91]

"I regard it as a duty to Captain Cook, who was one of the greatest men of our time, to give here as full and complete a description of him as possible...

"He was inexorable regarding the ships' regulations and the punishments connected with them – so much so, indeed, that if, when we were amongst the natives, anything was stolen from us by them, the man on watch at the time was severely punished for his neglect...

"He was scrupulously clean, and the example which he set in this direction had to be followed by every man on board. It was a regulation that every member of the crew should put on clean clothes every Sunday.

"Moderation was one of his chief virtues. Throughout the entire voyage no one ever saw him drunk. It was never permitted to the sailors to save up their brandy for several days and then get drunk, and if it happened at any time that a man was too drunk to carry out his duties he was severely punished...

"*Never was there a breath of suspicion in regards to his dealings with women.* While we were at *O-tahiti* and *O-waihi*, where all the men allowed themselves to be led astray by the attraction of the native women, *he alone remained clean and uncontaminated.* In all other enjoyments he loved equality, and on special

---

[91] Jillian Robertson uses Zimmermann's account to dig up evidence of what she paints as Cook's alleged violence and temper (*The Captain Cook Myth*, pp.89-93). Considering the praise Carruthers is able to cite from this source it may be that Zimmermann made greater allowance for the necessities of life onboard an eighteenth century sailing ship than did the twentieth century author. It certainly was a more brutal age, there were 200 offences for which capital punishment was the crime when convict transportation to Australia began – *Editor*.

occasions food and drink were served out to officers and men in equal portions.

"Fearlessness was his most outstanding characteristic. On the unknown coast of America the ships ran on foggy nights under full sail, and the Captain slept peacefully the while. But, on the other hand, when no one else had a suspicion of danger he often came up on deck and changed the course of the ship because land was near. This was so pronounced that everyone believed he had some secret source of foreknowing and avoiding danger. At least I can say with certainty that such occasions were frequent when he alone was sensible of the existence of land; and he was always right.

"I do not believe that England ever had a braver sea-officer than Cook. In times of greatest danger he was the bravest, the cheeriest, and the most resolute; and at such times his chief concern was to keep calmness and order on the ship. In this he was so successful that for the most part all eyes were fixed on him.

"He had an instinctive knowledge of how to deal with native peoples; and his pleasure in intercourse with them was self-evident. *He loved the natives, understood the language of many of them, and had the art of pleasing and charming them. It was on this account that he was so much respected by the islanders, and at times worshipped...*"

Another narrative by one of Cook's officers has recently come to light. It is that of Henry Roberts, a mate of the *Resolution*. Extracts from this were published in the *Morning Post* of London. Roberts was actually in charge of the pinnance which took Cook ashore on the day when he was killed.

Dr. Samwell, in his account, confirms this statement. This is how Roberts describes the temple ceremony:

"Captain Cook went on shore to meet the Chief *Karu Oboo* (Kalianopuu). Soon after they came on board together, the Captain having been presented with several cups, cloaks, cloth and other curiosities, with a number of hogs and every production of the Island, the whole given with great ceremony, and a pig burnt alive as a sacrifice, which we took for a peace offering, this was performed by their priest, with many prayers and songs, upon the occasion, and at times joined by whole in chorus."

Roberts says: "We took this as a peace offering." Evidently he and his fellow members of the crew of the *Resolution* did not regard the ceremony as one of worship of Cook; in fact, none of them were allowed within the temple walls.

Roberts's description of the death of Cook and the events ashore are similar to that contained in the official accounts. He says:

"His death occasioned concern and sorrow in every countenance. Such an able Navigator, equalled by few and excelled by none, justly styled the father of his people from his great good care and attention, honoured and beloved by those who knew or ever heard of him…"

One is justly entitled to place the testimony of men like Captain King, Captain Burney, Dr. Samwell and others – officers and scientists (Sir Joseph Banks and others) – as well as that of seamen such as Zimmermann and Henry Roberts before that of a disgruntled man as Corporal Ledyard was, and before that of other writers who collected material from young students and others who had only hearsay statements from unknown natives with a very limited point of view and with no actual knowledge of Cook's real worth and character as a man. One set of men, the first above mentioned, wrote at the very time the events happened, and the other set spoke, at the earliest, some forty years after when their memories must have weakened and when other minds than their own influenced them. The most widely quoted of these native stories are (1) the *Moolelo Hawaii*, published in 1838, or nearly sixty years after Cook died, and (2) the longer account by the native historian, S.M. Kamakau, published in 1867, or eighty-eight years after Cook's death. This repeats almost verbatim the *Moolelo Hawaii*.

In any Court of Justice which pays due heed to the rules of evidence founded on the wisdom and experience of a long line of great jurists, the statements of Cook himself, and of his officers and men, and of scientists and doctors on his ships, noted at the time when events were happening, would far outweigh the slipshod and haphazard collection of hearsay statements made from forty to eighty years after the events and edited by men whose ears were closed to any other side of the case, except that created by their limited knowledge founded on hearsay and faulty material.[92]

The earliest verified statements by natives are contained in the Rev. Wm. Ellis's work, *Travels in Hawaii*, 1820-1823, or forty-four years after Cook's death. These do not support either of the other accounts of natives to which I have referred. The Rev. Wm. Ellis, in my opinion, is more entitled to be accepted as a witness of the truth than the later writers. Ellis was a missionary of acknowledged high character, and his associates were American missionaries like Thurston, Bishop, and Goodrich, whose names and memories are venerated in Hawaii. Admitting even a bias towards Captain Cook, I think I am justified on the evidence available in saying that any man who reads both sides of the case will come to the same conclusion I do.

Finally I now quote from a fine article on Captain Cook, by David Hannay (appearing in *Blackwood's Magazine*, October, 1928, on page 499, Vol. CCXXIV), wherein he says:

"It is only certain that he (Cook) who has been accused of cruelty brought death upon himself by his humanity… His monument is the chart of the Pacific and we may leave a Frenchman to write his epitaph. M. Dumont d'Urville said of him:

"'To the sailors and geographers of the civilised world Cook's name will ever recall the most illustrious navigator of past or future times. No one

---

[92] Carruthers deeply believed in the burden of proof and the concept that an individual is innocent until proven guilty. This is one of the great problems of colonial history: evidence is scarce, much of it is hearsay, and in an effort to make up for the lack of native sources many people now rely on extremely tentative oral records. In such circumstances it is normally best to avoid passing judgement, particularly a negative or condemning judgement, but the very nature of "history" or "culture" wars make people feel that the present is at stake in the battle over the past, and to ignore such precautions – *Editor.*

rendered such service to navigation; and the actual extent of our knowledge would preclude one even more gifted than Cook from attaining the same height of fame. In him nature would seem to have formed the very model of a sailor, and no one has honoured as much the laborious profession, so irksome and so vexatious for one who could worthily fulfil all its demands. Viewed in this light Cook stands at the head of the navigators of all ages and of all nations.'"

That eulogium of a Frenchman, read with the words inscribed on a monument to him erected by his old friend and commander, Sir Hugh Palliser (see chapter twenty-one), should place the name of Captain Cook above reproach and above the attacks of men who never met him and never knew him in life.

14

Re alleged conduct of Captain Cook with the daughter of the High Chiefess of Kauai

Another matter to be dealt with is the charge that Captain Cook, at Kauai, in 1778, set an evil example to his crews in his conduct with regard to the daughter of the High Chiefess of that island.

The admitted facts are that when Cook discovered and landed at the island of Kauai, in 1778, the natives showed some hostility to the landing parties and a brief conflict occurred in which one native was killed. This was recorded in Cook's and King's Journals.

From native sources it has been gathered that a considerable section of the inhabitants held a meeting and decided to raid and seize the ships and divide them and their contents amongst the raiders. This news, reaching the ears of the ruling High Chiefess, she sturdily forbade any such hostile action, and gave orders that the strangers were to be treated in a friendly manner so that in turn their friendship would be secured. To emphasise her determination to carry out this peaceful policy, she intimated that she would send her own daughter with presents to the visitors. The native historians (if such a term as historian can be applied to those who wrote from hearsay accounts forty years after the events)[93] agree in stating that the High Chiefess carried out her

---

[93] The only full account by a native which I could find was that of S.M. Kamakau, published in 1867, in a native weekly paper *The Kuokoa* – eighty-nine years after 1778 - *Author.*

avowed intention and sent her daughter to Captain Cook (and in one account "daughters" are mentioned).

The gravamen of the charges subsequently made and founded on these statements lies in the implication that Captain Cook was personally involved in the reception of the daughter of the Chiefess, though how anyone in Cook's ships would know anything about the rank of any of the visitors before they had really landed or mingled with the natives is incomprehensible, and is rendered more so when one reads Captain Cook's own story on pp.179, *et seq.*, Volume II, of *Cook's Voyages*.

Cook gives a voluminous account of his arrival off this island on or about the 19th January, 1778. He tells how the natives put off from the shore in their canoes on the morning of 20th January, 1778. At first the natives were very full of fear and amazement, but finally some of them took courage and ventured on board as the ships lay off shore. From three to six *men* were in each canoe. Of those who came on board Cook states that they:

"were intensely curious and handled everything in sight and asked innumerable questions in their own way regarding each article. Then they began to steal whatever they got their hands on until the officers and crew convinced them that thieving was not tolerated. Finally, the natives found that watchful eyes were being kept over their actions, and they ceased to attempt to thieve."

At 9 a.m. Cook ordered three armed boats to go ashore, under the command of Lieut. Williamson, with the object of finding a landing-place and a supply of fresh water. Cook's orders were, that if Williamson found it necessary to land in search of water, not more than one man was to leave the boats with him. This final order of Captain Cook was given, to use his own words, "that I might do everything in my power to prevent the importation of a fatal disease into this island which I knew some of the men laboured under. With the same view I ordered all female visitors to be excluded from the ships" (p.181). In another passage Cook says: "Many women had come off in the canoes. They would as readily have favoured us with their company on board as the men: but I wished to prevent all connection which might, too probably, convey an irreparable injury to themselves and through their means to the whole nation." So Cook would not allow the women to come aboard. Another necessary precaution was taken, by "strictly enjoining that no person known to be capable of propagating the infection should be sent on duty out of the ships."

Corroboration of the facts that these orders were issued and were observed so far as humanly possible by the ships' officers is to be found in a similar statement published later by the Fleet surgeon, Dr. Samwell.

Further on in his diary Cook says that "about noon of the same day Mr. Williamson came back and reported that he had seen a large pond which, the natives told him, contained fresh water and there was good anchoring ground before it."

Williamson also reported that "his boats had been attacked by large parties of natives who attempted to take away the oars, muskets and, in short, everything they could lay hold of, and the natives pressed so thick upon the boats that Williamson was obliged to fire upon them, by which one man was killed."

In Cook's account he says, that on the previous day, 19th January, his ships had cruised along the islands looking for a haven and that the natives crowded on the overlooking headlands watching the ships, and a few canoes put off and came near to the ships and made offers to barter, but did not come aboard. At night, on the 19th January, the ships put out to sea until the early morning of the next day (20th January), when they again closed into the shore and when for the first time a landing party went ashore.

These facts possibly explain the story afterwards circulated by the natives, and later on recorded in the so-termed native historians' accounts, as to the High Chiefess's resolve. A meeting would naturally be held on the 19th of January to discuss the wonderful events of that day when the strange ships appeared to the wonder-stricken natives.

Then it was that the decision was arrived at, to raid the ships and to divide up the spoils; and possibly on that night to counteract that decision the High Chiefess would come to her decision in favour of friendly measures.

The events of the 20th January fell out just as might be expected. One section of the natives put into practice their resolve to raid and steal, but being worsted in their attempts with the loss of a life they gave way. Next, Cook's action in forbidding women from coming aboard his ships would also frustrate the intentions of the high Chiefess in sending her daughter and other women to the strangers.

A perusal of Cook's own narrative from this point shows that in the afternoon of the 20th January the ships (the *Resolution* and the *Discovery*) bore down towards the shore and anchored. Then between 3 and 4 p.m. the same day (after receiving Lieut. Williamson's report) Captain Cook went ashore with three armed boats and twelve marines "to examine the water and to try the disposition of the inhabitants." Says Cook: "The very instant I leaped on shore, the collected body of the natives all fell flat on their faces and remained in that very humble posture till, by express signs, I prevailed on them to rise." Then followed an exchange of presents, "many small pigs and plantains" from the natives and "such presents as I had brought with me from the ships" on the side of Cook.

Everything being satisfactorily arranged then for the supply of fresh water and for a trade in food supplies, Cook returned to his ship after making dispositions for an armed guard of marines on the beach "to protect the arrangements being made for the morrow's work."

The next day, the 21st of January, the supervision of the watering and procuring of supplies was left in charge of Lieut. Williamson; and the captain, with two other officers – Mr. Anderson and Mr. Webber – made an excursion into the country, followed by a voluntary train of natives, one of whom Cook made choice of as guide. Cook returned in the afternoon for dinner and sent Captain King to command the shore party until later on when the two captains, Cook and Clerke, intended to make another excursion into the country; but Cook records the fact that "as the day was too far spent we laid aside that intention." At sunset everybody connected with the two ships was brought aboard. These details are stressed because they show, from Cook's own statements, how keen he was to have everything done under proper supervision and how his crews were kept under the eye of authority. Every day a record was kept by Cook with meticulous care, as shown by his diary,[94] and no instance is given of any incident whatever which would give the slightest ground for the story that the High Chiefess had sent her daughter to Captain Cook or, at any rate, that such a person had ever visited him.

On the other hand, the native historian, S.M. Kamakua, in his writings very many years later, and based on hearsay evidence, states that the High Chiefess (Kamakahelei) and her family received Cook and exchanged presents with him on the day that he went ashore, but he does not mention that they visited the ships. Apparently, if this be true, Cook was ignorant of the exalted rank of the woman when he met her ashore (*see* Fornander, *Polynesian Race*, Vol. II, p.164).

It is worthy of note that Cook in his diary twice refers to the fact that he met no chief or person of rank at Kauai.[95]

Some possible corroboration of the statement by Kamakau is to be found on page 190, Vol. II, of *Cook's Voyages*, where Cook describes articles of

---

[94] Cook only landed on Kauai on the two occasions – on the 20th and 21st of January, 1778. His ships lay off the shore on the 22nd and 23rd January, in some jeopardy from strong winds and high seas. Communication with the shore was restricted to some trading for food and water, under the control of Lieutenant King (afterwards Captain) and Lieutenant Williamson. The ships left on the evening of the 23rd January. – *Author.*

[95] Captain Cook, in his Journal (Vol. VI of the *Three Voyages*), records that, although he did not meet any chief or other person in authority at Atooi (Kauai), yet Captain Clerke of the *Discovery* informed him that a chief, accompanied by a woman of rank (seemingly from his family), visited his (Clerke's) ship and stayed for some hours inspecting it and conversing with officers and men. He (Clerke) complained of the brutal and overbearing manner of this chief in his treatment of the common people, who humbled themselves in every way to him. This chief left before evening, evidently to the great satisfaction of Captain Clerke, who had no liking to his high-handed bearing. – *Author's Note.*

barter which he noticed – namely some wonderful cloaks of feathers, for which a musket was asked in exchange, and some similar cloaks, smaller and of less beauty, which were bought for some large nails. Inasmuch as these were articles solely possessed by those of chief rank and were strictly *tabu* to the common people, there is some ground to believe that unknowingly Cook or his officers on duty may have seen this High Chiefess and the members of her family during the day when they first landed. But as that day was crowded with events and Cook only landed between 4 and 5 p.m.[96] and returned to his ship after making arrangements for the work of the morrow, it was hardly likely that he would pay much attention to individual natives who would meet him.

Fornander in his work on the Polynesian race, which I have already quoted, devotes much space to the elaboration of the charge against Cook of violating the hospitality of the High Chiefess. The basis he accepts, viz., the belated stories of latter-day historians, cannot be accepted in contradiction of Cook's diary made day by day as events occurred. Fornander certainly does not accept the native story as conclusive, but he insists that because the native race became infected with disease after the visit of Cook's crews, this fact alone is proof that due care was not taken by Cook to protect the natives from infection, and to that extent supports the native versions. On page 165, Vol. II, of his work, Fornander sums up the case against Cook in these words:

"There is but one way to escape a dilemma between the varying versions, and that is to assume what was probably the fact, *though Cook does nowhere acknowledge it*, namely, that his order (to exclude women from the ships) was not properly carried into effect."

But Fornander's summing up of the matter in this way is faulty and, luckily, easily proved to be so. Cook's orders were twofold – directed to prevent infection being carried to the natives, viz.:

i.   Excluding women from the ships, and

---

[96]   Based on the earlier statement this should have been 3 to 4 p.m. but I have left it as the original had it – *Editor.*

ii.   Prohibiting members of his crew from remaining on shore
      where they might mingle with the women.

Disobedience of either order would create the risk against which
the orders were directed. Also accidents in regard to weather and sea
conditions might prevent orders being carried out.

Fortunately, Captain Cook, on page 199, Vol. II, of his *Voyages*, has
written this statement, which Fornander entirely overlooked and which
completely refutes Fornander's statement:

"On the 30th January I sent Mr. Gore ashore again" (not on the island
of Kauai, but on a smaller one – Nihau – lying about six miles to the
north) "with a guard of marines and a party to trade with the natives.
The surf increased so much that neither could I go ashore nor could
Gore's party return to the ships. The officer and twenty men, deterred
by the danger of coming off, were left ashore all night, and by this
unfortunate circumstance the very thing happened which, as I have
already mentioned, I wished so heartily to prevent and vainly imagined
I had effectually guarded against."

There, in his own words, Captain Cook put on record for all time his frank
acknowledgement of the unforeseen circumstances which prevented his
orders from being carried out. Yet Fornander, apparently in ignorance of
this acknowledgement, says that "nowhere does Cook acknowledge it."
If Fornander knew of this, then his criticism is inexcusable. Evidently
he overlooked this fact in Cook's own Journal.

Finally there stands in the way of acceptance of the native version about
the High Chiefess's daughter and Captain Cook one or two outstanding
facts which cannot be set aside.

First, Cook, by the accounts of his officers and crew and also of his other
English associates in life, was a man of admittedly high moral character
against which there was no doubt expressed, after eleven years of close
association on three long voyages.

Next, the practice of the British Navy (now an inflexible rule) was that

women were not *permitted* to remain overnight on one of the King's
ships in any point of anchorage, and only at sea in cases of rescue.

It seems, however, to be clear that occasionally some of the crews of the
ships under Cook's command got out of hand, and rules went by the
board even at the risk of punishment. Men in the King's Navy then,
and even nowadays, are not "plaster saints," nor are they without faults.
Sailors of every race and everywhere are hard to manage when in port;
and if captains are to be judged by the conduct of their men ashore, or
when their friends are on board the ship in port, then they will be put
in an impossible position.

When one remembers that Cook rose from the rank of A.B. to that of
Naval Commander – a rare thing – it will be realised how careful he
would have to be not to afford a shadow of doubt to be created in regard
to his character, as a man or officer, through any error, neglect, or wrong
behaviour on his part.[97]

I have endeavoured to make clear that no tangible grounds exist for the
slightest questioning of the high reputation of Captain Cook during the
last days of his life spent in the Hawaiian Islands, or when he visited
Kauai at the time of his discovery of the group.

---

[97] Here Carruthers' meritocratic lesson teaches the need for morality and propriety,
not just hard work alone – *Editor.*

15

Cook's humanity and the so-termed excesses of his crews

I think that any impartial critic will feel bound to admit, if he peruses every just account of the voyages of Captain Cook, that he sacrificed fewer lives, whether of natives of the places he visited or of his own crew, than any other discoverer-navigator before or since his days.

I am indebted to Mr. Quinn, the able Librarian of the Parliament of New South Wales, for a very carefully compiled summary of the cases where Captain Cook or his men punished the natives or inflicted harm in conflicts with them during his three voyages from 1768 to 1779, covering a period of eleven years, most of which was spent in newly discovered islands of the Pacific, where they came in contact with many thousands of the natives, either in large or small groups.

His instructions to his crew are set out on page 86 of Vol. I of his Journal as follows:

Rule 1. "to endeavour by every fair means to cultivate a friendship with the natives and to treat them with all imaginable humanity."

These words deserve to be engraven in gold on every monument erected to the memory of Cook, because they honestly express the spirit that actuated him right throughout the years of his voyages in the Pacific.

The following summary shows the deaths, casualties or punishment of natives or of his crews:[98]

At Otaheite (*vide* p.95 of his Journal, Vol. I):

1. "A native killed under a midshipman's orders to fire on
   him when he snatched a musket from a sentry whom he
   took unawares. For this action Cook severely censures the
   officer and the men for acting with fear, petulance or natural
   brutality."

2. At the same place "a native flogged for stealing nails" (p.143,
   Vol. I).

3. "A seaman flogged for stealing a bow and arrow from the
   natives" (p.149, Vol. I)

4. "Cook issues orders" not to fire on natives even when
   detected in theft, because it was against their own laws to
   punish such an offence with death, and we had no right to
   make such a law for them" (pp.150-1, Vol. I).[99]

5. "At Poverty Bay, N.Z. – Natives attack boats: two muskets
   fired over their heads, no effect, so no one killed" (pp.277-8,
   Vol. I).

6. "At New Zealand – Native grabbed hanger from an officer
   (Mr. Green) and ran away waving it exultingly: and then

---

[98] This list comes across as somewhat brutalist in the way it dismisses individual lives
in single lines of text. Carruthers is at least honest and upfront about the true cost
of Cook's voyages. His point that, given the life or death circumstances on both
sides of the equation, things went remarkably peaceful, is true. It is difficult for
us who now have so little experience with scarcity or privation to really appreciate
what it was like to be entirely reliant on securing a resupply from people you do
not know or even understand for survival. The natives were likewise dealing with
scarcity and the fact that they tended to be so generous with what little they had
suggests that a common humanity cut through – *Editor.*

[99] When making the case for Cook's alleged violence Robertson suggests that Cook
punished the natives for thievery despite their differing understanding of property
rights, and that this was unjust. This line suggests that Cook initially took that
view, and only became more strict as experience taught him the vital necessity of
protecting his limited possessions – *Editor.*

was joined by an insolent crowd. We then fired at them with small shot without effect, and they continuing to wave the hanger exultingly and defiantly, one was shot dead; when other natives seized the hanger and the natives crowded towards the ship's party, who felt it necessary to fire their muskets loaded with small shot to drive the hostile natives away. Two or three natives were wounded. The natives were very hostile and refused all overtures of friendship. Ships needed water very keenly at this time and place, and the natives were resisting every effort to obtain it" (p.280, Vol. I).

7. "New Zealand: Tupia (who spoke the natives' language) invited a canoe party to come aboard the ship, but the natives attacked with their weapons and stones. The party in the boat were forced in self-defence to fire, and killed four natives."

In this instance Cook, in his diary, censures himself and his men for having fired on the natives, but says in justification that the nature of his service demanded that he should become acquainted with the country that he was then visiting, and he therefore tried every friendly means to win the confidence of the natives and induce them to come aboard his vessel to help him in his service, but their hostile attitude forced a conflict in which, to his regret, lives were lost through excess of firing (pp.282-3, Vol. I).

8. "New Zealand: Musket fired over one party, one of which threw a spear."

9. "Botany Bay, Australia: Musket ball fired between two natives – then one wounded with small shot" (p.320, Vol. II).

10. "New Guinea: Small shot used after attack by natives, and they still came on, ball used and probably some wounded" (p.235, Vol. II).

11. New Guinea: Cook urged by officers to cause coco-nut trees to be cut down for sake of food and drink. Refused to permit this to be done as unjustifiable and calculated to breed resentment (pp.237-8, Vol. II).

12. "Otaheite: Musket fired over head of a thieving native" (p.158, Vol. III).

13. "Seamen punished for stealing from the natives" (p.247, Vol. III).

14. "Marquesas: Musket fired over head of cheating native" (p.299, Vol. III).

15. "Thief (native) killed at 3rd shot." Cook regrets that his instructions, not to fire at the native but over the canoe, were not heard, as the natives made too much noise (pp.299-300, Vo. III).

16. "Otaheite: Thieving native flogged as an example" (p.325, Vol. III)

17. "Tuana. Small shot fired at a thieving native, then a cannon fired over the canoe; no one hurt; done to show effect of firearms" (p.50, Vol. IV).

18. Tuana: Cook expresses view that the natives should be judged leniently for exhibiting a reluctance to permit his forces to explore the interior of their island; especially as they were otherwise friendly (pp.60-1, Vol. IV).

19. Cook expresses regret at a sentry shooting a native who was threatening him (pp.67-8, Vol. IV).

20. Cook censures the Europeans' treatment of native women (p.183, Vol. V).

21. Native shot with ball instead of small shot, contrary to his instructions.

22. Otaheite: Native punished and dismissed for thieving and apparently incorrigibility (p.93, Vol. VI).

23. Sandwich Islands- Alloi (Kauai):

    Unknown to Cook, one of his crew killed a native when he was attacked by a hostile crowd attempting to take cars, muskets and everything they could lay hold of. Cook only learnt of this occurrence after his ship left the island and he then surmised that the natives' curiosity and desire to barter had led them into a behaviour that contributed to a disaster (p.183, Vol. VI).

24. Cook expresses his admiration for the natives of Hawaii and their friendliness (p.464, Vol. VI).

25. At Eimeo, Friendly Islands: Cook punishes natives for stealing a goat and refusing to return it, by burning some of their houses after warning them that he should do so if they persisted in a refusal to restore the stolen animal (p.81, Vol. VI).[100]

From these facts it will be seen that in all his voyages Cook's crews killed only ten natives up to the time of the fatal affray at Hawaii, and wounded possibly six others.[101]

When one compares this with the fact (*vide "Sandwich Islands,"* by Manley Hopkins, 1862) that in the year 1789 at Oahu, one of the Hawaiian Islands, the Captain (Metcalf) of the American ship *Eleanor* killed over 100 Hawaiians in revenge for a stolen boat and for the death of one man, it will be seen that in a few minutes this Captain sacrificed ten times as many lives of natives as Captain Cook and his crews did in eleven years of their voyages.

---

[100] The Friendly Islands was the old European name for Tonga, so-called because of its cordial reception of Cook – *Editor.*

[101] This list does not include the unnumbered Hawaiians killed in the scuffle that took Cook's life. Four marines also died on that occasion – *Editor.*

Yet Cook is blamed for the excesses of his crews, when history actually teaches us that, by his orders and influence, they were restrained in the manner set out.

16
What became of Captain Cook's body and his bones after death

It may be taken as definitely established by native accounts, which are unanimous on this matter, that after Cook's death at Kaawaloa, in Hawaii, his body was carried some distance up the hill-side towards what is now the main coastal road from Kona to Napoopoo, where there was in 1779 a small *heiau*, or temple, the ruins of which still exist and mark the exact place. Apparently it was devoted to the preparation of the remains of any important chief or high personage.

There, the Hawaiian ceremony of respect was accorded to his body. It was subjected to fire in order to burn the flesh and leave the bones intact for cleansing. There is no ground whatever for associating this act of cremation with any cannibalistic practice. As I have stated before, the Hawaiians were not addicted to cannibalism but abhorred it. It is alleged in the *Moolelo Hawaii* (students' Hawaiian history) that some children, whose names are therein given, ate the heart and some entrails, mistaking them for those of a dog. Although this comes from native sources, it sounds improbable; but so it is recorded. (See chapter ten).

It is certain from the native accounts, verified by Captain King's journal and by other accounts written by members of the Expedition, that at least one hand was preserved intact and also a portion of the flesh on one of the limbs, both of which, with many of the bones, were taken to Captain Clerke by a friendly native the day after Cook's death.

The remainder of the bones were cleaned and were kept by the natives in accordance with their custom of preserving and honouring them as objects of veneration. Even after Cook's death the majority of the natives still regarded him as *Lono*, and wished to associate his remains with their superstitious ritual of *Lono* worship.

The Hawaiians had cultivated the cult of secrecy to an unusual extent in matters of this kind. Once a trust was committed to one or more individuals, it became an obligation to observe that trust under risk of the most severe penalties. Anyone attempting to interfere with these trustees in their duty was liable to meet his death. Native accounts show that some of the bones of Cook's body were given to trustworthy persons of high rank, either priests or chiefs. Their identity was known only to those highest in authority, such as the King or High Priest. At certain times and places and in certain ceremonies these sacred relics (for such they held them to be) were carried in procession, and the fullest respect was accorded to them.[102] After that, they were again secreted until the period once more came for a repetition of the ritual.

A rather remarkable confirmation of the foregoing is to be found in *Mariner's Tonga Islands* (by Martin) (Vol. II, pp.63-9), as follows:

"The people of the Sandwich Islands, although they actually did kill him (Captain Cook) have paid, and still continue to pay him, higher honours than any other nation of the earth. They esteem him as having been sent by the gods to civilise them, and one to whom they owe the greatest blessings they enjoy. His bones (the greater part of which they have still in their possession!) they devoutly hold sacred. They are deposited in a house consecrated to a god, and are annually carried in procession to many other consecrated houses, before each of which they are laid on the ground, and the priest returns thanks to the gods for having sent them so great a man.

"When the *Port au Prince* was at Woahoo (Oahu) – one of the Sandwich

---

[102] The bones of high ranking individuals were believed to possess *mana*, a spiritual power, central to the traditions of both Hawaii and Tahiti – *Editor.*

Islands – Mr. Mariner was informed of the above circumstances by an Englishman (or perhaps an American), who was a resident there: his name was Harbottle; he seemed a man of some information and respectability, and was formerly the mate of an American vessel that touched there, but, in consequence of some disagreement with the captain, he chose to remain at those islands, and acted in the capacity of harbour-master to the King, and pilot to all ships that arrived, from each of which he demanded five or six dollars for his services.[103]

"This person informed Mr. Mariner that the natives of Owhyhee (Hawaii) returned very few of the bones of Captain Cook, but chiefly substituted the bones of some other Englishman that was killed on that melancholy occasion; and that those of Cook were carried annually in the procession as above related. When Mr. Mariner afterwards understood the Tongan language, he conversed upon the subject with the natives of Owhyhee (Hawaii), who were with him at Vavaoo (Vavau); they corroborated everything that Harbottle had said, and stated, moreover, that the natives had no idea that Cook could possibly be killed, as they considered him a supernatural being, and were astonished when they saw him fall… Among the natives of Hawaii from whom Mr. Mariner heard this, one was a chief of a middling rank, the rest were of the lower order, but they all agreed in the same statement…

"They stated, moreover, that the King and principal chiefs were exceedingly sorry for the death of their extraordinary benefactor, and would have made any sacrifices in their power rather than so melancholy an accident should have occurred…"

In 1806 Mariner was marooned on the Tonga Islands, his ship, the *Port au Prince*, having been taken by the Tongans and most of the officers and men killed. He apparently was the only survivor and his life was spared. He became quite friendly with the Tongans and for several years lived with them, learned their language and studied their customs and history very closely. He managed to get away, and returned to England

---

[103] The date when this vessel and the Mariner were at Oahu was either late in 1805 or early in 1806, or twenty-six years after Cook's death – *Author's Note*.

early in the last century.

The Harbottle mentioned in Mariner's account was well known in the Hawaiian Islands, and his descendants still reside there.

There can be no doubt whatever that only a portion of the bones of Cook were handed to Captain Clerke. These, and the hands and the other scant portion of his remains, were committed to the deep by his old comrades close by where he died.

From time to time stories have gained currency that the remaining bones were found and either delivered or were ready to be delivered to his kin in England. Mr. W.H. Huntington, a well-known journalist of Sydney, Australia, prepared for publication a very fine account of the early history of Australia.[104] I have one of the few copies of it, which I received from Mr. Huntington before he died about thirty years ago. Reading over its pages I found the statement that King Kamehameha II of Hawaii, when visiting England in 1825, took with him some of the remaining bones of Captain Cook to give to his relatives there or to the nation.

Mr. Huntington says, on page 48 of his work:

"In July, 1878, Mr. W. Adams, of Cavendish Square, London, exhibited to several journalists an arrow supposed to contain a portion of the leg bone of Captain Cook, which was brought to England by Liholiho,[105] who received it from his medical attendant. This bone was shown to Mr. Ellis, the missionary, who thought the bone was not from Cook's body, from its being in an arrow and not wrapped in holy cloth, which fact showed a want of that respect and veneration which the natives had for

---

[104] Huntington had been a journalist for Henry Parkes' *Empire* newspaper and then the *Evening News*. He was a member of the Royal Australian Historical Society and was considered an authority on Australian history at the time. For the Kurnell Speech presented in the introduction, Carruthers had borrowed his copy of Cook's chart from Huntington – *Editor*.

[105] Liholiho, son of Kamehameha I, reigned as Kamehameha II - *Author*.

Cook's memory.[106] Some years ago Mr. Adams, to obtain confirmatory evidence of the bone having belonged to Cook, referred the matter to the Bishop of Honolulu (Bishop Stanley), who learned from the King of Hawaii, then a very old man, that the relic was probably what it was represented to be. Upwards of 20 years ago the king and queen of the Sandwich Isles died of the measles in England, and it is singular that, when leaving their native country, they had a presentiment that they would never return to their island home. The queen's last words to Mr. Ellis, as the ship was leaving the island, was, 'Good-bye, we will never return. Don't you think that they will remember that we killed Captain Cook?' In 1825, some of the officers of the British ship of war, *Blonde*," (which brought back the remains of the king and queen), "erected on the rock where Cook met his sad fate, a cross of oak 10 feet high, with the following inscription thereon – 'Sacred to the memory of Captain James Cook, R.N., who discovered these islands in the year of our Lord, 1778. This humble monument is erected by his countrymen in the year of our Lord 1825.'"

There are many relics and records which either still lie hidden in Hawaii or have been destroyed to prevent their falling into the hands of persons not inheriting a charge of trust over them.

For instance, the greatest historian and writer of the Hawaiian race, David Malo (whose work *Hawaiian Antiquities* is the classic of that language), is said to have written a history of the times of King Kamehameha I (The Conqueror) covering the period of Cook's visit and up to 1830.

Mrs. Lucy Peabody, an Hawaiian of high descent, who died at a ripe old age about 1927, told me in 1926 that she had seen and had Malo's manuscript in her hands many years previously. She said that Emerson and Alexander, two leading Americans in Honolulu, were translating this work for publication in English. One of them appealed to Mrs.

---

[106] In the early 2000s New Zealand and Australian scientists carried out a DNA test on the arrow and determined that it was not made out of the remains of Cook, but likely animal antler – *Editor*.

Peabody to help in translating some passages that were written by Malo in cryptic terms that were not understood by the translator. She was told that the manuscript was at a bookseller's store in Honolulu for her to peruse, if she would do so. She asked for a loan of it so that she might read it at her leisure. She was told that this could not be done, as the translators were bound by promise not to allow it out of their custody. She, therefore, complied with the request and called at the place indicated. There she saw the manuscript and read the passages that were mystifying the translators. She told me exactly what some of the passages were, quoting the Hawaiian words and giving her English translation. She said that the language used was metaphorical and needed special knowledge of the Court language to enable a proper rendition of the meaning in English. She had no opportunity to read much of the book, but she was informed that it was intended to publish the translation at some later date.

Dr. Harden (one-time resident of Honolulu and since in Australia), who was closely in touch with King Kalakua and Queen Kapiolani, forty or fifty years ago, told me that both these sovereigns informed him then that the manuscript and translation of Malo's History was in their possession but would not be published until after their death. When asked, "Why delay the publication? Why not publish now?" they answered: "the time is not yet right to publish. Titles and other personal matters would be in question and effect the living. It must stand over until there is no likelihood of harm to others who might suffer pain or loss."

The Malo History has never been published, and the manuscript remains hidden away in safe keeping or has been destroyed. Much search has been made for it without result.[107]

The point of all this is that, if Malo's History could be found, it would disclose a great deal about the events of 1778 and 1779, when Cook

---

[107] This manuscript remains lost, but enough of David Malo's work has survived for him to be considered a pioneer Polynesian historian, telling the Hawaiian story from their own perspective. Malo was also a Christian Minister and spent some time translating parts of the bible into the Hawaiian language – *Editor*.

was in the islands, and it would clear up many points now left in doubt.

Kamehameha was on Cook's ship, the *Resolution*, for two days before it reached Kealakekua Bay, and he was present when Cook arrived there, and he knew intimately all that happened there. He was a nephew of King Kalianopuu (who received Cook) and succeeded him on the throne.

It is quite possible that this missing link of history will yet be found. What has happened has only added one more proof of how religiously an Hawaiian will fulfil a trust and preserve secrecy if enjoined to do so.

Carruthers addressing the Gathering at Kaawaloa, where Captain Cook died

17

The introduction of diseases which decimated the native population in Hawaii; confusion of two diseases, yaws and syphilis; yaws not definitely proved of venereal origin; communication with other islands and visits of foreigners; Bishop Restarick's address; Dr. Storie Dixson's views

In dealing with the matter of the introduction of venereal diseases into the Hawaiian Islands one is faced with this difficulty, viz., that Captain Cook in his Journals practically pleads guilty to the charge that his crews were responsible for this, despite his strict orders.

It is, therefore, an almost hopeless task to attempt to clear away this charge in the face of such a plea. It is only open to one, under the circumstances, to submit known facts and expert opinions to prove that, despite Cook's own admission, there is very grave doubt in the matter.

It is undoubtedly clear that venereal disease did exist in the Society Group, when Cook called at Tahiti on his third voyage. The surgeon of the expedition (Dr. Samwell) also admits that some of the crew were infected and uncured when Kauai and Hawaii were visited in 1778 and 1779.

It is well known that a disease known as *Yaws* was very prevalent in all the islands of Polynesia visited by Cook. It was, and still is, rampant, right through the Pacific from Fiji up to Hawaii, except where modern methods have resulted in its control. This disease presents features making it hard to distinguish from syphilis in a certain stage. Moreover, it is curable only by the same remedy (Salvarsan) that cures syphilis. It was and, in many places, is still as common with Polynesian children as measles with European. Mothers deliberately infect young children with yaws in order to get them over it in early life, as any attack of the disease in later years may be severe.[108]

For over 150 years medical men have almost unanimously regarded yaws as connected with syphilis, or as a variant. Only in the last four or five years has it been definitely established that it is neither a venereal disease nor a form of syphilis. In chapter twenty-one will be found a fuller reference to this matter, showing that Captain Cook was the first man to hold an opinion that yaws was not an effect of venereal contagion; and he alone amongst his surgeons and officers seemed to hold that opinion. Keen observer as he was, it is more than possible that he was unable at all times and places to distinguish between the visible effects of yaws and venereal diseases respectively, when meeting natives of the various islands. Undoubtedly, no other man in his ships did distinguish a difference.

Hence it is certain that La Perouse and Dr. Samwell were confused at Hawaii as to the identity of the disease that natives, especially children, were suffering from who presented symptoms identical with that of both yaws or syphilis. In their narratives they speak of syphilis being common when most probably the disease was yaws. Natives themselves and Europeans, such as missionaries and travellers, in the early days of settlement were completely misled by these two very similar diseases. Hence a widespread and long-persisting confusion as to the prevalence of venereal or syphilitic diseases in the Hawaiian Islands.

---

[108] This seems odd considering there is still no vaccine for yaws. The disease can be contained through effective treatment and hygiene and is now largely confined to Ghana, Papua New Guinea, and the Solomon Islands. The World Health Organisation had set a target for the eradication of yaws by 2020 but this has not yet been achieved – *Editor.*

The most common disease, certainly, was yaws – yet the one term of "venereal" was applied alike to that and to the other disease.

From this may have arisen the legend of a grave wrong done to the Hawaiians through the introduction of venereal disease by some of the crews of Cook's vessels. To make Captain Cook responsible for this wrong was only part of the process of exaggeration and calumniation directed against him and his memory.

It is apparent that a section of the Hawaiians, fearful of condemnation for killing him, whether through premeditation or from sudden impulse, looked around for some grounds of justification or extenuation of their crime; and they were encouraged or abetted in this by others not of their race. Hence the charges of idolatrous worship, of sacrilege, and of spreading vile diseases became part of persistent propaganda directed against Captain Cook's moral character and his good name and fame.

Cook in his Journal says:

"No matter what precaution I took to protect the natives from the disaster of evil consequences of introduced diseases, I found too often that all these precautions went astray."

I think it will be admitted that, in order to justify a charge against Cook of responsibility for the introduction of these diseases, it must be proved that Cook, as a commander, neglected to take proper precautions against such.

On p.182, Vol. VI, of Cook's own narrative of his Voyages, he says:

"The order not to permit the crews of the boats to go on shore was issued, that I might do everything in my power to prevent the importation of a fatal disease into this island which I knew some of the men laboured under. With the same view I ordered all female visitors to be excluded from the ship. Another necessary precaution was taken by strictly enjoining that no person known to be capable of propagating the infection should be sent upon duty, out of ship. Whether these regulations, dictated by humanity, had the desired effect or no, time only can discover. I had been equally attentive to the same object, when I had first visited the Friendly Islands. Yet I afterwards found with real concern that I had not succeeded, and I am very much afraid that this will always be the case in such voyages as ours, whenever it is necessary to have a number of people on shore. The opportunities and inducement to an intercourse between the sexes are then too numerous to be guarded against, and however confident we may be of the health of our men, we are often undeceived too late."

This statement of Captain Cook is absolutely supported by the account published by Surgeon David Samwell, Medical Officer of the *Discovery*, from which I quote the following:

"I bear testimony, for I was then in the *Resolution*, to the particular care taken by Captain Cook to prevent any of his people, *who were not in perfect health*, from having communication with the shore and *also to prevent women from coming on board the ship.*

"As this humane precaution answered the intended purpose we had great reason to believe, for not one of those who did go on shore was afterwards in the Surgeon's list, or known to have any complaint; which was the most convincing proof we could have of their being well at the time."

Samwell then proceeds to state that

"on the second visit to the Hawaiian Islands, eleven months from the discovery of them, we then fell in with two islands- Mooewee (Maui) and Owhyee (Hawaii) – which we had not seen before, and very soon found that the venereal disease was not unknown to the natives. This excited astonishment amongst us, and made us anxious to ascertain, whether or not, so dreadful a calamity had been left at Kauai by our ships on their previous visits. But the scanty knowledge we had of their language made this a matter of great difficulty, and rendered the best intelligence we could get but vague and uncertain."

It is more than probable that what Samwell saw on these two islands was the disease now known as "yaws."

Samwell refers to the fact that both Cook and King seemed to accept the natives' story, that the disease had come from the crews of Cook's ships. He therefore tested the natives, so as to check their story, and found that, to every question asked, they returned the invariable answer – "Yes." So he then took the step of checking their statements as follows:

"I asked them," he says, "if they did not receive the disease first from Oahu, a neighbouring island *which we had not touched at, when we were in these parts before.* The man directly answered that they had, and strenuously persisted in the same answer every time the question was put to him either by myself or by another officer who was with me."

Thus the native was prepared to insist that the disease had been introduced from an island on which Cook nor any of his men had ever been before, and nearly 200 miles distant, and between which island and Kauai there was a war at the time.

Samwell then says:

"Such contradictory accounts as these prove nothing but our ignorance of their language, and consequently we are apt to be misled by inquiries of this sort.

"Yet those who have maintained that we left the disease at the Sandwich Islands, have no better foundations than this to rest their opinion upon."

Samwell points out that it appears there had been little intercourse with the Island of Kauai and the islands to the windward, such as Oahu and Hawaii, some hundreds of miles apart. War was a chronic affair then and before and after for years between the inhabitants.

He further says that – "At the time, their inhabitants rarely visited each other, except for hostile purposes." Then he goes on to say:

"But even were we to allow that there is a frequent intercourse between them, which from the distance alone was highly improbable, yet it is hardly possible that the disease should have spread so far and so *universally* as we found it at Hawaii in the short space of time that had intervened between our first and second visit to the Sandwich Islands."

This universal disease could only be yaws, unless a miracle had happened.

On the same supposition he says:

"It will appear very extraordinary that we should have found it more common by far at Hawaii, where we had never been, than at Kauai, the place where we were supposed to have first left it."

"That this was the case, however, from my situation at that time as Surgeon of the *Discovery*, I am able to announce with some certainty. The priests pretended to be expert at curing them, and seemed to have an established mode of treatment, which by no means implied that it was a recent complaint amongst them, much less that it was introduced only a few months before."

Does this not clearly indicate that the disease was yaws?

What does the term "established mode of treatment" imply – unless that the disease was long prevalent?

Then Samwell sums up the position in these words:

"Whence, or at what time, the inhabitants of those Islands received the disease, or whether or not it be indigenous among them, is what I do not pretend to ever guess; but from the circumstances above mentioned, I think myself warranted in saying that there are by no means sufficient proofs of our having first introduced it, but that, on the contrary, there is every reason to believe that they were afflicted with it before we discovered those Islands."

No medical man of to-day can come to any other conclusion than that the prevalent disease with which the natives were afflicted before and after the discovery of the Islands was yaws. If it was a venereal disease, then it was not introduced by Cook's crews.

I now call attention to a work by Dr. Martin Wall, entitled, *Dissertations*, *letters, etc., by Martin Wall, M.D.,* Oxford, 1786.

Wall states that the *Dolphin*, under Byron, left England in 1764 and visited Tamar and returned to England in 1766.

In the latter year Wallis in the *Dolphin* accompanied by Carteret in the *Swallow*, left England. Wallis discovered Tahiti in 1767 and returned to England in 1768. In 1766 (November 21), Bougainville sailed from Brest and touched at Tahiti in 1768.

On 26th August, 1768, Captain Cook in the *Endeavour* was despatched to the South Seas, and called at Tahiti, and he again visited it in his two subsequent voyages.

Dr. John Reinhold Forster in his *Observations made during a Voyage round the World*, p.488, said:

"When Captain Cook came, in the year 1769, in the *Endeavour* to O-taheitee, he found that half his crew when he left the Society Isles (of which O-taheitee is the principal and most central) were infected with the venereal disease, and it was then suspected that M. de Bougainville's ships' crews had communicated this disease. M. de Bougainville, in his turn, suspects the English in the *Dolphin* to have first introduced it, and the gentlemen in the *Dolphin* assert that they never had one man infected with the least venereal symptom whilst they were at O-taheitee or afterwards."

With all these contradictory statements and denials, is it not possible that whatever the disease was, it was indigenous to the Society Islands? It is certain that yaws was an endemic disease there.

But perhaps the most important statement is that made by La Perouse. In the publication, *Voyage de La Perouse – Autour du Monde*, Paris, 1797, Vol. II, La Perouse refers to:

"the support which his statements obtained from the observations of M. Rollin, the enlightened Chief Surgeon of his Expedition. He paid a visit to several persons on this Island, Owhyhee, who were attacked by venereal disease, the development of which would have required in Europe a period of 12 to 15 years. He also saw children of seven or eight years smitten with this disease, who could have contracted it only in their mother's womb."

This statement clearly indicates yaws. La Perouse then remarks that "Captain Cook on the first occasion only touched at Kauai and nine months later, on his return from the North, he found that the natives of Moouee (Maui) who came aboard were nearly all affected by the disease." As Moouee is 180 miles distant from Kauai, the course of the disease seemed to La Perouse to be too rapid not to raise a doubt." Then La Perouse concludes by saying:

"If one adds to these observations the fact of the former communication between the Spaniards and these Islands, it would doubtless appear probable that they have for a long while shared with other people the ills that menace the human race."

The last statements of La Perouse are only explicable when one considers the confusion arising from the similarity of yaws and syphilis. In my opinion, based on some study of the subject, there is no doubt that prior to Cook's visit to the Sandwich Islands, communication had been established, although of a very casual character, between mariners of the maritime races of the Pacific, including the Polynesians.

There is indisputable evidence that there was communication between the Sandwich Islands and Tahiti, for centuries prior to Cook's visit. In point of fact, the language of the two groups of islands is practically the same. Therefore, as a similar disease was noticeable at Tahiti in 1769, it is probable that, at the same time, it was also prevalent in the Sandwich Islands.

The ground for attributing to Captain Cook and his crew the introduction of these diseases is largely based upon the admissions of Cook and King in their narratives. Why they made these admissions, one can only conjecture, especially when they must have realised they would be used against them. But the very fact that they made these admissions shows how honest they were in what they wrote. They certainly made no effort to cloak any mishaps or wrongdoings, and their frankness in this respect is entitled to be treated more as in their favour, than against them.

It stands out, however, in bold relief, that Cook did everything that was humanly possible to prevent his crew from communicating the disease; and no human being could do more than that. Yet, in some accounts[109] which have been so sedulously spread abroad from local sources in the Hawaiian Islands, no credit whatever is given to Cook for his efforts in attempting to prevent the introduction of the disease.

During my visit to the Hawaiian Islands. I spoke to the captain of one of the large boats on which I travelled between the islands. He was an officer who had blood relationship, through his ancestors, with the Hawaiian people. I asked him how he would like to be held responsible for what his crews did when they landed at one of the ports at which he traded. He answered me readily: "I wouldn't keep the job for five minutes if I were to be *held* responsible for what my crew did when they went ashore. No captain," he said, "could honestly accept such a responsibility."

If I were to permit the case to rest on the foregoing facts in this chapter, my conclusions might be discounted on the ground of an unconscious bias either in myself or my authorities cited.

I will therefore adduce American evidence, and refer to an address recently delivered at Honolulu (1927 or 1928) by the President of the Hawaiian Historical Society (the Rt. Rev. H.B. Restarick, retired Bishop of Honolulu). No one in the islands, or in America, will impugn the high character or the veracity of Bishop Restarick, even if one may not agree with his conclusions.

In his address (published in full as a pamphlet) he says that yaws and syphilis in certain stages are indistinguishable except by microscopical

---

[109] This does not apply to all accounts, as many recent American writers, notably Bishop Restarick, have stressed the fact that Cook's orders were not obeyed despite his great efforts to see that they were complied with - *Author*.

examination by a bacteriologist. He refers to the unjust charge "that Cook brought a terrible disease to Hawaii and was thereby its worst enemy," and says that this charge is unfounded and that blame is unjustly attached to Captain Cook. He quotes Seaman Zimmermann, Dr. Samwell, and even Ledyard (the American corporal of Marines), to prove that not only did Cook issue strict orders "forbidding anyone to have any dealings with native women," but also "insisted on rigid medical examination of any man going ashore... threatened heavy punishment to those who violate the orders... and talked to the men in a body on the subject."

Further in his address Bishop Restarick cites not only La Perouse, but M. Rollin, his surgeon-major, to prove that the disease which they saw was in such a stage and so universal that Cook's crews could not possibly have been responsible for it.

Then he says:

"Bruce Cartwright, on his recent visit to Samoa, found that yaws was very common, especially among the children, and being interested in the subject wrote to Dr. Storie Dixson,[110] an eminent authority in Sydney, Australia. His reply is here given in full:

"'The question is, did Cook's crew introduce venereal disease to the Hawaiian Islands? Samwell seems to have noticed the disease upon Cook's arrival. This would imply it was evident to the eye and therefore a very evident skin disease, thus excluding gonorrhoea. There is a disease not syphilitic which engenders ulceration, but men would not typically be allowed ashore with it. In any case this tropical ulcer is very common in hot climates and would hardly be considered venereal. Hence the question, is there any skin disease which prevailed in the east, including the Pacific islands, which resembles syphilis and long antedates Cook? I may say here that I have had much acquaintance with syphilis and have seen its *alter ego* yaws in cases from the islands in white and coloured folks.

"'Let me quote from that authoritative work by Bryan and Archibald

---

in three volumes, *Practice of Medicine in the Tropics*. In Vol. II, p.1291, we read:

Yaws: This disease greatly resembled syphilis and is caused by an infection with a spirochaete, spironema pertenue, which is indistinguishable morphologically from spironema pallidum of syphilis, but is as distinct from syphilis as varicella (chicken-pox) from variola (small pox). Patients suffering from syphilis may contract yaws and those suffering from yaws may contract syphilis.

"'Yaws is more common among children than adults. The similarity of tertiary yaws to syphilis is very great, and Howard, who has wide experience of both diseases in Africa, considers that many of the manifestations of tertiary yaws are indistinguishable from tertiary syphilis.

"'Is there any evidence that Cook's men introduced syphilis? On the contrary Cook was, I may say, meticulously careful as regards allowing any man on shore who had any signs of disease, hence his distress when, through confusion with yaws, extensively present in the tropics, including many Pacific islands, and almost certainly the Hawaiian islands. It was to Cook's credit that he was ready to accept responsibility that through what he considered disobedience to his instructions, this dread disease was spread. Cook's specific instructions are too clear and were thoroughly understood by all on the Society group. To sum up, Cook's doctors would easily get confused between syphilis and yaws. The special notice of the very experienced French doctors with Bougainville, as regards the presence on children of symptoms which could only be due to infection, if syphilitic, gained from the mother some years before, made him doubt that what he saw very like syphilis really being such. To spread the disease in nine months from Kauai to Hawaii is to my mind impossible.'"

(Signed) "T. Storie Dixson."

Finally Bishop Restarick says:

"If Hawaiians were to accept the theory that Cook's men gave the disease to the Hawaiians, and that it spread from Kauai to Maui and Hawaii in nine months, it involves the belief that promiscuity between the sexes was such that the disease spread like wildfire. Captain King remarks that Hawaiians were very jealous of their wives with respect to men of their own race, and Campbell, who lived on the islands in 1809, says the same thing.

"From all I can learn it is impossible to believe that conditions were such that disease could have spread, as Cook found it in nine months, or in fact a very much longer period. I have a better opinion of the Hawaiians than to accept the idea that they lived a life of utter promiscuity, which it would be necessary to accept if we were to believe that Cook's men left disease at Waimea, Kauai, where they remained only four days, and that before the end of the year it was a veritable plague on Maui and Hawaii."

I hope that the evidence I have adduced in this chapter is sufficient to convince my readers:

i.   That there is at least very grave doubt about the charge that venereal diseases were first introduced into the Hawaiian Islands by Cook's crews.

ii. That the evidence definitely proves that yaws was prevalent, and was not distinguishable from syphilis: and that its prevalence confused the minds of not only Surgeon Samwell, but of Captains Cook and King, and of later visitors.

I think, too, that it is clear that Captain Cook was far from responsible for the misconduct of his men but, on the contrary, was deeply mortified that his orders had miscarried (as at Nihau) or had been disobeyed elsewhere.

18
The decline of the Hawaiian race and the causes contributing to it

The statements which have been persistently made, "that the decline in the population of the Hawaiian Islands is mainly attributable to the spread of these vile diseases, introduced by Europeans," will not bear analysis.[111]

I quote the following extract from Stanford's Compendium of Geography, Australasia, Vol. II, by F.H.H. Guillemard, and A.H. Keane, pp.538-9:

"What is the immediate cause of the depopulation of these and other islands of Polynesia, it is very difficult to say. Neither the diseases nor the ardent spirits introduced by Europeans are sufficient to account for it. By many writers who cannot be accused of bias, it is considered to be due in part to the missionaries, who, in their zeal to rescue the uncivilised natives, have not always gone to work with the necessary discretion. The repressive measures alluded to on a former page have entirely altered the life and customs of the native, and have been instrumental in depriving

---

[111] It is important to note that here Carruthers is not dismissing the importance of European diseases, which he acknowledges in the coming paragraphs, merely that they were not the only factor at play.

This is one of the most emotionally complex chapters in this book, as it deals with the loss of numerous indigenous lives both in Hawaii and across the Pacific. It reveals both Carruthers' strengths (in his deep and genuine empathy, his dismissal of the prevalent myth of dying races, and his ability to identify the wrongs of missionaries and other European actors) and his weaknesses (in the somewhat condescending tone he takes and the racial language he uses) - *Editor*.

him of his former light-heartedness and freedom, which, among an undeveloped, child-like race, is no small matter.

"The Hawaiian Consul-General, Mr. Manley Hopkins, considers that 'the oppressive system of government, the discontinuance of ancient sports, and consequent change in the habits of the people, have been powerful agents in this work of depopulation; and the ill-judged enforcement of cruel punishments and heavy penalties for breaches of chastity have much aided it, by giving an additional stimulus to the practice — always too common among Polynesian females — of causing abortion, of which practice sterility is the natural result.'"

The Rev. Wm. Ellis, in his Journal written in 1823, states that Cook's estimate of the population of the Sandwich Islands was very much above the mark. Cook estimated 400,000. Ellis estimates that that was about one-third too high. In 1823 Ellis estimates the population at about 150,000, and he distinctly says that the cause of the declining population was the practice of infanticide – he might have added "and the constant warfare between the islands."

I quote his own language in which he states, after alleging that the practice of infanticide was more common in Hawaii than in any other of the Pacific Islands, that:

"Among the Sandwich Islanders, the infant, after living a month, or even a year, was still insecure, as some were destroyed when nearly able to walk. It is painful to think of the numbers thus murdered. All the information we have been able to obtain, and the facts that have come to our knowledge in the neighbourhood where we resided, afford every reason to believe, that from the prevalence of infanticide two-thirds of the children perished.

"We have been told by some of the chiefs, on whose word we can depend, that they have known parents to murder three or four infants, where they have spared one. But even supposing that not more than half the children were thus cut off, what an awful spectacle of depravity is presented! How many infants must have been annually sacrificed to a custom so repugnant to all the tenderest feelings of humanity, that, without the clearest evidence, we should not believe it would be found in the catalogue of human crimes."

If I may venture a layman's view, I would say that a very material factor in causing the very regrettable decline of the Hawaiian native population was the introduction of some very common European diseases such as dysentery, measles, and (with the wearing of clothes) pulmonary complaints. These diseases are endemic amongst European people who are so immunised as to make them more or less proof against severe attacks. Whereas, the native people are not immunised, but present, in their bodies, a very fertile field for the activity of the germ life of European diseases which take a virulent form with them (the natives).

There is no doubt, from the accounts given by early historians, that shortly after the islands were open to European civilisation they were twice visited by widespread pestilence. I have not been able to ascertain definitely what these so-called pestilences were, but I do know that in the South Sea Islands, which were also visited at the same time by pestilence, they were known to be *dysentery and measles*. For one European in a thousand to be carried off by a disease of this kind, there would probably be a hundred times as many of the native population. Not only would these diseases be more severe with the natives than with the Europeans, but, unfortunately, the natives adopted remedies calculated to kill rather than to cure. Later on, by the introduction of skilled treatment by European doctors and nurses, the native death-rate has been diminished.

Even to-day, speaking from my personal observations on the Island, I found that the pure Hawaiian population was still declining. I was told by many keen observers, good friends and admirers of the native race, that the Hawaiians were dying out, mainly because they were giving way to, rather than battling against, their fate. Certainly they are marrying out of their race and there are more half-castes than full-bloods.

At an address which I gave at the Hawaiian Civic Club in Honolulu, at the request of some of its members, I sought the advice (before speaking) of several of the best Hawaiians of my acquaintance there. That advice was, to urge the natives to get to work, to take a greater interest in the affairs of life, and not to give way to a spirit of the inevitable. Thus, in my address, I stressed this point in as kindly a fashion as I could. The natives appreciated my advice, or at least I think so, by their applause and by the way they spoke to me afterwards. But the difficulty is that they seem to have it in their souls that their race is doomed.

I remember that some thirty years ago, when I was visiting Tasmania, I made inquiries as to the cause which had led to the complete wiping out of the native race in Tasmania.

I was then very much struck by the statement of medical and scientific men who had studied the question much more closely than I could pretend to have done, that the main contributing factor to the extinction of the Tasmanian natives was that they had "lost the will to live." When they were removed in a body to neighbouring islands – King Island and Flinders Island, in Bass Straits – where there was no contaminating influence of the whites and where they could have reverted to their ancient mode of living if they had so chosen, the doctors attending them found that the natives were dying in a mysterious way, and with great rapidity, and they attributed their deaths to the fact that they had absolutely extinguished, by their attitude to life, all resistance to sickness of any kind. It was said of them: "They died simply because they wanted to die and had lost the will to live."

I will not go to this extent in my judgement of the Hawaiian native race. They are undoubtedly a much finer race than the natives of Australia, and are quite the equal of the best of the Samoans, New Zealanders and the Maoris. Physically they seem to be a very strong people, taking them individually; and when they engage in work they are spoken of highly by those who know and observe them. They are a very musical people, but throughout their music, which charms and enchants, there runs a sad strain, and everything is in a minor key, which typifies their frame of mind. They are a very generous people and would give away all they had to benefit others. Thus, they have impoverished themselves; and they have seen their islands passing away into the possession of the white, the yellow and the brown people, whilst they themselves, or at least many of them, are living on the ragged edge of poverty.[112] On the other hand, if the native Hawaiians could only live up to their opportunities, as the Japanese and Chinese in their midst do, the race could recover from its decline and could once more get on the up-grade.

A more hopeful view is expressed by Dr. Lambert of the Rockefeller Institute in his pamphlet *Medical Conditions in the South Pacific*. He says:

"Popular opinion is that Pacific races are dying out. Actually there is little evidence of it. The eastern groups which met the first shot of western civilisation, are slowly recovering and are on a fairly stable basis now, except for the Marquesas. Some others show a slow but steady gain and a divergence over a period of the birth and death lines in reassuring directions."

As a matter of fact, the Samoans in American Samoa are steadily increasing, whilst those in Western Samoa are slightly on the up-grade, despite severe losses in recent outbreaks of influenza.

The Tongans, thanks to the wise government of their native Queen, are increasing.

The New Zealand Maoris are definitely over the crisis of race decline.

The Fijians show an increase of 8,000 or 10 per cent. in the last census. They are free from venereal disease and are slowly becoming immunised to European introduced diseases.

The evidence now available with up-to-date vital statistics proves distinctly that in all these races there has been a terrible mortality of children, attributable almost entirely to mal-nutrition caused by improper feeding after the weaning period. The birth-rate is high, but

---

[112] Elsewhere in his writings Carruthers describes Hawaii as a highly successful society where the various ethnic groups worked together so harmoniously that it made him question the white Australia policy. This is an example of where the dated racial language can mask a reasonable point, though at other times it is genuinely pernicious – *Editor*.

only a small percentage of the infants live to adult age.

With modern organisation of child welfare movements in these Pacific Islands there is reason to believe that the present terrible mortality of child life will be arrested. Then the Pacific Island races will be saved.

19
Europeans at the Sandwich Islands prior to Cook

Many authors have given good reasons for the belief that Europeans had landed at some of these islands before the time of Cook's arrival there. The Rev. William Ellis refers to it at length in his Journal, and quotes the natives' statements to him on this point. Cook also refers to it in his account. I will only add this additional statement by the Rt. Rev. H.B. Restarick.

Bishop Restarick says that he found a clue as to the nationality of the seven men who arrived in Kealakekua Bay "in a painted boat with an awning over the stern," and one of them had a *pahi* or sword. These men remained in Hawaii, married natives and were made chiefs (*vide* the native historical statements given to Cook, Ellis and others).

The clue he has discovered is as follows:

In 1598 Dutch merchants fitted up eight vessels for a voyage to the Indies, three to sail by the Cape of Good Hope, and five to proceed through the Straits of Magellan. The chief pilot engaged for the five ships was an Englishman named Will Adams.

They passed through the Straits in April, 1599. One hundred and twenty men died in the winter of that year. In the spring two of the ships gave up the venture and returned to Holland. The other three ships agreed to steer separately and to meet at a point on the coast of Chile, 47° south latitude.

Adams, on the *Charity* (a vessel of 126 tons), with 110 men, reached the proposed rendezvous and waited 28 days for the other ships. The *Charity* then sailed north to the Island of Mocha, near the Chilean shore, and about 39° south latitude.

Disaster occurred here and 23 armed men landed, but the whole of them were killed, amongst them being the brother of Will Adams.

The *Charity* then returned to an island near Mocha, where they found one of their companion ships – the *Hope* – whose commander and 27 men had been killed in an attempt to get food.

Among the sailors with Adams was a Portuguese who had been to Japan, in which land his countrymen had carried on trade for fifty years. Acting on his advice, the two ships determined to sail for Japan, which they did on 27th November, 1599. They took a north-westerly course, taking advantage of the trade winds. The *log* of the voyage is in the Bodleian Library at Oxford.

In the route to Japan from the Island of Mocha, it bisects Hawaii, and Adams kept his course, between three or fourth months sailing some five thousand miles, and, as the record of the *log* states, they encountered a group of islands about 16° north latitude. With the imperfect observations of the day, that is near enough for the southern part of Hawaii. In point of fact, there are no other considerable islands within 2,000 miles.

Adams states in his *log* that eight men ran off with the ship's pinnace; one man was captured, but seven got away.

If this theory is correct – and it seems to be on the facts stated – the *Charity* and the *Hope* sighted the Hawaiian Islands about the end of February, 1600. The two ships continued their course without capturing the seven deserters. The *Hope* was never heard of again, but the *Charity* reached Japan in April, 1600.

I have in my possession a copy of this narrative of Will Adams, who is spoken of as the first Englishman in Japan, and which supports to an extent Bishop Restarick's statements.

There can be no reasonable doubt that some foreigners, long prior to Cook's discoveries, did at times land in these islands, never to return to their own country. Who they were and of what nationality, there is no clear evidence.

That they left their mark on Hawaiian history is evident. Some of the natives 150 years ago evidenced a white cross in the breed. That, and the admitted presence of some European articles, is only to be accounted for by the fact that foreigners had landed on the islands and remained there for a time.

The *Heiau*, or Temple, in which Cook's
bones were buried after his death

20

A frank admission of misrepresentation by an English writer who, in 1788, falsely impugned the United States First Continental Congress as ordering the capture of Captain James Cook notwithstanding Benjamin Franklin's earnest recommendation to the officers of the American Navy to spare him and his ships

Whilst I am endeavouring to clear away every calumny affecting the memory of Captain Cook it is only just that I should act similarly in regard to a false accusation made against the American Government and Legislature. We must do as we would be done by, by acknowledging any wrong on our side and repairing the error.[113]

Once more I owe thanks to my friend Victor Houston, of the U.S. Congress (1929), in furnishing me with the material to enable this to be done.

I now proceed to quote portions of an article appearing in the *Washington Historical Quarterly* of April, 1929, Vol. XX, No. 2, by Edmond S. Meany, University of Washington, under the heading of "The Congress – Captain Cook Falsehood":

---

[113] Carruthers has a gentlemanly sense of fairness, but considering his successful defence of Cook would ultimately facilitate alliance building between the Americans and the British Pacific, there were good strategic reasons to be chivalrous – *Editor.*

"One of the most persistent falsehoods relating to the Continental Congress declares that Congress ordered the capture of Captain James Cook, the great English discoverer, during the War for American Independence...

"At the outset it was quite clear that the offensive charge [*sic*] emanated from the *Life of Captain Cook* by Andrew Kippis, an English dissenting minister and author, whose life span was from March 28, 1725 to October 8, 1795. If he did not originate the falsehood complained of, he at least, through his book (published in 1788) gave it wide publicity and persistence. This fact is shown by the many subsequent editions of his book and quotations from it, as well as by the immediate denial of the falsehood at the time of the book's first publication.

"In order to ascertain any possible source from which the first story could have originated, it was determined to have a search made in the records of the Continental Congress for the dates involved. An appeal was sent to Dr. J. Franklin Jameson, Professor of American History in the Library of Congress and formerly Director of the Department of Historical Research in the Carnegie Institution of Washington. His reply... contains a... complete denial of the falsehood...

"Some ten years ago the Department of Terrestrial Magnetism of the Carnegie Institution of Washington asked for information about the Continental Congress and Captain Cook. The Department of Historical Research furnished what information could be found and it was published in full in the journal called *Terrestrial Magnetism* for September 1918, Volume XXIII., beginning at page 143. A brief summary of that article was published in the Year Book, No. 17 (1918), pages 262-263. Those dependable publications by the Carnegie Institution of Washington are now available for any student of this event in history. For those who love the name and fame of Captain James Cook it is well to reproduce here some of the information thus collected and saved.

"In the *List of the Benjamin Franklin Papers* in the Library of Congress, page 66, is found under date of March 10, 1779, the following entry:

'Franklin to all captains of United States armed vessels. Safe conduct for Capt. Cook. Autographed drafts signed.' There is a notation here that his letter to the captains is printed in John Bigelow's edition of *Franklin's Works*, Volume VI., page 321. In that same volume (*List of the Benjamin Franklin Papers* in the Library of Congress), page 199, there is mention of a draft, written by Franklin, of a letter to some unknown American publisher, apparently in 1789, thus described: 'Refutation of calumny of Americans in Dr. Kippis's *Life of Cook*; David Henry's refutation; English authorities' recognition of Franklin's action.' Such citations are ample to show how instant was the refutation of the story published by Andrew Kippis in his *Life of Captain Cook.*"

Corroborative testimony is further set out in Professor Meany's article from no less an authority than Charles Thomson, Secretary of the 1st Continental Congress from its beginning to 1789, when the new Constitution went into effect.[114] Evidence is adduced that the name of Charles Thomson in his time was synonymous with "truth." The Delaware Indians adopted him into their tribe and gave him a name meaning "Man of Truth."

The article continues:

"*The New York Historical Society's Collections* for the year 1878, pages 254-256, contains the draft of a letter by this truthful and well equipped Secretary Charles Thomson, dated March 9, 1795, after he had ceased to be Secretary. He quoted from a letter from Dr. Jeremy Belknap who had himself quoted the objectionable statement from the Kippis book. The Thomson letter goes on to say:

"'Though on reading these remarks I could not hesitate a moment in contradicting them, because Congress never did express a disapprobation of the directions issued by Doctor Franklin, nor did they ever direct that especial care should be taken to seize Capt. Cook if an opportunity

---

[114] Thomson was secretary of the Continental Congress through its entire existence from 1774 until 1789 when the present U.S. Constitution came into effect. He is in many respects an unsung hero, facilitating history for which others would be remembered – *Editor.*

of doing it occurred, yet I thought it might not be improper to pause and try to find from what source this misrepresentation sprung. Was it an inference drawn from subsequent proceedings of Congress? It is true that on the 2nd day of May, 1780, Congress passed a new form of commissions for private vessels of war, and new instructions to the Captains or Commanders of the said private armed vessels, in which the ships or vessels, together with their cargoes, belonging to any inhabitant or inhabitants of Bermuda, and other ships and vessels bringing persons with an intention to reside within the United States, are expressly exempted from capture, and no notice is taken of Captain Cook. But at that time of passing these Acts Congress had no information of the directions issued by Doctor Franklin. From March, 1779, to that time they only received from him two letters, one dated 30 Sept. 1779, which was received and read the 23 Feb., 1780, and the other dated 4 Oct., 1779, which was received and read 4 March, 1780, neither of which mentioned anything of these directions. It may be seen by reference to those letters now in the Secretary of State's office.

"'This circumstance not being known publicly, and no notice being taken of Captain Cook, an inference might be drawn that Congress had reversed the orders which their Ambassador had given; in fact they had not in view nor knew anything of them. But there is nothing in the commission or instructions, nor in any Act of Congress, which will warrant the assertion. With regard to Doct. Kippis' note of his having obtained the account from Sir Joseph Banks, as S. J. could not have given it from his own knowledge, 'that it was directed by Congress that especial care should be taken to seize Capt. Cook if an opportunity of doing it occurred,' some other source must be looked from which this has come. Sir Joseph Banks could have had no personal knowledge of this; he must have had information from others. And all this proceeded from a false notion that - it would be injurious to the U.S. for the English to obtain a knowledge of the opposite coast of America. I am therefore led to conclude that this has arisen from misinformation, or from some of those spurious pieces which were fabricated and published within the enemies lines as Acts and Resolves of Congress, with an intent to vilify

Congress or to answer some hostile purpose.'"

Dr. Jameson (mentioned above) is quoted by Professor Meany in these words:

"Dr. Jameson says he was helped in gathering the citations and quotations by Dr. Edmund Cody Burnett, a member of the staff of the Department of Historical Research, Carnegie Institution of Washington. Dr. Jameson says that Dr. Burnett 'knows more about the Continental Congress and its doings than anyone else does or ever did.' Dr. Burnett has lately been working again through all the proceedings of the Continental Congress for 1780. He has assured Dr. Jameson 'that no action on their part relating to action of naval vessels respecting Captain Cook is in existence.'"

It appears clear from the foregoing statements of men most qualifies to speak with authority on the action of the Congress of the date, that there is no foundation in fact for the statement published by Kippis in his *Life of Cook*.[115]

---

[115] Benjamin Franklin's intervention to protect Cook is just the first of a number of acknowledgements of the scientific importance of Cook's work by the American Government. After the Challenger Space Shuttle disaster of 1986, a competition was held to name its replacement. During a poignant speech consoling his nation President Reagan had compared the Astronauts to Sir Francis Drake and the earlier age of exploration. In the subsequent competition a large group of entrants suggested the name Endeavour, both because of Captain Cook and because of how well the term captured the spirit of NASA's mission. The Americans went so far as to include the "u" in Endeavour, to make it clear that they were paying tribute to the British Navigator. Considering that the Sesquicentennial Celebrations (covered in the third section of the book), which included commemorative coins and stamps, did much to popularise the memory of Cook in the United States, Carruthers may have played an indirect role in the choice of name.

21

Cook's education and training; Americans notice absence of honourable recognition of his services; the answer to this; the London statue 1910; the ordinary Englishman's casualness regarding Cook; Australian sentiment of deep gratitude; Cook's natural genius in some matters; his sea instinct and his great skill as a navigator; "yaws" and his keen perception of what it was

Captain James Cook was in some respects a born genius. Moreover, he seemed marked by Fate to do great deeds.

He is reputed by most accounts to have been a man of little education and that of the Dame School type.[116] I have seen statements which incline one to the belief that he had at least a very fair education. I refer to the Souvenir issued by the County Borough of Middlesbrough on the occasion of the Bi-Centenary Celebrations arranged in the Cleveland District. Stewart Park at Marton has passed into the possession of the above Borough, and in the grounds there is a granite vase marking the

---

[116] Dame Schools were rudimentary private schools, generally run by women or even just one woman in her home. They provided relatively affordable and flexible education, so much so that as early as 1789 convict Isabella Rosson would set one up in Sydney Cove, the first school in Australian history – *Editor*.

site of the cottage where Cook was born. Easby, Whitby and Great Ayton are close by and these districts, as well as others associated with Cook's early days, joined in the celebrations.

It is recorded that Cook's grandfather was a pious Scot and an elder of the Kirk. When his son (Cook's father), after whom Captain Cook received his Christian name, went to live in Yorkshire, the grandmother said to him: "God send you Grace." At his new home he met his future wife and her name was Grace, thus fulfilling the grandmother's parting prayer. She became the mother of the great Captain. So there was Scottish blood in him as well as English.[117]

Cook was first taught at the village Dame's School; then at Great Ayton the lad was put to school under the village dominie, George Pulleyn. Young Cook was keen, and his application, particularly in mathematics, led Mr. Skottowe, the father's employer, to defray the youngster's school fees. The boy's thirteenth year saw the end of his school-days however. Later on, when at work, he attended evening classes and read and studied assiduously. It is manifest that he had a good grounding in mathematics when he went to sea. He lost no opportunity to acquire a knowledge of navigation and astronomy. With his fine intellect he was bound to digest whatever he was taught at school or learnt from his own studying.

He became a first-rate seaman and navigator, a first-rate astronomer, and a first-rate officer. Above all he was a first-rate man and a natural gentleman. His wage as captain of his ship, with the rank in the Navy of First Lieutenant, was five shillings a day plus his allowances as an officer. It is just as well in these days, when the union wage in Australia and America varies from one pound to three pounds per day, to remember that the greatest discoverer and navigator of all time did his job magnificently on "five bob" a day and never made a murmur about

---

[117] Carruthers was of Scottish descent, as were many other contemporary liberal politicians like George Reid. It is noteworthy that despite this he still occasionally uses "England" to refer to the whole of Britain – *Editor*.

his pay.[118] More, he kept a wife and family and a home on that pay. Of course a shilling in those days was worth fully half a crown in these days. Money was dear in 1768 and goods were cheap.

For that small pay, and equipped with no great education, Captain Cook did his work that the French explorer, La Perouse, told Captain King, in 1788, that Captain Cook had done so well as to have left nothing further for him (La Perouse) to do, but to admire his work.

During the Sesqui-centennial Celebrations in Hawaii, in 1928, an American said to me that the one thing that had contributed mostly to the formation in America of a wrong opinion about Cook's work and reputation was the fact that, during his life and after, his own countrymen and his own King and Government had shown no marked respect for him or his services, conferring no honour and only a paltry pension on his widow and family. "What is your answer to that, Sir Joseph?" was the direct question put to me. This is the reply I gave and it is worth recording as it will fortify others in facing that question in America and elsewhere. I said:

"Neither I nor any other man of my race feels proud of the way that England regarded Cook's memory and services just when he died. But remember that a pension of £200 a year in 1779 means in value what a pension of £500 a year would be worth to-day. Moreover, there were some allowances made for the young children (£50 a year to each son). Most important, however, is the fact – little known nowadays – that Mrs. Cook, the widow, was allowed one half of the clear profits from the sale of Cook's *Third Voyage*, which amounted to £3863 9s. 4d. up to 1794 and exceeded £4000 up to 1801." (*Vide* George Nicol Trustee, Letters to Mrs. Cook, Jan. 7, 1795, and Jan. 14, 1801, in Grey Collection, Auckland Library, N.Z.)

"It seems certain that from this source there was an annual income to

---

[118] Carruthers had initially supported the union movement, but over the years he had grown frustrated at its increasing demands and the institutional power it had monopolised within a rigid industrial relations system. These issues would only be exacerbated with the advent of the Great Depression – *Editor.*

Mrs. Cook above her share of the £4000 mentioned. As a matter of fact, Captain Cook's widow was placed above want and in comfortable circumstances for her life."

"But," said my interrogator, "Cook or his widow received no honour in or after their lives from their Sovereign." I replied:

"That is a matter of shame felt by us who have benefitted so much from Cook's life work. Surely it does not detract from Cook's reputation, that his contemporaries and his Government did not fully appreciate it. Is it not all the more reason why we, with the light of days gone, should put Cook's name where it should be – high up on the Roll of Honour for Great and Famous Men?"

Let Englishmen especially realise this American point of view. They know and we know that England honoured Marlborough, Wellington, Nelson, and a host of other great soldiers and sailors, with dukedoms or peerages and with large grants from the public purse.

Cook, the greatest missionary of Peace for England and our greatest Empire Builder, received no honour save the Copley Gold Medal of the Royal Society for his care of the health of his crews; and only a small pension to his widow and sons. Add to this a medal struck and a posthumous coat-of-arms by the British Government.[119]

In the great City of London – the Mother City of our great Empire – one that abounds in thousands and thousands of monuments and tablets to the memory of the illustrious dead, there was not one monument or tablet to the memory of Cook when I visited it in 1908. I was prompted to write to the London *Times* in that year, reproaching the people of the metropolis for this utter neglect of one of the greatest of Englishmen. As I have said, this reproach was speedily removed and a fine statue is erected now in a most suitable position in London.

---

[119] People who believe that there is a "mythology" surrounding Cook are still apt to cite this neglect as proof that his later fame was constructed. Just prior, Carruthers admits to his underlying goal of building up Cook, but there is certainly no inherent nefariousness in this intent – *Editor.*

Dealing with the matter of statues to Captain Cook (a subject often referred to by Americans when speaking to me):

Facts reveal that shortly after Cook's death a public movement was initiated to erect a suitable monument to him at some appropriate place in England, and subscriptions were called for. It is unfortunately clear that this appeal received only scant support and nothing tangible eventuated. Thus for years no public monument was erected to his memory.

But this default by the nation that he served so well and faithfully, was atoned for to some extent by the fine action of his old patron and commander, Admiral Sir Hugh Palliser, who rose to the rank of Controller of the Royal Navy. He was, in Cook's life, his most sincere friend and an ardent admirer of his work. He knew him better than did any other of his contemporaries.[120]

Towards the end of the eighteenth century Sir Hugh Palliser erected a monument, to the memory of Captain Cook, in the park of his house, *The Vache*, at Chalfont Saint Giles.

Even this fine act of a comrade in recognition of Cook's magnificent work in his period of service of King and Country, seems to have escaped the notice of Cook's biographers and of his fellow-countrymen for many long years. Until so late as 1913 the notable inscription remained without any reference until it was published in full by commander J.A. Rupert-Jones in the *Hydrographic Annual* of that year.

The inscription, at some length, recounted Cook's claims to recognition of his work as a navigator and naval officer, but is too long for reproduction on these pages. One or two portions of it deserve to be set out and are as follows:

---

[120] Cook had served with Palliser on the H.M.S. *Eagle* during the 1750s. Both were later involved in the Siege of Quebec (1760) which helped to secure Canada as a British possession. Carruthers tried to include Canada as one of Cook's legacies, but the Canadians would never revere the Captain to the same extent as their antipodean cousins – *Editor.*

On one side are the words:

"To the memory of Captain James Cook, the ablest and most renowned navigator this or any other country has ever produced."

Mark these words from the man who, in his life, knew Cook better than any other of his contemporaries as his commander, comrade, and friend.

This inscription concludes in these words:

"If public service merits public acknowledgement, if the man who adorned and raised the fame of his country is deserving of honours, then Captain Cook deserves to have a monument raised to his memory by a generous and grateful nation."

Later on other monuments were erected at and near his birthplace. Tardily other similar recognition has come in other lands and in the heart of the Empire – London itself.

I must not omit, however, to mention that after the news had been received of the death of Captain Cook the British Government caused a memorial medal to be struck, and the Royal Society, by private subscription from its members, also caused a gold medal to be struck commemorating his service, one of which was presented to each subscriber. The British Government also granted a posthumous coat-of-arms to the dead commander, the central feature of which was a globe showing the main courses of his voyages in the Pacific, and a motto *Nil Intentatum Reliquit*.[121] The crest was an arm with the British flag displayed in the fist.

It would be unjust to be hypercritical of these honours which show at least the spirit in which they were accorded. I think, however, it will be admitted that they do not compare favourably with the recognition usually accorded to men who have done great deeds which have made

[121] This translates to "he left nothing un-attempted". The posthumous granting of arms was quite unusual and therefore amounted to a significant honour. It was as if this low-born sailor had finally earned his place amongst the ranks of the aristocracy – *Editor.*

our Empire what it is.

Looking at these facts it stands out with all the greater significance that the noblest memorial to Captain Cook is his unblemished reputation, a life well spent, and a work well done. His visible monuments are a continent and great dominions added to the British Empire.

I meet hundreds of Englishmen in official positions in Crown Colonies in the Pacific, and in the Dominions, as well as scores of them travelling in palatial liners in the Pacific. The best of them, when I remind them of Cook's fine work as the man who "blazed the track" for them, warm up and enthuse and take one to their hearts for reminding them of what we owe to him and to the crews of his little ships of 300 or 400 tons. But another set of men seem bored to be reminded of such a man, and possibly most of them have never troubled to read or learn what he did for King and Country.

In Australia I once took a trip through our noble north coast rivers with a dear old friend, "Daddy Rust" (W.E. Rust, an old English sailor-man who "made good" in Australia). He was amazed at the glorious country that he saw, studded with prosperous homes on dairy farms, or with cane fields, sugar mills, and dairy factories. Said he to me: "Australians ought to go down on their knees every night before they go to rest and say: 'Thank God for Captain Cook!'"[122]

So I repeat that sentiment and say that every Englishman should do the same. To Cook and England we owe Australia, New Zealand, a multitude of fertile islands in the South Seas, and thereby a securer hold upon our other possessions north of those seas. Nearly ten millions of people of English, Irish, Scottish, and Welsh blood hold these southern dominions and colonies of our Empire now. In another century's time, please God, and if we keep our trust, we shall have eighty to one hundred

---

[122] Appreciation of Cook became a de facto appreciation of Australia, just as modern criticism of Cook is now generally a de facto criticism of contemporary Australian society. This is both a blessing and a curse, but it is part of Carruthers' legacy. He wanted Cook to be the icon because he felt that the Captain was a positive role model whose emulation would make Australian society better – *Editor*.

million people, mainly of the fine Anglo-Saxon breed, in these lands. Mind you, the United States of America in the last one hundred years have similarly increased their population which is, however, only about 52 per cent. of Anglo-Saxon origin.

I began this chapter with the remark that Cook was a natural genius. Read Zimmermann's statement, that he had an uncanny instinct for the landfall. Where the charts showed no land he instinctively sensed that it was near. Only once – on the Barrier Reef – did his ships receive damage in about eleven years of voyaging in these little cat-built craft of from three to four hundred tons, slow sailers, doing at best an occasional nine knots an hour. In every case these ships reached their home port safe and sound after voyages of over three years' duration.

How well he cared for his crew at a time when other commanders would lose two-thirds of their men! Once he made the long voyage without the loss of one man from disease on his ship – a marvellous record.

Then take his observations on the disease of "yaws" in Tonga in 1769, or thereabouts. Cook, in his diary, gives his reason for his view, that it was a disease similar to syphilis yet not that complaint. That was 160 years ago, and since then medical men by the thousands have insisted that yaws is a form of syphilis, whilst a few have said it was not.

In a publication (*Medical Conditions in the South Pacific*) by Dr. S.M. Lambert, Deputy Central Medical Authority, Western Pacific High Commission, the writer states:

"In Cook's Voyages we find a most intelligent description of yaws and the first query I have seen as to its identity with syphilis. This was in connection with his two visits to Tongatabu. Cook states:

"'They have another disease of a more mischievous consequence, which is also very frequent, and appears on every part of the body, in large broad ulcers, discharging a thin, clear pus, some of which had a very virulent appearance, particularly on the face. Some, however, appeared to be cured of it and others mending; but it was generally attended with the loss of the nose or a considerable part of it. It being certainly known and even acknowledged by themselves, that the natives were subject to this disease before they were visited by the English, it cannot be the effect of venereal contagion, notwithstanding the similarity of the symptoms; unless we adopt a supposition that the venereal disorder was not introduced here by our people in 1773...'"

Finally, within the past four or five years, after a keen controversy amongst the scientific medical investigators, Captain Cook's view has been proved to be correct and it is definitely accepted that the two diseases are distinct, yaws not being a venereal disease and not related to venereal disease, though curable by the same remedy.

22

The last survivor of Cook's expedition; the tortoise at Nukualofa, Tonga

Although there is no mention of the matter in Cook's journals, there is, from Tongan sources, handed down from generation to generation, the tradition that Captain Cook left two tortoises at Haapai, one of the islands in the Tongan group, during one of his two visits there between 1774 and 1777. Of these, one still survives and is an honoured guest in the grounds of the Royal Palace at Nukualofa, in the Island of Tongatabu.[123]

There is no doubt about the tradition, which was committed to writing as soon as the natives were able to do so. I received a copy of this from the Rev. R. Page, Chairman of the Tongan Wesleyan Mission in 1927, when I first visited the Tongan Islands. I then also met the Prince-Consort Tungi, the grandson of the Chief to whom Cook gave the two tortoises. At the Royal Palace Prince Tungi showed me the tortoise, now partially blind and considerably battered as the result of bush fires (in which it was three times caught) and of an injury from a heavy limb of a tree falling on it and partially crushing its shell. Otherwise the tortoise was doing as well as could be expected at his age, possibly 200 years and certainly more than 160 years.

The Prince said there was no question that Captain Cook left it in the

---

[123] "'Tu'i Malila" lived until 1966, having in 1953 even received a visit from Queen Elizabeth II, which keeps alive a connection between past and present. It was reported to be 188 years old when it died – *Editor.*

islands. He also showed me a roll of very fine red cloth and other things which were given to his and the Queen's ancestors 150 years ago. The cloth had been well cared for and it was as good, when I saw it, as on the day it was manufactured. A piece of this cloth was presented to the British Museum by the late King of Tonga. I see no reason to doubt the truth of the story handed down to, and repeated by, the present generation of Tongans. Cook called at the Cape of Good Hope on each of his voyages, and took in all manner of animals for use, and for gift purposes.

I find no trace in his journals of the two tortoises being received by him, but that was not a matter of concern needing official notice. This small variety of tortoise, weighing probably 80 to 100 lb., was not difficult to procure in Cook's time, either at the Cape or at some of the smaller islands off the S. American coast.

Whilst one cannot speak positively, I think it can be assumed on the above facts that this old tortoise is the sole survivor of Cook's voyages, and as such I have deemed it worthy of this notice and also of the reproduction in these pages of its photograph with its present owner, Prince Tungi – a fine gentleman, educated at Newington College, Sydney, Australia. Queen Salote is a worthy ruler of her people. She is young, of commanding presence and pleasing appearance, and is every inch a Queen.

The native legend of the tortoise is as follows:

The Story of the Tortoise

Tu'i Malila (The King of Malila)

One story is that Captain Cook brought this tortoise as a gift from Tu'itoga (the King of Tonga). Another story is that Captain Cook brought it to Haabai, and the chiefs of Haabai got possession of it; and that, when the Tu'itoga heard about it, he had it brought to him. The first story, however, is more likely the true story, as we do not hear anything about it in Haabai.

Two tortoises were brought, but one died. The other, Tu'i Malila, is still alive. The name originated from the residence of the Tu'itoga, that name of which was Malili; and the name, "The King of Malila," was given to the tortoise, which had the free run of the grounds. The tortoise was cared for by the people, just as if it were a chief; and it went where it pleased in Tonga. If it came to a pit of Tongan bread, it would stay there and feed on the bread; and, although people might be grieved, they would not hurt it, because they regarded it as a chief. It would go to Hihifo and to Nukualofa; and the people would present kava to it and give it food. It would often be in difficulties out on the plains. The plains would often be fired, and the fire would pass over the tortoise. After the fire died out, it would return. It still bears on its back the mark where it was burnt on one occasion. It is very blind and very old, but it still goes about with ease, and eats and drinks. It eats all sorts of things, Tongan bread, bananas, paw-paws, and different fruits, and grass; but it does not care much about European food, probably owing to its unfamiliarity.

After the Tu'itoga died, the tortoise lived with his successors and their families. The children of this generation, however, are not really aware of the true position of this chief, and are often disrespectful to it. The Sisters were very kind to it and kept it in their grounds, and the school children took care of it. One day the Queen heard about it, and she ordered that Tu'i Malila be taken to the Palace grounds and kept there. Ever since then, Tu'i Malila has been in the Palace grounds, and may be seen at any time, as it has the freedom of the grounds.

Another animal first introduced to the islands by Captain Cook deserves a passing notice. Thousands of lean, long-snouted, reddish pigs abound in Tonga, where they are called by the natives "Captain Cookers." They are the progeny in a long line of descent from those brought to the islands by Captain Cook on his second and third voyages, and they have long helped to vary the diet of the natives in a land where animal food is scarce, though fish, fruits, and vegetables were abundant.[124]

---

[124] We have a justifiable tendency to focus on the negative effects that European contact had on native peoples. Much like modern globalisation, it was a more complicated picture of costs and benefits – *Editor.*

Prince Tungi of Tonga and Cook's Tortoise

Part III

The Sesqui-centennial Celebrations in the Hawaiian Islands in 1928

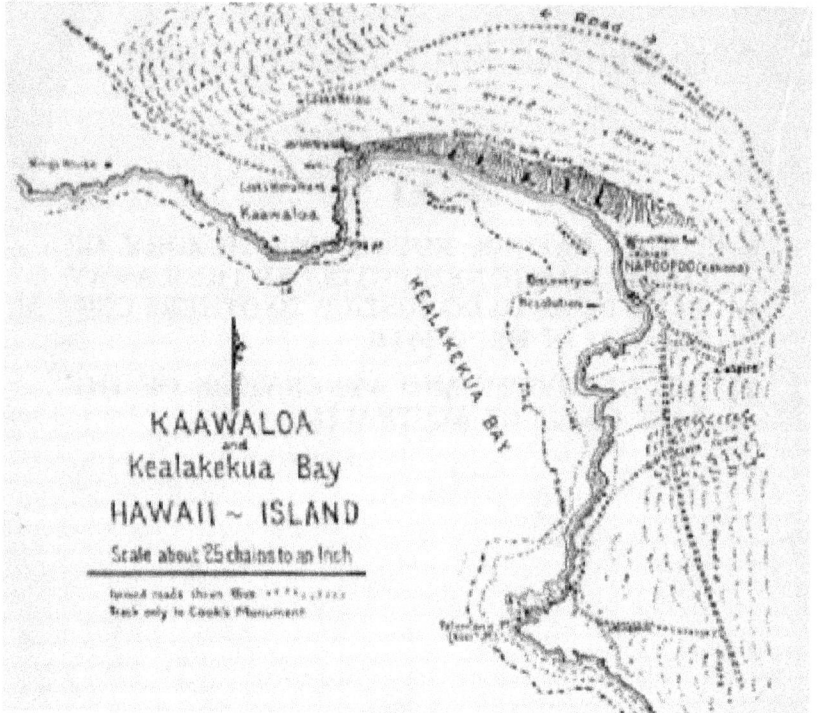

Kaawaloa Map
(taken from US Navy Charts, 1929)

23

The Sesqui-centennial celebrations of the discovery of the Hawaiian Islands (1778) celebrated by the Federal Government of the United States and the Territorial Government of Hawaii in the Islands of Kauai, Oahu, and Hawaii, on the 17th, 18th, and 19th of August, 1928

Captain Cook discovered the Hawaiian Islands on 20th January, 1778, when he landed at the Island of Kauai and, on the 23rd January, paid a brief visit to the Island of Nihau. He then, on 2nd February, 1778, sailed away to the northern coasts of America, touching at one point on the western coast of California, but finally staying at what he called Nootka Sound, in the neighbourhood of the present cities of Victoria and Vancouver, in Canada.

He again visited the islands towards the end of that year without landing until he reached Maui (Mooewe) and after a brief stay, Hawaii, which Island he circumnavigated, took off provisions at one or two points and finally came to Kealakekua Bay in what is now known as the district of Kona, in the southern part of the Island of Hawaii. At Kaawaloa in this Bay he was killed on 14th February, 1779.

Hence the Cook Sesqui-centennial Celebrations of 1928 were held in three places, namely:[125]

i. At Waimea, which is now a prosperous village and is the site of Cook's landing on Kauai.

ii. At Honolulu (Oahu), the seat of Government of the Islands; and

iii. At Kealakekua Bay, at Kaawaloa, Hawaii where Cook was killed.

A commission had been appointed by the U.S. Federal and Territorial Governments concerned for the purposes of organising and carrying out these celebrations. The commission consisted of:

Col. Curtis P. Iaukea, chamberlain to their late Majesties King David Kalakaua and Queen Lydia Liliuokalani (Chairman);

The Rt. Rev. H.B. Restarick, former bishop of Honolulu, and president of the Hawaiian Historical Society;

Bruce Cartwright, Esq., past president of the Hawaiian Historical Society;

Dr. Herbert E. Gregory, director of the Bishop Museum, Honolulu;

Albert P. Taylor, Esq., Librarian of the Archives of Hawaii; and

Edgar Henriques, Esq. (Executive Secretary of the Commission).

The greatest credit was due to these commissioners for the very thorough way in which they did their work. The programme which they

---

[125] The third section of the book focuses almost exclusively on the ceremonies held to commemorate the 150th anniversary of the discovery of the Hawaiian Islands and of Captain Cook's death. It contains a number of speeches that offer deep insight into how we should remember Cook and the overall legacy of European "discoveries". It is also historically fascinating, because here you have the Americans and the British Pacific coming together in a show of their intimate connection just over a decade out from Pearl Harbour. It encapsulates one aspect of a psychological shift fundamental to our history, as Australians would increasingly look to America for protection over the coming years. If the Americans could let Revolutionary War bygones be bygones and come to respect Cook, it in turn made it easier for Australians to respect the United States – *Editor.*

submitted and was approved of by their Governments and concurred in by others consulted, was as follows:

i.   A celebration on the first day at Waimea (Kauai) and the unveiling of a monument commemorating Cook's discovery in 1778 (*see* Appendix A).

ii. The reading of papers or delivery of speeches in a public building in Honolulu (the capital), and

iii. An appropriate celebration on the spot where Captain Cook was killed at Kaawaloa, Kealakekua Bay, Hawaii, including the unveiling of a submerged tablet on the spot where he fell and died (*see* Appendix B).

This programme, to be carried out in three days, entailed a lot of travelling from place to place. Waimea, for instance, is about fourteen hours' journey by fast steamer from Honolulu. Being in the Tropics and the height of summer-time, it was expedient that the celebrations should take place very early in the morning. From Waimea there was a journey back to Honolulu to participate next day in celebrations there. Then, on the afternoon of the Honolulu function, one had to make the steamer journey to Hawaii, about 250 miles south. Again there was an early ceremony (8 a.m.) at Kaawaloa and a host of other functions on the Island of Hawaii, taking up the day and night.

It was found that the most convenient time for these celebrations would be in the month of August, which would be the mid-way between the two dates, of the discovery and of Cook's death respectively.

Suggestions made long previously to the British Government and to the Commonwealth Government, that they should send warships, were acceded to. Great Britain sent one of her new warships just launched, the H.M.S. *Cornwall*, 10,000 tons, commanded by Captain the Honourable W.S. Leveson-Gower, with about 1,000 officers and crew.[126] The Commonwealth of Australia was represented by the best cruiser available, H.M.A.S. *Brisbane*, under Captain G.C. Harrison, with a complement of about 650 officers and men.[127] New Zealand sent the very fine cruiser H.M.S. *Dunedin* (500 complement), under Commodore G.C.T.P. Swabey, who, ranking as Senior Officer, was the Officer in charge of the British and Australian Squadron.[128] The United States of America was represented by the battleship *Pennsylvania*, with a complement of somewhere about 1,000.[129] A number of other smaller war craft of the United States Navy joined in the celebrations at the various places and a fleet of airplanes carried out evolutions over the scenes of the ceremonies at Waimea and Kealakekua Bay.

The Federal Government of the United States was very ably represented by the Honourable Dwight F. Davis, Secretary of War. The Territory of Hawaii had official representation by Governor Farrington. Australia was represented by myself as sole Commissioner for the Commonwealth, and Captain Harrison and his Officers of the *Brisbane* assisted me in my task. New Zealand had a delegation consisting of Commodore Swabey, the Honourable Maurice Cohen, and Dr. Peter Buck (a Maori); and Canada was represented by Judge Howay, F.R.S.C., a well-known historian. Captain Leveson-Gower (H.M.S. *Cornwall*) was the chief

---

[126] The *Cornwall* would be sunk by a Japanese aircraft carrier on 5 April 1942 near Ceylon. These British lives lost near Australian waters should disprove the harmful myth that during WW2 Britain essentially abandoned her Pacific Empire (and above all us) and left them to their fate – *Editor*.

[127] The *Brisbane* was one of the first Australian cruisers, along with her sisters the H.M.A.S. *Sydney* and H.M.A.S. *Melbourne*. Launched in 1915, the ship's main role in WW1 was patrolling the Pacific, looking for the German raiders *Wolf* and *Seeadler*. It would be decommissioned in 1935 - *Editor*.

[128] Not to be confused with her contemporary British namesake, the H.M.S. *Dunedin* had the most ignoble history of any of these ships. Not only did she not see action in either World War, but she is primarily remembered for being sent as a show of force against the Mao independence movement in Samoa. It was for condemning New Zealand's authoritarian treatment of Western Samoa that Carruthers earned a censure in that nation's Parliament – *Editor*.

[129] The *Pennsylvania* was one of the luckier ships during WW2. She survived the attack on Pearl Harbour largely because she was in dry-dock. Despite being launched in 1915 and therefore bordering on the obsolete, she subsequently saw action a number of times before being taken out (but not sunk) by a Japanese torpedo bomber at the Battle of Okinawa – *Editor*.

representative of Great Britain, whose Consul in Honolulu took part in the celebrations.

A very large gathering participated in the function at Waimea (Kauai): and I was able to secure fine photographs showing the celebrations in progress, also a few, taken from the air, of the scenes there, which latter enable one to visualise where Cook's ships anchored, and where he met the natives in the village square.

These celebrations at Kauai were carried out under the chairmanship of Judge C.N.B. Hofgaard, a very fine gentleman who ably played his part in the opening address and in conducting the proceedings. With others I have the liveliest recollection of the splendid hospitality of the Judge and his good lady during the course of the day.

The landing from the ships at Waimea Bay was difficult. Usually the sea there is comparatively calm, but on this occasion, unexpectedly, there was a very heavy ground swell, which made the landing by the ships' boats not only difficult but dangerous. However, the natives who were steering the craft were experts, and everybody got ashore without accident.

Large contingents of the naval forces – American and British – landed and lined the area where the celebrations took place. It was the first time in 150 years that British Naval men were permitted to carry arms on Hawaiian shores. The bands of the *Pennsylvania* and the *Dunedin* were present and livened up proceedings, playing the National Anthems of the United States and of Great Britain. What most pleased the native element was the kilted piper from the New Zealand Cruiser *Dunedin*, as he marched at the head of the marines from the bay to the park where the monument was erected. A large choir of the villagers, chiefly Hawaiian, also entertained the gathering with beautiful songs.

The principal speech on this occasion was made by the Honourable Victor Houston, Delegate to the United States Congress from Hawaii. To him I am indebted for a full report of the various celebrations, which he submitted to the United States Congress on Thursday, 14th February,

1929. It was a very appropriate day for him to do so, being the 150th anniversary of the death of Cook at Kaawaloa in Hawaii.

That report is contained in a later chapter. I consider it worthy of full reproduction here because, coming from such a source, it is unusually valuable. It denotes the first occasion upon which the United States has officially celebrated any of Captain Cook's great deeds. That exceptional act may well be one of those links which everybody desires to see forged in the chain which will bind together in friendly sentiments the English-speaking people of the United States and of the British Empire.

Resuming my narration, from which I digressed:

The gathering at Waimea numbered between ten and twelve thousand people including those from the warships and from the steamers which carried large numbers of passengers from the other Islands.

After the official speeches and the unveiling of the monument, the Committee at Kauai took the visitors for a tour round the greater part of the Island and to a port near Lihue on the opposite side of the Island of Waimea. Many places of interest were seen, including an improvised fort constructed by Russian adventurers who, in the year 1816, seized and occupied a disused *heiau* (or temple).[130] That improvised fortification still remains as evidence of their visit. The Russians remained only two years, then vanished never to return.

The hospitality of the people was unbounded and visitors were treated with much kindness.

The Island of Kauai bears testimony to some fine results which followed on Cook's discovery. It is in reality an Island Paradise. The country is very fertile with rich volcanic soil, the greater portion of which has been used for agricultural and productive purposes. The population is industrious,

---

[130] Georg Anton Schäffer was a German trader who launched a bizarre expedition to seize Hawaii on behalf of the Russian Government. The escapade was eventually repudiated by that Government, helping to bankrupt the Russian-American Company of which Schäffer was a part. Had that company been more successful there is good reason to believe that Russia may not have sold Alaska to the United States in 1867 – *Editor*.

consisting of Hawaiians, Japanese and people of other Eastern races, with a considerable number of Americans and other white people.

The Hawaiian population, pure blooded and mixed, in the whole territory of Hawaii is about 60,000. They have not been dying out so much as they have been marrying out of their race. Everyone admits that their admixture with either the Caucasian or the Asiatic race has resulted in no physical or mental deterioration of the offspring, but rather in an improvement.

I may here interpose, before describing the ceremonies at the other parts, that it was pointed out to me by Commodore Swabey, on behalf of the British Naval units, that the programme of ceremonies involved too much steaming about, anchoring and moving from anchorage to anchorage within a short space of less than three full days. This would entail a little too much strain on the staff of the ships and on the crews. It had been proposed that there should be a procession of the British Naval forces in Honolulu on the second day: but at our suggestion this was omitted. Instead of that, on the following Sunday, after the celebrations were over, a very fine Church Parade was held and the men, numbering many hundreds, marched through the streets of Honolulu and thence to the Episcopalian Cathedral and to the Roman Catholic Cathedral. The band of the H.M.S. *Dunedin* was permitted to play at the close of a splendid service conducted by Bishop De la Mothe in the Episcopalian Cathedral. It was very fine indeed to hear in that beautiful edifice the National Anthems of America and England.

The Honolulu ceremony, which the Americans called "Exercises" but which we would call "Addresses," was carried out in the large hall of the Army and Navy Y.M.C.A. in the centre of the city. There the Honourable Dwight F. Davis delivered his principle speech which was followed by an address by the Honourable Wallace R. Farrington (the Governor of the Territory). Papers were read on behalf of Sir Henry Newbolt, Official Naval Historian of Great Britain, and by Judge F.W. Howay, and others.

There was a very large assemblage at this gathering and an American lady presented a beautiful plaque commemorating Captain Cook's visit to the islands. This plaque is being placed in one of the public institutions in Honolulu.

24
Further account of the sesqui-centennial celebrations – particularly at Kaawaloa, Hawaii

I now come to the last and probably the most important of the official celebrations. This took place at Kealakekua Bay (Island of Hawaii). Twenty-four hours of sailing were necessary for the fleet to reach there. It included all the warships, one large passenger steamer, accommodating about 800 visitors, and a very large fleet of sanpans and native craft of all kinds, including small launches which came from parts of the islands.

The gathering was scattered, inasmuch as Kaawaloa (where the main celebration took place) is on the opposite side of the bay to where the port town lies. That town is now called Napoopoo (the old name is Kakooa), a very flourishing town indeed and the centre of the thriving coffee plantations of Kona. Embarkation across the bay from Napoopoo, a distance of about 1 ½ to 2 miles, had to be made by small boats. The consequence was that a large number of people remained at Napoopoo to meet the visitors and to enjoy the celebrations there.

But at Kaawaloa a crowd, which I estimate at anything from eight to ten thousand, gathered, consisting of the visitors from America and parts of the British Dominions and from other parts of the Hawaiian Islands, these numbering some thousands. The gathering included also a very large number of Japanese, Hawaiians and Chinese residing in the populous neighbourhood which abuts on this port. At Napoopoo, when the crowd gathered from all parts for the local ceremony, there must have been an assemblage of between twenty and twenty-five thousand people.

The ceremony at Kaawaloa was most impressive. The Australian Government had sent three fine wreaths from Australia to be placed on the monument at Waimea and on the monument where Cook fell at Kaawaloa. They were embellished with eucalyptus leaves and with English roses, and bore the colours of the various parts of the Empire. Inscribed in letters of gold on the ribbons were the words: - "In Loving Remembrance of Captain Cook." These wreaths were placed on the above two monuments by the representatives of Great Britain, Australia and New Zealand. Canada placed a beautiful wreath of autumn leaves on the Kaawaloa monument. Other wreaths were placed on that monument by the residents of Kona, by Americans, by the women from Australia, and by people of all nationalities who were represented at the ceremonies. It was a very moving experience.

The little piece of land where the monument to Cook stands (erected in 1874) is British property and was deeded to England by the then owner and by the then Government many years ago, long prior to the American annexation of the Territory (*see* Appendix C).

Proceedings were opened at Kaawaloa by an address from Dr. Gregory, of the Bishop Museum, Honolulu, who explained the history of the monument and of the various memorial tablets which had been placed from time to time at places adjacent, associated with Cook's death.

After that a move was made to a place about fifty yards further out towards the Pacific Ocean at a spot which, according to all accounts, is identified as the actual place where Cook fell when he was struck by the club and the spear. He fell with his head in the shallow water and there he died. Here a tablet of uncorrodable metal had been securely affixed into the rock. The tidal waters submerge this to a depth of a foot or two.

The unveiling ceremony of the tablet was performed by the Honourable

John Carey Lane, a Hawaiian of high rank and the Head of the Order of Kamehameha. Mr. Lane delivered his address in the Hawaiian language. It was a fine utterance and impressed the natives very much. He has been a great leader of his race in all movements for their good and for the promotion of a spirit of amity between his people and the American community.

Australia was honoured, as well as I, when I was invited to deliver the principal address right by the spot where Cook died. What I then said appears in the Congressional Report contained in chapter twenty-five.

As soon as I concluded my address, six buglers from the British Squadron, standing close alongside of the tablet, sounded the beautiful and impressive strains of the Last Post – that sublimely affecting Funeral Call of the bugles, which honours the dead soldier or sailor who has served his country.

Cook died on the 14th of February, 1779. At sunset five days later, those few of his bones which were restored by the natives were committed to the deep. A naval service was then celebrated and ten-minute guns were fired by the ships whilst the colours were half-staff up.

But right down the 150 years which have since elapsed, no military or naval honour to the Great Dead Hero had ever been paid similar to that when the Last Post was sounded by the British and Australasian buglers on 18th August, 1928. It was a soul-stirring and inspiring moment, which none of those who participated in the proceedings at Hawaii will ever forget. The vast majority had never heard the Last Post played: and few, if any, had heard it as those naval buglers played it that day. Everything seemed to fit in worthily. The blue waters of the Pacific Ocean on one side of us were just rippled by the softest breath of wind; the sky over our heads was a canopy of un-flecked blue; on the shore-side towered the craggy cliffs of the Kona, honeycombed with the burial caves of the old Hawaiian feudal chiefs. The bugle notes were softly re-echoed from these cliffs, and when the last drawn-out tones of the call were sounded – "Come to rest; Come to rest; Come to rest;" – the echo repeated them very slowly and softly as though a spirit were responding. It seemed to many of us as if the spirit of Cook might have been there listening and answering the call.[131]

Whilst the bugles played, everyone stood bareheaded, or at the salute, and when the last notes ceased, for some five minutes after not a soul moved from the place, but all stood in respectful silence until the boom of the cannon on the ships was heard as they gave the salute for the dead. There were many whose feelings were so stirred that tears dimmed their eyes, and amongst all the crowd there was a prevailing sentiment worthy of the great occasion.

I say deliberately that we ought to be drawn closer to our American cousins because of their action in so worthily honouring a Great Englishman like Cook in the manner that I have attempted herein to describe. It was just that one touch of nature which makes the whole world kin.

I must not omit to say that when the warships and other craft sailed into Kealakekua Bay in the morning they were met by a fleet of Hawaiian out-rigger canoes, of the type of those which Cook saw 150 years before, and manned by native Hawaiians, wearing their chief's capes or dressed in the garb common amongst the natives of that time. This water pageant was admirably carried out. It reproduced vividly the reception of Captain Cook and his ships when they sailed into port in January 1779.

Other celebrations followed close by at Napoopoo (Kakooa). There a huge gathering had assembled in the neighbourhood of the old temple (*heiau*), the scene of the alleged worship of Cook and near to the beach

---

[131] It seems fitting that final tribute was payed to Cook via the Last Post, considering that haunting song's centrality to Australian Anzac traditions. It appears that Carruthers wanted the site of Cook's death to become a place of pilgrimage for Australians in the manner that Gallipoli Cove and the Kokoda Track have since. While many today would not place Cook's sacrifice on the same footing as our war dead, the fact that Carruthers got the Commonwealth Government to contribute funds to the upkeep of the site was arguably an important precedent for our current arrangements with Turkey and Papua New Guinea – *Editor.*

where Cook's boats, in 1779, were landing day by day in the course of their labours. Here another fine ceremony was carried out in the unveiling of a monument in the form of an obelisk with a suitable bronze tablet affixed to it, commemorating the fact that a seaman, William Whatman, of Cook's Expedition, died and was buried there in 1779. That was the first Christian service to be celebrated on Hawaiian soil, and Captain Cook read the burial service.

Fine addresses were delivered here by the Rt. Rev. Henry B. Restarick, former Bishop of the Episcopalian Church, Honolulu, and by the Rev. D.D. Wallace, Episcopalian Vicar of the Parish of Kona.

A visit was next made to Honaunau, the City of Refuge, of historical importance, and the most perfectly preserved relic of bygone days in the islands. These cities of refuge occur in different parts of the Hawaiian Islands. They were sanctuaries during times of war and of strife. It was visited in 1779 by Cook and many of his officers and crew.

After that, a five or six miles' road journey, through beautiful scenery on the hill-side, studded with villages and coffee plantations and small ranch holdings, was taken to the main village of Kona Weana. There a *luau*, or native feast, was prepared for 4,000 visitors, that number comprising the official visitors, the officers and men from the warships, local committees, and those who has assisted in carrying out the celebrations. It was quite a wonderful feast. An enormous shed, roofed in but open on all sides, was erected in the school grounds at Kona Weana. Probably it was a permanent building erected for the children to play in during wet weather, but, of course, the 4,000 could not be accommodated in that. A large number had to seat themselves outside; but tables were set which would accommodate four or five hundred of the principal guests in the structure mentioned. Tables were laid with viands – native dishes, meats, vegetables, and fruits, of every kind – and all of them were tasty, and the meats, etc., were well cooked and prepared. No knives, forks or spoons were provided, although an occasional spoon was here or there to be got. One had to eat with the aid of one's fingers, and it was amusing to see a United States Minister, the Governor, Delegates from the various parts of the Empire, the Commanders of the various warships and the ladies, all busy with their fingers helping themselves. Plates, or banana leaves, were provided, but everyone seemed to be able to produce something to help the fingers in the feeding process. Everybody took it good humouredly and played the part for the occasion. It was a question of "when in Rome do as Rome does." The main thing was that everybody got a real good lunch, for there were very many good "eats" and the fruits were magnificent, including mangoes, pine-apples, paw-paws, Hawaiian water-lemons (a variety of passion fruit), oranges, bananas, mountain apples, and many other native and local fruits which some of the visitors tasted for the first time, and liked. The vegetables included taro, yams, kumara (a variety of sweet potato), bread-fruit, avocado pears and others hard to identify. Also there was plenty to drink. America being a prohibition country it was all non-alcoholic; and I can testify that right throughout the proceedings I saw no hip-flasks and no alcoholic drinks.[132]

After this ceremony, which took one back to the native way of eating and feasting 150 years ago, yet still in vogue, a move was made for an 80-mile journey to the volcano of Kilanea, where quarters were prepared in the fine Volcano House. The journey was over beautiful roads; in fact, all the roads in the Hawaiian Islands are first-class, and the motor-cars up to date. One could not help being forcibly reminded, when travelling, whether in automobiles or on great modern steamers, of the difference of now and when Cook went three times around the world in a little craft only about 400 tons, without any other means of propulsion except the wind in the sails; and how most of his food was salt beef and stale biscuits, and the malt which he carried to avoid scurvy, and the occasional supply of vegetables which he was so careful to obtain in the places that he visited. It is well for one just for a moment to compare the circumstances then and now.

---

[132] While he was a modest drinker, particularly compared with many of his political contemporaries, Carruthers was an early advocate for Australian wines which he had spruiked at the Franco-British expedition in London in 1908. Prohibition was a significant barrier to a potentially profitable Australian export – *Editor.*

That concluded the ceremonies on the Island of Hawaii. The party returned the next day to Honolulu; and on the evening of that day a very fine play was presented, with some hundreds of Hawaiian and local white participators. It was a dramatisation and representation of the times of the islands 150 years ago, and of the scenes that occurred when Cook arrived. It had been prepared by Mr. James A. Wilder and the appropriate title was: "Hawaii 150 years ago."

It was an excellent work of art and was performed in the open air in a natural setting midst groves of palms and native trees. The old villages and huts were represented down to the last item, just as they were when Cook came. The acting was in accord with the times gone by; and the words of the play showed the poetic talent of the author. It was a fine conception put into appropriate language. The dialogue had dignity, the situations were natural and developed one out of another in a natural way. This represented Cook's landing; the surprise and consternation amongst the villagers and the people when his ship was first seen and when he arrived and, finally, the friendship which was displayed to him, and the old-time ceremonies of welcome to the strangers. The performance drew vast audiences for the two nights.

Only one thing more remains to be mentioned in this chapter. The landing-place is very bad at Kaawaloa where Cook died, and tends to make it difficult for visitors to go ashore to pay their tribute of respect. The Government of Australia, however, authorised me to convey to the Governor of Hawaii an offer to defray the cost of constructing a stone jetty of approved design, so that passengers in small boats could easily land without danger or difficulty right alongside the monument, and step ashore on the land which had been given to and was to be owned by the British Government. Governor Farrington was pleased to accept the offer, and plans are now being prepared preliminary to the carrying out of the work, which should be completed in 1930.

In connection with the celebrations the United States Government issued a special 50-cent coin. The issue was limited to 10,000. A special surcharged Hawaiian stamp was also issued. The coins were sold to the public at a charge of two dollars each, and the stamps at face value.[133] The profit on the sale of the coins went to the Celebrations Commission and, I am informed, realised almost 15,000 dollars, whilst the play, "Hawaii 150 years ago," added considerably more to that sum.

Grants towards the celebrations had been made by the Territorial and Federal Governments, so that ample funds were available to carry out the task of the Commission. I can testify to the efficiency and thoroughness exhibited in the performance of that task. A brochure which will include a full report of the proceedings is in course of printing and will be made available to any who would like to obtain this valuable record of America's fine effort to remind people of what Cook did and how he died 150 years ago.

Mr. A.P. Taylor, Librarian of the Archives, Honolulu, prepared and is in charge of this publication. He was most helpful in every way, not only to me but to all visitors who approached him for guidance or help whilst the celebrations were being carried out.

---

[133] The coins featured Cook, labelled the "discoverer of Hawaii", on one side and a Hawaiian Chieftain in a noble pose on the other. They are now highly valued by currency collectors, at the time of writing there are several listed online for over 2000 USD - *Editor.*

25

The United States Congressional Record; Report of the Captain Cook Sesqui-centennial Celebrations held in Hawaii, August, 1928, submitted to the United States Congress and the Senate by Mr. Victor Houston, Delegate to the United States Congress from Hawaii, August, 1929, and printed in the U.S.A.

Congressional Record

Mr. Welsh of Pennsylvania. – Mr. Chairman, I yield ten minutes to the Delegate from Hawaii [Mr. Houston].

Mr. Houston of Hawaii. – Mr. Chairman, I shall address my remarks to the Hawaiian Sesqui-centennial, and I ask unanimous consent to extend my remarks by including therein the speeches of the President's special representative, Secretary Davis, Governor Farrington, certain of the foreign delegates, and my own.

The Chairman. – Without objection, it is so ordered.

There was no objection.

Mr. Houston of Hawaii. – Mr. Chairman, it is only a matter of 450-odd years since Christopher Columbus penetrated the unknown vastness of the oceans, braving the perils of nature and eventually reaching to this great continent of ours, to his everlasting fame and glory.

Explorers and discoverers have followed in his footsteps, both on land and sea. Recently, that intrepid breed have taken to the air, and who here does not recall the thrill we felt when it was known that our own Lindbergh, alone, had winged his way across the broad Atlantic?

We are too prone to soon forget such exploits when, as time flies by, these extraordinary undertakings are repeated and come to be the everyday occurrence. Those who have not braved the deep in sailing vessels, or even small steamers, cannot conceive the perils and dangers that beset the captains when sailing unknown and uncharted seas. Even now, with the seas charted and weather forecasts being sent out twice daily by radio, we hear almost daily of innumerable difficulties besetting those that go down to the Seas in ships.

One hundred and fifty years ago this date—February 14, 1779—there died one such captain, one of the band of unafraid whose name, even then, was honoured, and who has since been acclaimed and recognised as one of the world's great navigators, discoverers, scientists, and humanitarians—Captain James Cook, of the Royal Navy.

The life of Captain James Cook makes a special appeal to us in America. Like so many of our successful men, he was of lowly origin, self-taught, and by his own endeavours rose to a high position and received some recognition for his attainments.[134] We admire such traits because of the qualities of initiative and perseverance which they imply.

This man of the people, a product of that great naval service which has served so to mould the traditions of our own naval service, as commander of an expedition of two small sailing vessels three times circumnavigated the globe. He penetrated into the Arctic Ocean through Bering Straits, exploring the waters of our present Territory of Alaska; he sailed beyond the Antarctic Circle, where our own Commander Byrd is now engaged in completing the work. He was head of an astronomical expedition to

---

[134] This certainly seems to indicate that Houston had been influenced by Carruthers' image of Cook. It also highlights the natural connection between two settler nations who had to idolise meritocracy and effort if they were to build new and prosperous societies – *Editor.*

observe the transit of Venus. He surveyed the approaches to the Gulf of St. Lawrence and took part in the campaign of General Wolf against Quebec. His services and explorations brought into the fold of the British Empire the continents of Australia and New Zealand. Last, but not least to us of Hawaii, this Captain courageous made known to the world the Hawaiian Islands, that glorious Territory in the mid Pacific— integral part of the United States—whose aspiration it is in the future to be represented in the union of the flag by a new star whose brightness none will surpass.[135]

America can well associate herself with the rest of the world in recognising the worth of Captain Cook's labours. Besides discovering what is now part of our country, it is worthy to note that his exploring expeditions were carried out during a time when we were still struggling with the mother country in the War of Independence. Though beset with the tribulations that come to a country under such circumstances, yet the work of this man was of such an outstanding character that Benjamin Franklin, then our minister plenipotentiary from the Congress of the United States to the Court of France, found time to address a letter to all captains and commanders of armed ships of the United States of America, then in war with Great Britain, recommending to such commanders that the expedition of Captain Cook, his people, ships, and goods, should be treated with all civility and kindness, and that they should be assisted in their return to England:

To All Captains and Commanders of Armed Ships, Acting by Commission from the Congress of the United States of America, Now in War with Great Britain:

GENTLEMEN : A ship having been fitted out from England before the commencement of this war to make discoveries of new countries

---

[135] Houston would not live to see his dream as Hawaii would be accepted as the 50th state in August 1959, just three weeks after he died. The Hawaiian state flag is unique in that it features a Union Jack combined with red, white and blue stripes. It had first been designed during the War of 1812 when the King wanted to indicate that he remained friendly to both sides. Carruthers' actions in spreading a positive image of Cook and the British influence throughout the islands may have played some small role in its survival – *Editor.*

in unknown seas, under the conduct of that most celebrated navigator and discoverer, Captain Cook; an undertaking truly laudable in itself, as the increase of geographical knowledge facilitates the communication between distant nations in the exchange of useful products and manufactures and the extension of the arts, whereby the common enjoyments of human life are multiplied and augmented and science of other kinds increased to the benefit of mankind in general. This is, therefore, most earnestly to recommend to every one of you that in case the said ship, which is now expected to be soon in the European seas on her return, should happen to fall into your hands, you would not consider her as an enemy nor suffer any plunder to be made of the effects contained in her, nor obstruct her immediate return to England by retaining her or sending her into any other part of Europe or to America, but that you would treat the said Captain Cook and his people with all civility and kindness, affording them, as common friends to mankind, all the assistance in your power which they may happen to stand in need of. In so doing you will not only gratify the generosity of your own dispositions but there is no doubt of your obtaining the approbation of the Congress and your other American owners.

I have the honour to be, gentlemen, your most obedient, humble servant,
B. FRANKLIN,

Minister Plenipotentiary from the Congress of the United States to the Court of France.

At Passy, near Paris, this 10th day of March, 1779.

In Hawaii Captain Cook died, still in the prime of manhood, and last year as a consequence of an act of the territorial legislature, supported by a joint resolution of this Congress, and with the Secretary of War representing the President, the occasion was marked by ceremonies, memorial of his passing away, and also in commemoration of the rebirth of the Hawaiian Islands and their entrance into the family of nations.

Great Britain was represented by three men-of-war, and delegates from the Empire and the Dominions interested in the explorations of this great man. A monument was dedicated on the island of Kauai at the point where Captain Cook first landed and a tablet was unveiled at the spot where he died. A historical tableau and literary exercises brought the ceremonies to a close in the city of Honolulu.

Time has softened the feelings on one part and the other, so that the angry passions of 150 years ago are replaced by a feeling of friendliness, by that spirit of aloha for which the Hawaiian has come to be so well known. I am hopeful that these ceremonies will have done their little share toward advancing that better understanding between the English-speaking peoples for which we are ever striving. [Applause.]

Address of Hon. Dwight F. Davis, Secretary of War, as official representative of the Government of the United States at the Sesqui-centennial of the discovery of the Hawaiian Islands, at Honolulu, 15th to 20th August, 1928[136]

Through the commemoration of significant events in our history we dedicate milestones by which we may measure the course of our progress. At the same time we are afforded an opportunity for a retrospection which never fails to serve as an inspiration for further progress.

The importance of the discovery of the Hawaiian Islands has increased with each of the 150 years since Captain James Cook landed upon these shores. The value of his discovery has been enhanced by succeeding generations of its inhabitants. Consequently, to-day when we commemorate the arrival here of Captain Cook we honour his accomplishment the more if we evaluate the progress of Hawaii and depict the possibilities of its future.

The Government of the United States has commissioned me to come and express to you the congratulations of the Nation upon your accomplishments and to join with you in a celebration of the fortuitous

---

[136] Dwight F. Davis was Secretary of War in the Coolidge Administration and later Governor-General of the Philippines. He is best remembered for founding the Davis Cup tennis tournament in 1900, initially a competition limited to the United States and Great Britain. We were represented by a combined "Australasian" team from 1905 – *Editor*.

occasion of the introduction of this highly endowed land and people to the acquaintance of the world. The Federal Government does not join in these exercises solely because they are of consequence to the people of an integral part of the United States. The participation is more intimate. The occasion affords an opportunity for an expression of national appreciation of the good fortune which brought to the attention of mankind these islands which have become an important element of our great Union.

Scientists have depicted the formation of the universe in accordance with the basic natural phenomenon of the attraction between masses. They visualise the action of a cosmic, inherent force which, operating to join innumerable particles, gave permanence to the creation we know to-day. We gain an impression of some similar attraction when we view the years of political progress which led to the union of our States with Hawaii to form the present United States of America. We are conscious that here is an example where peoples gravitated steadily to a peaceful combination much as though they, too, were drawn together by an inherent and irresistible force of nature. The union was accomplished and has been maintained as a normal step in the destinies of those geographical elements which now constitute the United States of America.

Prior to the visit of Captain Cook to these islands two great leaders were engaged in constructive and similar efforts in two distantly separated parts of our present large domain. On the Atlantic seaboard George Washington was marshalling the scattered forces by which he eventually gained independence and a political entity for our colonies. Here in Hawaii, Kamehameha I was engaged in those lifelong efforts which resulted in political unity. Unknown to the rest of the world he was exhibiting those qualities of leadership and statesmanship which entitle him to high recognition among all great men.

Since those days there have come representatives of many nationalities to join the original inhabitants and settlers in both our island and continental territories. Everywhere there has resulted a considerable fusion of the blood of our founders. However, regardless of the numerous elements which have entered into our society and have influenced our customs, there has been preserved the liberty and unity secured through the efforts of Washington and the first Kamehameha.

Captain Cook found in these beautiful islands a race of stalwart, sport-loving, and lovable people who had developed an aristocracy and many courtly graces. He was received with a remarkable hospitality—a trait which has continued to the present day as an especial characteristic of Hawaiians. Unfortunately, for the first 40 years after 1778 many of the visitors to these shores appeared to have abused their welcome. Not until 1820, with the advent of the missionaries, does there appear to have been much altruism in those who came here either to bargain or to live.

With the arrival of the missionaries there came to these lands an influence which became a most potent factor in their destiny. The record of a majority of those devout men and women constitutes a notable example of constructive service to mankind. They brought from our oldest States on the Atlantic seaboard the good will which ever since has characterised the relations between our peoples. Furthermore, they introduced here their customs and ideals so that, with the passage of time, laws and practices became similar in Hawaii and in our States. Thus to the missionaries more than to any other social group must we give credit for the basic qualities which ultimately occasioned a natural fusion of our population.

It must be a matter of satisfaction to us all that prior to the incorporation of the Territory of Hawaii into the United States our Federal Government had proved repeatedly its friendliness to Hawaii as an independent State and its unwillingness to undertake any form of coercion. Commencing with the negotiations of Captain Thomas Catsby Jones, United States Navy, in 1826, the relations of the two countries always were based on mutual respect and confidence.

Thus in 1842 the American Government made it clear that it did not desire any exclusive control or advantage and advised the King of Hawaii through his commissioners as to the method of approach to England and France in diplomatic negotiations to secure treaties for the guaranty of independence and neutrality. The action of the United States a year later in expressing disapproval of the occupation of Hawaii by a British naval commander undoubtedly had considerable effect toward recognition of Hawaiian independence by England and France and in their joint agreement in 1843 never to take possession even under a protectorate.

In December, 1849, there was concluded between the United States and Hawaii a treaty of friendship, commerce, navigation, and extradition. Two years later the benevolent Kamehameha III sought the protection of the United States by the preparation of an instrument whereby he might cede his monarchy to the United States should his power be put in jeopardy by any other nation. The attitude of the United States was expressed by Daniel Webster, Secretary of State, as follows:

"The government of the Sandwich Islands ought to be respected; that no power ought to take possession of the islands either as a conquest or for the purpose of colonisation; and that no power ought to seek for any undue control over the existing government or any exclusive privileges or preferences in matters of commerce."

From time to time, between 1853 and the accomplishment of annexation in 1898, there arose proposals in both the United States and Hawaii for the unification of the two countries. The long delay in the accomplishment of this aim is proof of the sincere intention of our Federal Government to act only in accord with the wishes of the Hawaiian people. Indeed, after the new provisional government of Hawaii in 1893 had raised the American flag and applied for entrance into the United States, President Cleveland appears to have delayed his acquiescence entirely by reason of a concern lest the action of an American naval force had been prejudicial to the success of the rebellion against the Hawaiian monarch.[137] Finally, however, the Spanish-American War carried the Stars and Stripes beyond the North American Continent, and public opinion rapidly consummated the union.

So much for the past. Let us now consider the future.

The frontiers of civilisation have moved steadily westward through the ages. With that progress there has occurred a westward displacement of the world centre. From Athens to Rome and to London has moved the hub of the world. The Mediterranean gave way in importance to the Atlantic. Now the Pacific Ocean steadily gains as an avenue of world progress.

We have seen these islands steadily increase in prestige with the improvement of transportation and intercommunication between the peoples of the world. First came the replacement of sails by steam power. Then came steady improvement of engines to facilitate travel and improve commerce. As science overcame handicaps the continents were brought closer as regards time which is the true gauge of distance. With each forward step this "Crossroads of the Pacific" received an added incentive to progress.

Were industry and trade the sole reasons for Hawaiian importance, and were the sea the only medium of access to these islands still your dominating position would assure you complete participation in the benefits which appear destined for the countries of the Pacific. However, we find here attractions for other than the industrialist and the trader. You have contrived to enhance the bounteous attractions of nature with a comfort which emanates from excellent hospitality dispensed with a natural and charming cordiality. Hawaii has become a goal for all travellers, and each year in greater numbers they come in quest of

---

[137] Grover Cleveland was a hero to Carruthers and his political colleagues as the only Free Trade politician to have real success in the Protectionist stronghold of the United States. Indeed, Reid claimed it was the 1892 American election which convinced him to support federation, as he believed that it proved protectionism was dying. Cleveland's attitude towards Hawaii shows that he was deeply concerned that the United States should not become an imperial power, but his immediate successors had less qualms – *Editor.*

recreation and the enjoyment of this beautiful land where are combined the attractions of the Orient and Occident.

Nor do we longer limit our conception of transoceanic travel to ships of the sea. Little more than a year ago two officers of the Army, Lieutenants Maitland and Hegenberger, first negotiated the flight to these islands from San Francisco—a feat in which I take especial pride—since it was undertaken as a military venture under my approval as Secretary of War. Since then, other daring aviators also have proved the practicability of such flights. Quite recently you welcomed the intrepid crew which stopped here on the epochal journey by air from California to Australia. We cannot say when or how such travel may become a common practice. We only know that if aviation continues its astounding progress of the past few years, these islands will become one of the most important airports of the world. In any event, the future lies bright before Hawaii.

This celebration has been given an especial importance through the gracious participation of many of those countries which have been associated with the development of the lands of the Pacific and the Hawaiian Islands. Though the exploits and accomplishments of Captain Cook have been of advantage to all nations, they remain a glowing example of the results which have accrued from the far-flung interest and initiative of his own country. Therefore, on this occasion of honour to the services of Captain Cook, we extend our compliments to Great Britain and to Australia and New Zealand. We thank them for their courtesy in sharing with us in these honours to their countrymen who caused their flag to be the first sighted from these shores.

The Government of the United States feels a debt of gratitude to Captain Cook. His introduction of this "Paradise of the Pacific" to the society of nations has proved of inestimable benefit to our Nation. On behalf of the Federal Government, I voice appreciation for this opportunity to participate in these exercises and to express the thankfulness of the Nation for the advent of Hawaii to the knowledge of mankind.

Address by Gov. Wallace R. Farrington, of Hawaii, at Honolulu, 18th August, 1928

Captain Cook Celebration – Greetings to Delegates

Every period of history has given us men fired with an ambition to break through into the unknown.

Especial honour is given to the comparative few who, as they went out, charted a course so that others might follow. Such leaders have usually made the greatest contributions, and it is noted that with their courage they have possessed a sense of responsibility to others that is quite apart from reckless daring.

Captain James Cook, the explorer and geographer, in whose honour the representatives of the English-speaking nations are here assembled, had the ambition, the courage, and the capacity for contagious inspiration that qualified him to be a successful leader destined to leave a permanent record. Few men in history have contributed more than he in placing new lands and new opportunities within the grasp of his own and succeeding generations.

In this year 1928, 150 years after Captain Cook and men of his ships' company set foot on these islands, the descendants of the discoverers and of the discovered join happily in appropriate ceremonies to honour his memory.

The people of Hawaii, through their legislative assembly, elected under universal suffrage, officially requested that the Government of the United States, of which this Territory is an integral part, extend an invitation for the meeting here of the representatives of English-speaking nations and dominions. We are all beneficiaries in the new worlds opened up by Captain Cook. While we unite in the tribute of honour to an heroic figure of the past, we may find in this new inspiration for achievement in the present and for the future.

Captain Cook opened the eyes of the then civilised world to new fields the extent and conditions of which had not been pictured in the visions of even the dreamers. His charting of the hitherto unknown ocean and shore brought to Hawaii's people new counsellors. Barbarism was wiped out. Free scope was given to the normal friendly instincts of the native Hawaiian people. In a remarkably short period Hawaii and the Hawaiians moved into a position where they have exercised a reciprocal influence in fostering a more practical and sincere friendliness among all the peoples of the islands and the lands in and about the Pacific.

Other speakers will sketch the steps in the path of historical events that have brought us to the generally happy conditions of the present time. My pleasant duty and privilege is to extend the welcome, the aloha of Hawaii, on behalf of the citizens and residents of the Territory of Hawaii, and especially of the citizens of native Hawaiian ancestry.

The years immediately following the arrival of Captain Cook were for Hawaii years of upheaval and turmoil. When conditions began to settle down and orderly methods took the place of chaos, it is interesting, and we hope significant, to note the spirit of friendly cooperation that characterised the relations of the Hawaiians and the men and women of the English-speaking nations.

The Hawaiian monarch, Kamehameha I, retained John Young, who helped very materially in the successful battles fought by the King.

As time went on and constitutional government was finally established, the ruler of Hawaii called to his assistance the Hon. Robert C. Wyllie to serve as Minister of Foreign Affairs. Mr. Wyllie was a British subject who accepted Hawaiian citizenship and loyally served his adopted nation. The premier and adviser of equal authority in this period was Dr. Gerrit P. Judd, a citizen of the United States, who linked his fortunes with the Hawaiian Kingdom. He gave the best years of his life in loyal service.

These men were united in their purpose to support and maintain the integrity of the Hawaiians.

About this time the Hawaiian people, moving into the sphere of international relations, adopted a national flag. You see this flag to-day in the Territorial emblem. It is a union of the British and the American flags. The British flag was the first national banner known to the Hawaiians. The Union Jack was used. The eight stripes of the flag represent the eight principal islands of their kingdom, following the stripes of the flag of the United States representing the thirteen original States.

There is no historical record that this design was ever changed or even the subject of any bitter differences of opinion that are so often reflected in a national emblem.[138]

When the United States accepted the petition of Hawaii for annexation there was no breath of opposition to the adoption of the former national flag as the emblem of the Territory.

All along the course of events that has made history in the Pacific the Hawaiians, the British, and the Americans of the United States have been in hearty accord. Not to suggest that never were there differences of opinion. Residents of these islands 150, 100 years, and 75 years ago were quite human. They were active and vigorous in the expression of their opinions. We honour them for the balanced judgment that finally prevailed and for the good standard established to influence and largely control subsequent events.

In Captain Cook's time the venturesome men were seeking physical worlds to conquer.

To-day our central thought is to discover the most approved routes for arriving at permanent friendly relationships. Having learned through Captain Cook how large is our world, we are engaged in the great adventures involved in learning that the world is big enough for all to live comfortably, with a fair share for each of the reasonable prosperity that assures contentment.

---

[138] The controversy surrounding Cook certainly demonstrates the divisions engendered, or perhaps more accurately encapsulated, by national icons – *Editor.*

The disaster in Captain Cook's last voyage to Hawaii is not without a guiding thought.

Ignorance and misunderstanding, superstition and fear, shaped the incidents that led up to the death of the great explorer. Looking back, we have a feeling of pity for the benighted people who first deified as their great god *Lono*, the visitor from the great unknown; then, finding their mistake, destroyed him.

In the perspective of a century and a half we can understand the folly of it all. Looking out upon the future we have reason to highly resolve that the understanding and friendships that have become traditional along the ocean routes of the Pacific shall be emphasised.

The late Lord Bryce, in his *Modern Democracies*, quotes from Disraeli, where a character in one of his novels says, "Few ideas are correct ones, and what are correct no one can ascertain; but with words we govern men."

The "aloha" of Hawaii, the word of friendliness, has had continuing power. Suspicion and intrigue have scored destructive failures.

As the people of Hawaii voice the national greeting of a kind hearted race, it carries the thought that this meeting and your stay in these islands will be more far-reaching than a mere pleasant memory.

A timely word can control the minds of men. Courage to strike out into new fields in human relationships may well be expressed in a determination to use words and be prompt to perform the deeds that will strengthen old friendships and build new friendships. Profiting by the past, we will exercise the intelligence born of our present-day enlightenment so as to make those friendships permanent landmarks for charting the progress of the new world of our day.

Address of C.B. Hofgard, president of Kauai Historical Society and Chairman of the Kauai Cook Celebration Committee, at Waimea, Kauai, 17th August, 1928

Ladies and gentlemen, 150 years ago that illustrious navigator, Captain James Cook, Royal Navy, who had already made two voyages round the world, sailed from the island of Bolabola, one of the Society Islands, to explore the west coast of the American Continent and to find a passage north of America, which last part of the plan has just been accomplished in our time after numerous unsuccessful attempts.

He sighted Oahu, but on account of unfavourable wind kept sailing northwest and saw Kauai and sailed along the south coast and landed on the beach of Waimea on the 20th of January, 1778.

We hail Captain Cook as the discoverer of Hawaii, although Spanish navigators had a nebulous information of some islands near here. Captain Cook recorded his discoveries and scientifically located Hawaii on this terrestrial globe. He is entitled to all the honour of discovery as much as that other intrepid navigator, Christopher Columbus, who discovered America, although other Europeans had visited America as much as 400 years before his time.[139]

We, the people of Kauai, under the auspices of the Kauai Historical Society, have raised a monument in commemoration of the one hundred and fiftieth anniversary of the discovery, which I as president of the Kauai Historical Society have the honour and pleasure to present to the county of Kauai.

---

[139] This echoes Carruthers in its argument that making good on a discovery, both scientifically and through future contact, is what matters more than trying to arbitrarily decipher who was first – *Editor.*

Sir Joseph Carruthers, Official Representative of the Government of Australia to the Captain Cook Sesqui-centennial Celebration, at the scene of the death of Captain James Cook, Kaawaloa, Kealakekua Bay, Hawaii

We stand to-day on ground sacred to the memory of one of the bravest and best of men, Captain James Cook, of the Royal Navy of Great Britain. It was on this very spot that his life's blood ebbed away 150 years ago. He died leaving an imperishable name that as the ages roll on shall never be forgotten by those who honour and revere him for those fine qualities of courage, of devotion to duty, and of humanity, as well as for his outstanding ability as a sailor and as a leader of sailors.

When the news of his death was brought to England a public monument was proposed, yet it did not materialise until long years after.

But his closest and best friend, his former commander and patron, the man who knew him most intimately, Sir Hugh Palliser, erected at his own expense at his family seat, Mache Park, Buckinghamshire, a square block of stone surmounted by a globe and inclosed by a neat but simple roofed building. On this monument Palliser caused to be inscribed these words:

"To the memory of Captain James Cook, the ablest and most renowned navigator this or any other country has ever produced."

That inscription from such a man as Palliser, who rose to the high rank of comptroller of the navy, constitutes the most valuable testimony to his great reputation amongst his contemporaries, who knew him best from actual and long association with him.

Since that time—about 148 years ago—many monuments have been erected, amongst others a very fine one at the Admiralty in London, which I was mainly instrumental in securing as the result of a letter to the London *Times* which I wrote and published in 1908. Monuments now abound right through the Pacific as well as in England and Australasia to commemorate Captain Cook's great work.

In St. Paul's Cathedral, London, there is a tablet to the memory of Sir Christopher Wren with these words upon it:

"If you seek his monument, look around you."

So if you seek Captain Cook's monument, travel, as I have done, in the Pacific and look around you.

Then you will see the great Continent of Australia, with its 7,000,000 people of one race, who are on the way to found a great and a united nation of happy and prosperous people that will in the course of the present century be in the south Pacific just what the United States are in the north. Next look and see the Dominion of New Zealand, with over 1,000,000 people of the British race, happy, prosperous, and contented. See also the many other islands which he discovered or visited—Samoa, Tonga, the Cook Islands, New Caledonia, and, last but not least, these beautiful Hawaiian Isles, the outpost of the United States.

Look also at the Pacific States of the United States, which sprang into existence as the direct sequence of Cook's discovery of these islands; and if you look still farther north, see Canada and realise that it was Cook who charted the course for General Wolfe which resulted in the capture of Abrahams Heights and thereby laid the foundation of what is now the Dominion of Canada.

These are the monuments to Cook's life and work, and they are imperishable.

Captain Cook was a most humane man, as witness the fact that in 11 years of exploration in unknown parts where he came in contact with lands having millions of untutored races less than 1 man for each of those 11 years perished as the result of any conflicts. About 10 natives were killed in unavoidable conflicts in 11 years of his voyaging. There has never been, in all the world's history, such a record of peaceful methods of dealing with strange people. Compare that record with the conquest of Southern and Central America and of Mexico by the Spanish. Even in North America there was a trail of almost interminable bloodshed in the early days of colonisation and discovery.

Why did Cook leave such a unique record? Simply because he deliberately set himself to the task of avoiding conflicts with the natives, whilst aiming at winning their friendship by peaceful means.

Cook's death would never have occurred in February, 1779, but for the fact that he went ashore on this place, trusting to his ability to gain the good will of the Hawaiians by peaceful means in a period of difficulty. At a critical moment when his men in the boats lying close to here fired a volley into the ranks of the natives menacing him, Cook turned his back on the natives, held up his hands to his officers and men, and ordered them to desist from firing. That very act of humane feeling cost Cook his life, for with his back turned he was clubbed and killed.

I have studied more thoroughly than most living men the whole of the recorded facts, and I unhesitatingly say that the events which led up to the death of Captain Cook on that fatal day were the result of a complete and mutual misunderstanding that suddenly arose. The very action of Cook in striving to avoid bloodshed resulted in the sacrifice of his own life.

Many untrue statements have been made and have passed into current history without justification regarding the events leading up to the death of Captain Cook. I am satisfied that with a more complete and impartial study of the ample evidence available, the memory of Captain Cook will be found to be free from any stain of wrongdoing on his part.

May I say here and now that these proceedings to commemorate the events of 150 years ago with which Captain Cook was associated will be regarded throughout Great Britain, throughout Australia and New Zealand, and in all other parts of the Empire of which I am a humble citizen, as a splendid gesture indicative of the friendship which exists between the people of the United States and those of the British Empire. May that friendship forever continue for the benefit of humanity and as an enduring influence for the peace of the world.

Just now the whole world is being gladdened with the welcome tidings that the nations which compose the British Empire have entered into a bond with the United States of America and with France and Italy to outlaw wars of aggression. Happily that event synchronises with the one hundred and fiftieth year of Cook's death and with the two hundredth anniversary of his birth.

The spirit of James Cook has largely contributed to that accomplishment inspired as it has been largely by the English-speaking people of the world. My fellow countrymen in Australia are thrilled with a feeling of joy and of fraternity by these celebrations inaugurated by their big brother Jonathan, the United States.

I feel it to be an honour to the young communities of Australia and of New Zealand that we are here associated with the people of the United States and of this Territory in these historic proceedings.

In sending me here as her envoy Australia wished most appropriately to be associated with these proceedings.

Our history comprises three periods:

"First. Cook's discovery of Australia and its first settlement.

"Second. The grant of representatives, institutions, and responsible government.

"Third. The foundation of the United Australian Commonwealth."

Largely because for over 40 years I have served as minister and legislator in the second period and am one of the few surviving founders of our Federal constitution, I was selected and have been appointed as the first envoy under the terms agreed upon at the last Imperial Conference, which conferred the right on every dominion of direct representation in another country.[140]

---

[140] This was a significant milestone for Australia's emergence as a fully independent nation, retaining the same sovereign as Great Britain as a just acknowledgement of our former sentiments – *Editor.*

Thus, the link is preserved which connects Australia with its first foundation.

Australia was discovered and founded without the shedding of one drop of blood.

The inspiration of Cook's spirit has ever been with us. Loyalty, service, justice, and humanity in all our doings.

As to loyalty, William Charles Wentworth in his poem, "Australia," wrote:

"And thou, Britannia, shouldst Thou cease to ride,

Despotic Empress of old ocean's tide,

May this, thy last-born infant, then arise

To greet with gladness thy parent eyes,

And Australasia float with flag unfurled

A new Britannia in another world."[141]

That spirit of loyalty and service caused us in the hour of peril to send over 400,000 of our sons across the seas to fight for a great cause when 60,000 of our bravest and best made the supreme sacrifice.

The spirit of Cook inspired that loyalty and that service. That spirit is not dead. It will never die.

I may be forgiven perhaps if I single out one man who above all others has nobly wrought to bring about this day. And that man is Governor Farrington, who has played his part as a leader of men from first to last in advocating and accomplishing this good work.

I do not believe that we should allow these proceedings to pass by

---

[141] If there was any rival to Cook as "founder of Australia" in Carruthers' mind it would have been William Wentworth, the man conceived on a convict ship who had gone on to win trial by jury, a free press, university education, and self-government for the country in which he was born – *Editor.*

without reflecting on what is our duty to those fine though simple races in all these Pacific lands. I hope that we shall take stock of the position and endeavour to make provision to save and uplift these races for our honour and credit and for their preservation in happiness and content.

That would perpetuate the spirit of Cook and his consistent sense of humanity to these people.

Our hero, Captain Cook, is dead.

"Life's fitful fever o'er, he sleeps well."

But his spirit lives forevermore. It is for us to remember those sweet lines which so eloquently breathe what is our duty:

"Of those who in the dust do dwell

May there kindly mention be

When the birds that build in the branches tell

Of the planting of the tree."

Address By Hon. John C. Lane, of Hawaii, at the unveiling of a bronze tablet set just beneath the water at the spot where Captain James Cook was killed, at Kaawaloa, Kealakekua Bay, Island of Hawaii, on 14th February, 1779, delivered at the spot on 18th August, 1928

Secretary Dwight F. Davis, of the United States War Department, personally representing President Coolidge in the Territory, His Excellency the Governor of Hawaii, Gerald H. Phipps, His Britannic Majesty's consul, other distinguished guests, and fellow citizens, on this hallowed ground 150 years ago, Captain James Cook, the discoverer of these beautiful islands, met his death here in Kaawaloa, and we are assembled to-day to pay homage and honour to his memory.

Whatever may have been the hard feelings engendered in the past, time has softened and effaced them. To-day we stand near the very spot where he expired, with hearts full of gratitude for the good rendered by him to mankind, and with feelings of appreciation for the knowledge he gave to navigation.

Civilisation acclaims him a great discoverer and scientist, and this Territory our benefactor.

His name will always be repeated by the young in schools, and by the old, admired for his achievements as a navigator.

I need not dwell at length with the life of this man, the main speaker of the day, Sir Joseph Carruthers, has furnished us in full. Mine is the honour, as an Hawaiian, to unveil the bronze tablet, and therefore in the name of the Hawaii of old and the Hawaii of to-day, I hereby do perform this honourable duty gladly.

(Here unveil).

Fellow citizens, in removing the old Crown flag of the monarchical days of the Hawaiian Islands from this memorial bronze tablet, I find these words inscribed thereon:

"Near this spot Capt. James Cook, R. N., was killed 14th February, 1779."

Let the people of the Territory behold these beautiful and historical surroundings—the world told of the celebration held in these far-distant isles, where the two great powers of our modern age, Great Britain and America, have joined hands on this occasion, and thereby promote feelings of friendship.

From this day henceforth, let the aloha of the Hawaiian race penetrate the soil of this sacred and hallowed spot, and let God lead us all, to do what is right and just, one race to another race, in the affairs of mankind.

Reply by Commodore G.T.C.P. Swabey, D.S.O., Royal Navy, to the address of welcome to the visitors made on behalf of the Kona Civic Club at Kaawaloa when the Captain Cook monument was decorated on Saturday, 18th August, 1928

Mr. Secretary, ladies, and gentlemen, standing here on this little bit of British territory, and speaking on behalf of the officers and men of the British warships here assembled for this memorable ceremony, I would like to thank the speaker very much for the words of welcome he has addressed to us.

We of the British Navy are very proud of Captain Cook and of his great achievements and of the high traditions for which he and other great sailors of the past have stood.

It is therefore a matter of great satisfaction to us that it has been found possible to assemble here to-day three British cruisers to do honour to this great occasion—*Cornwall*, representing Great Britain; *Brisbane*, representing the Commonwealth of Australia; and *Dunedin*, representing the Dominion of New Zealand.

We are very proud that this tribute is being paid to a great Englishman and a great sailor by the citizens of the United States of America, and we are very grateful for the invitation which has been extended to us to take part with you in these memorable celebrations.

Delegate Houston's Address, 17th August

Civilisation in Hawaii at the time of Captain Cook's Discovery

Following is the address of Delegate Victor S. K. Houston at the unveiling of the monument to Captain Cook at Waimea, Kauai, erected by the Kauai Historical Society:

We are met to celebrate the one hundred and fiftieth anniversary of the discovery of the islands of the Hawaiian group, since erected into a Territory of the United States, and to do honour to the achievement of

---

one of the greatest navigators of the world, the discoverer.

On the 18th of January, 1778, Captain James Cook, of the Royal Navy, in command of a scientific and exploring expedition, sent out by the British Admiralty, first sighted the island of Oahu, and named the group, of which Oahu was one, the Sandwich Islands.

Captain Cook was one of that hardy race of mariners of which Great Britain has been so prolific. His fame rests not alone upon this one discovery. His is the renown that comes to men invading the deep blue sea and opening up new worlds. His is the glory that rewards application, perseverance, and that stoutheartedness that carries certain men into the unknown. He filled in the blank spaces on the world's map and established a reputation as a scientist that is second only to his position as an explorer.

I could not add to his reputation—it is already so solidly founded. Other speakers during this celebration will make known to us details of his life and character, which it is well in this day we should know. But as a Hawaiian, I believe it will not be out of place if in this short paper I should address myself to the subject of the people whom this great man discovered, and by means of a collection of quotations and extracts from the Reports of the Voyage to show the state of civilisation in which they were found.

One hundred and fifty years is but the briefest period in the life history of any people. But into this particular period there has been crowded the development of this people, reaching from its stone age to an assimilation of modern civilisation. When Captain Cook arrived they had neither metals nor pottery, no textile of any kind, no written language, and apparently they had been isolated in the midst of the vast Pacific for ages untold.

When into this garden spot—now aptly termed the paradise of the Pacific—there erupted these hardy mariners, product of a gradually developed civilisation, thousands of years old, it is not strange that the habits and customs of the Hawaiians should have startled and astonished them. It would be the same had any of us been carried back to the times of the Pharaohs or to that age which appropriately is known in history as the stone age.

As a consequence, the Hawaiians were frequently referred to as savages and barbarians. That they were primitive may be readily granted, but that they were wild, untamed, uncivilised, or uncultured—the equivalent of the word so often used—is simply a statement of comparison rather than of fact. That they were barbarians is equally untenable, for they were not cruel, or brutal, but were, as I hope to show, kindly and hospitable, friendly and frank. If the word is taken in its narrow sense, such as it was used by Greeks to mean non-Hellenes, or as used later by Latins— even now by Italians to mean foreigners in a deprecatory sense—the word is undoubtedly applicable. I like to feel that the terms were rather thoughtlessly applied.

Abraham Fornander, who 50 years ago wrote the *Polynesian Race*, said of the Hawaiian, "… a people whom none knew until 100 years ago, and whom no one even now recognised as a chip off the same block from which the Hindu, the Iranian, and the Indo-European families are fashioned." He claimed that they were descended from a people that was agnate to, but far older than, the Vedic family of the Aryan race; that it entered into India before these Vedic Aryans; that there it underwent a mixture with the Dravidian race, which, as in the case of the Vedic-Aryan themselves, has permanently affected its complexion; that there also, in greater or less degree ; it became moulded to the Cushite-Arabian civilisation of that time; it established itself in the Indian Archipelago at an early period, and thence was probably forced into the Pacific.

Fornander assumes the following steps in this later migration:

a)   At the close of the first and during the second century of the present era, the Polynesians left the Asiatic Archipelago and entered the Pacific, establishing themselves on the Fiji groups and thence spreading to the Samoan, Tonga, and other groups eastward and northward.

b) During the fifth century, Polynesians settled in the Hawaiian Islands and remained there comparatively unknown until—

c) The eleventh century A.D. when several parties of fresh immigrants from the Marquesas, Society, and Samoan groups arrived at the Hawaiian Islands, and for the space of five or six generations, revived and maintained an active intercourse with the first-named groups.

d) From the close of this era, about 21 generations ago, Hawaiian history runs isolated from other Polynesian groups till 1778.

Now, if you will kindly bear with me, I will make use of a collection of extracts and quotations from the published reports of the voyage, which will, I hope, give you a picture of the people whose civilisation was of no mean order, whose characteristics were marked by kindness and hospitality, and whose capacity and ingenuity was such that in the course of the last 150 years they have been able, to a very large extent, to assimilate and adapt themselves to the revolutionary changes brought about by contact with the rest of the world.[142]

I apologise for the manner of their presentation. The time at my command has been brief. Extracts and quotations may be somewhat mixed, and I may not have been consistent in my spelling of native names. My efforts have been to collate in sequence the varied references to matters not so well known as they are found in the voyage report. I have purposely omitted geographical data and detail reference to matters that are better known through later study, such as the feather

---

[142] "Bear with me" may be apt sentiment here, for the remainder of this chapter is an anthropological survey of the Hawaiian people that is longer than any other single item included in the original book. It is certainly worthwhile as it describes both the Hawaiians as Cook and his crews met them and the violent chaos that followed Cook's death. It even contains the first description of surfing; that Hawaiian past-time that has become an integral part of Australian culture. The extracts are primarily from Captain King's journal – *Editor*.

cloaks, heiaus, religion, etc.; I have also omitted generally matters that were not the result of direct observation.

Captain Cook and his collaborators were keen observers, and the facts they observed, not always their conclusions, are the most valuable contributions to our knowledge of this race. For the changes in customs and habits came with lightninglike rapidity thereafter, and later students were not always able to make the proper distinction as between the old standards and the new modifications.

I hope that a study of this data will lead to a more sympathetic attitude with respect to this race, to an understanding of the psychology of the people, and to a feeling, perhaps, that after all they were neither savages nor barbarians. The Romans at the time when Christians were pitted against wild beasts in the arena of the Coliseum are not classed as such: then why should our people be so classed because of religious sacrifices. The religious wars in Europe and the burning of witches in New England—many more parallels could be offered to show savagery perhaps in other lands—I simply wish a broader understanding of our people of whose history we feel we have a right to be proud.

General Appearance

"These people did not exceed the ordinary size and were stoutly made. Their complexion was brown; and there appeared to be little difference in the casts of their colour, there was a considerable variation in their features. Most of them had their hair cropped rather short; a few had it tied in a bunch at the top of the head; and others suffered it to flow loose. It seemed to be naturally black; but the generality of them had stained it with some stuff which communicated to it a brownish colour. Most of them had pretty long beards. They had no arms about their persons; nor did we observe that they had their ears perforated. Some of them were tattooed on the hands, or near the groin; and the pieces of cloth which were worn by them round their middle were curiously coloured with white, black, and red. They seemed to be mild and good natured; and were furnished with no arms of any kind, except small stones, which they had manifestly brought for their own defence; and these they threw into the sea when they found that there was no occasion for them.

"From what continent they originally emigrated, and by what steps they have spread through so vast a space, those who are curious in disquisitions of this nature, may, perhaps, not find it very difficult to conjecture. It has been already observed that they bear strong marks of affinity to some of the Indian tribes that inhabit the Ladrones and Caroline Islands; and the same affinity may again be traced amongst the Battas and the Malays. When these events happened is not so easy to ascertain; it was probably not very late, as they are extremely populous and have no tradition of their own origin but what is perfectly fabulous; whilst on the other hand, the unadulterated state of their general language, and the simplicity which prevails in their customs and manners, seem to indicate that it could not have been at any distant period.

"The inhabitants of the Sandwich Islands are undoubtedly of the same race with those of New Zealand, the Society and Friendly Islands, Easter Islands, and the Marquesas. This fact, which, extraordinary as it is, might be thought sufficiently proved by the striking similarity of their manners and customs and the general resemblance of their person is established beyond all controversy, by the absolute identity of their language.

Physical Appearance

"The natives of these islands are, in general, above the middle size and well made; they walk very gracefully, run nimbly, and are capable of bearing great fatigue; though, upon the whole, the men are somewhat inferior, in point of strength and activity, to the Friendly Islanders, and the women less delicately limbed than those of Otaheiti. Their complexion is rather darker than that of the Otaheitans, and they are not altogether so handsome a people. However, many of both sexes had fine open countenances; and the women, in particular, had good eyes and teeth, and a sweetness and sensibility of the look, which rendered them very engaging. Their hair is of a brownish-black, and neither uniformly straight, like that of the Indian of America, nor uniformly curling, as amongst the African negroes, but varying in this respect like the hair of Europeans. One striking peculiarity in the features of every part of this great nation—I do not remember to have seen anywhere mentioned—which is that, even in the handsomest faces, there is always a fullness of the nostril, without any flatness of the nose, that distinguishes them from Europeans.

"The inhabitants of Kauai are of the middle size, and in general stoutly made. They are neither remarkable for a beautiful shape nor for striking features. Their visage, particularly that of the women, is sometimes round; but others have it long, nor can it justly be said that they are distinguished, as a nation, by any general cast of countenance. Their complexion is nearly of a nut-brown colour; but some individuals are of a darker hue. We have already mentioned the women as being little more delicate than the men in their formation; and we may add, that with few exceptions, they have little claim to those peculiarities that distinguish the sex in most other parts of the world. There is, indeed, a very remarkable equality in the size, colour, and figure of the natives of both sexes; upon the whole, however, they are far from being ugly, and have to all appearances few natural deformities of any kind. Their skin is not very soft, but their eyes and teeth are for the most part pretty good. Their hair, in general, is straight; and though its natural colour is black, they stain it, as at the Friendly and other islands. We perceived but few instances of corpulence, and these more frequently among the women than the men; but it was principally among the latter that personal defects were observed, though if any of them can lay claims to a share of beauty it appeared to be more conspicuous amongst the young men.

"They are active, vigorous, and most expert swimmers, leaving their canoes upon the most frivolous occasion, diving under them and swimming to others, though at a considerable distance. We have frequently seen women with infants at their breasts, when the surf was so high as to prevent their landing in the canoes, leap overboard and swim to the shore without endangering the little ones.

"They appear to be of a frank and cheerful disposition, and are equally free from the fickle levity which characterises the inhabitants of Tahiti, and the sedate pose which is observed among those of Tongatabu. They seem to cultivate a sociable intercourse with each other; and except the propensity to thieving, which is as it were, innate in most of the people we have visited in these seas, they are extremely friendly to us. And it does no small credit to their sensibility, without flattering ourselves, that when they saw the different articles of our European manufacture they could not refrain from expressing their astonishment by a mixture of joy and concern that seemed to apply the case as a lesson of humility to ourselves; and on every occasion they appeared to have a proper consciousness of their own inferiority; a behaviour that equally exempts their natural character from the ridiculous pride of the more polished … or of the ruder natives…

"The inhabitants of these islands differ from those of the Friendly Islands in suffering almost universally their beards to grow. There were, indeed, a few, amongst whom was the old King, that cut it off entirely, and others that wore it upon the upper lip. One peculiar fashion though, they sometimes cut it close on each side of their head to the ears."

"The same superiority which is observed in the persons of the Aliis through the other islands is found also here. Those whom we saw were, without exception, perfectly well formed, whereas the lower sort, besides their general inferiority, are subject to all the variety of make and figure that is seen in the populace of other countries. Instances of deformities are more frequent here than in any of the other islands. While we were cruising off Hawaii two dwarfs came on board, one an old man 4 feet 2 inches high, but exactly proportioned, and the other a woman, nearly of the same height. We afterwards saw three natives, who were humpbacked, and a young man, born without hands or feet. Squinting is also very common among them; and a man, who they said had been born blind, was brought to us to be cured. Besides these particular imperfections they are in general very subject to boils and ulcers, which we attributed to the great quantity of salt which they eat with their flesh and fish. The Aliis are very free from these complaints."

"The chiefs exercise their power over one another in the most haughty and oppressive manner …"

"The people of these islands are manifestly divided into three classes; the first are the Aliis, or chiefs, of each district, one of whom is superior to the rest, and is called at Hawaii Alii—Taboo and Alii Moi. By the first of these words they express his absolute authority, and by the latter all are obliged to prostrate themselves (or put themselves to sleep, as the word signifies) in his presence. The second class are those who appear to enjoy a right of property without authority. The third class are the Towtows, or servants, who have neither rank nor property."

Character

"None of the inhabitants we ever met with before in any other island or country were so astonished as these people were upon entering a ship. Their eyes were incessantly roving from one object to another, and the wildness of their looks and features fully indicated their ignorance with respect to everything they saw, and strongly marked to us that they had never, until the present time, been visited by Europeans nor been acquainted with any of our commodities except iron."

They called iron koi or hamaiti, and "on asking them what iron was they immediately answered 'we do not know; you know what it is, and we only understand it as koi or hamaiti.'"

"They were in some respects naturally well bred, or at least fearful of giving offense, asking whether they should sit down, whether they might spit on the deck, etc., … at first they endeavoured to steal everything or later to take it openly…"

"We met with less reserve and suspicion in our intercourse with the people of this island than we had ever experienced among any other tribe of savages. They frequently sent up into the ship the articles they meant to barter, and afterwards came in themselves to traffic on the quarter deck."

The Tahitians, whom we have so often visited, have not that confidence in our integrity. "Whence it may be inferred that those of Hawaii are more faithful in their dealings with each other..."

"It is but justice to observe that they never attempted to overreach us in exchanges nor to commit a single theft."

"... rather than dispose of them at an undervalue, would carry them to shore again."

"A large village is situated on this point (South Point of Hawaii), many of whose inhabitants thronged off to the ship with hogs and women."

"These people merited our best commendations in their commercial intercourse, never once attempting to cheat us, whether ashore or alongside the ships." At first "... they thought, that they had a right to everything they could lay their hands upon; but they soon laid aside a conduct which we convinced them they could not persevere in with impunity."

Speaking of the guides that accompanied one of the ship's parties into the interior to obtain timber for repairs, "they bestowed high commendations on their guides, who not only supplied them with provisions but faithfully protected their tools."

"... They rise with the sun, and after enjoying the cool of the evening retire to rest a few hours after sunset. The making of canoes and nets forms the occupation of the Altis; the women are employed in manufacturing cloth, and the Towtows are principally engaged in the plantations and fishing."

"... notwithstanding the irreparable loss we suffered from the sudden resentment and violence of these peoples, yet in justice to their general conduct it must be acknowledged that they are of the most mild and affectionate disposition, equally remote from the extreme levity and the fickleness of the Tahitians and the distant gravity and reserve of the inhabitants of the Friendly Islands. They appear to live in the utmost harmony and friendship with one another."

During certain parleys a chief came off and told us from the King "… that the body was carried up the country, but it should be brought to us the next morning. There appeared a great deal of sincerity in his manner, and being asked if he told a falsehood he locked his two forefingers together, which is understood amongst these islands as the sign of truth, in the use of which they are very scrupulous."

"Their natural capacity seems in no respect below the common standard of mankind." …"The eager curiosity with which they attended the armorers and the many expedients they had invented, even before we left the islands, for working iron they had procured from us into such forms as were best adapted to their purposes were strong proofs of docility and ingenuity."

Treatment of Women

"It must, however, be observed that they fall very short of the other islanders in that best test of civilisation, the respect paid to their women. Here they are not only deprived of the privileges of eating with the men but the best sort of food is tabooed or forbidden them. They are not allowed to eat pork, turtle, several kinds of fish, and some species of the plantains; and we are told that a poor girl got a terrible beating for having eaten on board our ship, one of these interdicted articles. In their domestic life they appear to live almost by themselves, and though we did not observe any instance of personal ill treatment, yet it was evident they had little regard or attention paid them."

"The young women were no less kind and engaging; and till they found, notwithstanding our utmost endeavours to prevent it, that they had reason to repent of our acquaintance, attached themselves to us without the least reserve."

"In justice, however, to the sex, it must be observed that these ladies were probably all of the lower class of the people; for I am strongly inclined to believe that, excepting the few whose names are mentioned in the course of our narratives, we did not see any women of rank during our stay amongst them."

Care of Children

"It was pleasing to observe with what affection the women managed their infants, and with what alacrity the men contributed their assistance in such a tender office; thus distinguishing themselves from those savages who consider a wife and child as things rather necessary than desirable or worthy of their regard and esteem."

"The women who had children were remarkable for their tender and constant attention to them, and the men would often lend their assistance in those domestic offices with a willingness that does credit to their feelings."

Hospitality

"He experienced great kindness and civility from the inhabitants in general, but the friendship shown by the priests was constant and unbounded."

At Kealakekua the "party on shore were daily supplied by them (priests) with hogs and vegetables, sufficient for our subsistence, and to spare; and canoes laden with provisions were as regularly sent off to the ships. Nothing was demanded in return, nor was the most distant hint ever given that any compensation was expected."..."We had, indeed, less reason to be satisfied with the behaviour of the warrior chiefs than with that of the priests. In our intercourse with the former they were always sufficiently attentive to their own interests; ... the priest who supplied the excursion party with everything is spoken of as follows: "His conduct on this occasion was so delicate and disinterested that even the people he employed were not permitted to accept of the smallest present."

"The great hospitality and kindness with which we were received by them has been already frequently remarked. The old people never failed to receive us with tears of joy; seemed highly gratified with being allowed to touch us, and were constantly making comparison as between themselves and us, with the strongest marks of humility."

Gratitude

After Captain Cook's death, and in the fighting that followed, several of the natives were shot in making their escape from the flames; and our people cut off the heads of two of them and brought them on board, and … at this time an elderly man was taken prisoner, bound, and sent on board in the same boat with the heads of his two countrymen. I never saw horror so strongly pictured as in the face of this man, nor so violent a transition to extravagant joy as when he was untied and told he might go away in safety. "He showed us he did not lack gratitude, as he frequently afterwards returned with presents of provisions and also did us other services."[143]

Greetings

It is not improbable that this (fullness of the nose) may be the effect of their usual mode of saluting, "which is performed by pressing the ends of their noses together."

Ceremonies

When Captain Cook first landed, "the very instant he stepped on shore the collective body of the natives fell flat on their faces, and remained in that very humble posture till by expressive signs I prevailed upon them to rise; they then brought a great many small pigs, which they presented me with plantain trees…"

"The 4th of February being fixed for our departure, Kalaniopuu invited Captain Cook and Mr. King to attend him on the 3rd at Kaoo's residence. On our arrival there we saw large quantities of cloth scattered on the ground; abundance of red and yellow feathers fastened to the fibres of coconut husks; and plenty of hatchets and ironware, which had been received from us in barter. Not far from these was deposited

---

[143] This is truly gruesome and demonstrates how Carruthers' list of casualties has a significant omission. Cook could not be held responsible by this point however, hence the author's discretion. The seemingly perverse title of "gratitude" comes from the Congressional Report written by Houston (who was of Hawaiian descent), rather than being a choice of the author – Editor.

an immense quantity of various kinds of vegetables, and at a little distance a large herd of hogs. We supposed at first that the whole was intended as a present for us, but we were informed by Kaireakeea that it was a tribute to the King from the inhabitants of that district. And we were no sooner seated than the bundles were brought and laid severally at Kaireakeea's feet, and the cloth, feathers, and iron were displayed before him. The King was perfectly satisfied with this mark of duty from his people, and selected about a third of the iron utensils, all of the feathers, and some pieces of cloth; he ordered them to be set aside by themselves, and the remainder of the cloth, hogs, vegetables, etc., were afterwards presented to Captain Cook and Mr. King. The value and magnitude of this present far exceeded anything that we had met with."

"Between 10 and 11 o'clock we saw a great number of people descending the hill which is over the beach in a kind of procession, each man carrying a sugar cane or two on his shoulders and breadfruit, taro, and plantains in his hand. They were preceded by two drummers, who, when they came to the waterside, sat down by a white flag and began to beat their drums, while those who had followed them advanced one by one and deposited the presents they had brought and retired in the same order. Soon after Eappo came in sight, in his long feather cloak, bearing something with great solemnity in his hands, and having placed himself on a rock, made signs for a boat to be sent him. Captain Clerke, conjecturing that he had brought the bones of Captain Cook, which proved to be the fact, went himself in the pinnace to receive them, and ordered me to attend him in the cutter. When we arrived at the beach Eappo came into the pinnace and delivered to the captain the bones, wrapped in a large quantity of fine new cloth and covered in a spotted cloak of black and white feathers. He afterwards attended us to the *Resolution*, but could not be prevailed upon to go on board, probably not choosing, from a sense of decency, to be present at the opening of the bundle."

Fighting

"Throughout all this group of islands, the villages for the most part are situated near the sea; and the adjacent ground is enclosed with stone walls about 3 feet high. These, we at first imagined, were intended for the division of property; but we now discovered that they served, probably were principally designed, for a defence against invasion. They consist of loose stone, and the inhabitants are very dexterous in shifting them, with great quickness, to such situations as the direction of the attack may require. In the sides of the mountain, which hangs over the bay, they have little holes or caves, of considerable depth, the entrance of which is secured by a fence of the same kind. From behind both these defences the natives kept perpetually harassing our waterers with stones; ..."

"...and the men were soon clad in their mats, and armed with spears and stones. One of the natives having provided himself with a stone and a long iron spike, advanced toward the captain flourishing his weapon in defiance and threatening to throw the stone. The captain requested him to desist; but the islander repeating his menace, he was highly provoked and fired a load of small shot at him. The man was shielded in his war mat, which the shot could not penetrate; his firing, therefore, served only to irritate and encourage them. Volleys of stones were thrown at the marines; and one of the Aliis attempted the life of Mr. Phillips with his pahoa dagger; by not succeeding in the attempt, he received a blow from him with the butt end of his piece. Captain Cook immediately discharged his second barrel loaded with ball and killed one of the most violent of the assailants. A general attack with stones succeeded ... The natives, to our great astonishment, received our fire, with great firmness; and without giving time for the marines to charge again, they rushed in upon them with dreadful shouts and yells..."

"After the fighting ... a small boat, manned by five of our midshipmen, pulled toward the shore where they saw the bodies without any signs of life, lying on the ground; but judging it dangerous ... they returned to the ships, leaving them in possession of the islanders."

"...the men put on their war mats and armed themselves with long spears and daggers. We also observed that since morning, they had thrown up stone breastworks along the beach where Captain Cook had landed; ... but as soon as we were in reach they began to throw stones at us with slings..."

"The bravery of one of these assailants well deserves to be mentioned. For, having returned to carry off his companion amidst the fire of our whole party, a wound which he received made him quit the body and retire; but in a few minutes he again appeared, but again wounded, he was obliged to retreat. At this moment I arrived at the Morae, and saw him return there the third time, bleeding and faint; and being informed of what had happened I forbade the soldiers to fire, and he was suffered to carry off his friend; which he was just able to perform, and then fell down himself and expired."

Flag of Truce

"...And went on with a small boat alone, with a white flag in my hand, which, by a general cry of joy from the natives, I had the satisfaction to find was instantly understood. The women immediately returned from the side of the hill, whither they had retired; the men threw off their mats, and all sat down together by the water side, extending their arms and inviting me to come on shore."

Religion

"The religion of these people resembles in most of its features that of the Society and Friendly Islands...Their religious notions are derived from the same source."

"In a bay to the southward of Kealakekua a party of our gentlemen were conducted to a large house, in which they found the black figure of a man, resting on his fingers and toes, with his hand inclined backward, the limbs well formed and exactly proportioned, and the whole beautifully polished. This figure the natives called Maee, and round it were placed 13 others of rude and distorted shapes, which they said were the akuas of several deceased chiefs whose names they recounted… They likewise gave a place in their houses to many ludicrous and some obscene idols like the Praipus of the ancients."

"The temples, idols, sacrifices, and sacred songs all were found similar to those of the Society and Friendly Islands. As to the taboo, the word 'taboo' implies laying restraint upon persons and things. Thus, they say the natives were tabooed, or the bay was tabooed, and so of the rest. This word is also used to express anything sacred or eminent or devoted. Thus the King of Owyhee was Alii Taboo, a human victim—Kanaka Taboo… The women are said to be taboo when they are forbidden to eat certain kinds of meat."

Villages

"Throughout all this group of islands the villages for the most part are situated near the sea, and the adjacent ground is enclosed with stone walls about 3 feet high."

"We passed several villages, some situated near the sea and others farther up country…We saw no wood, but what was up in the interior, except a few trees about the villages, near which we could observe banana plantations and sugar-cane and spots that seemed cultivated for roots."

Houses

"The houses are scattered about without the least order. No fortifications. Some are large and commodious, from 40 to 50 feet in length and 20 or 30 feet in breadth… They are well thatched with long grass, which is laid on slender poles. Their figure resembles that of haystacks… "The entrance is either made in the end or side, and is an oblong hole, extremely low; it is often shut up by a board of planks… which serves as a door… No light enters the house except by this opening; and though such close habitations may be a comfortable place for retreat in bad weather, they seem ill adapted to the warm climate of the country. They are kept remarkably clean, and the floors are strewn with dried grass over which mats are spread to sit and sleep on." "…The method of living among these people was decent and cleanly." "They had an opportunity of observing the method of living amongst the natives, and it appeared to be decent and cleanly."

Animals

"The only tame or domestic animals that could be found were hogs, dogs, and fowls, which were of the same kind we met with at all the islands of the South Pacific."

"There were also small lizards and some rats, resembling those of every island which we had hitherto visited. The quadrupeds are confined to three sorts—dogs, hogs, and rats. The dogs are of the same species with those of Otaheiti, having short, crooked legs, long backs, and pricked ears. I did not observe any variety in them, except in their skins; some having long and rough hair, and others being quite smooth. They are about the size of a common turnspit; exceedingly sluggish, though perhaps this may be more owing to the manner in which they are treated than to any natural disposition. They are in general fed and left to herd with the hogs; for I do not recollect any instance in which a dog was made a companion in the manner we do in Europe. Indeed, however, the custom of eating them is an insuperable bar to their admission into society... The number of dogs in these islands do not appear to be nearly equal in proportion to those in Otaheiti. But on the other hand, they abound much more in hogs; and the breed is of a larger and weightier kind."

"The birds of these islands are as beautiful as any we have seen during the voyage and are numerous, though not various." The report speaks of a large white pigeon.

"...fish and other products of the sea were, to appearance, not various."

Food

"The food of the lower class of people consists principally of fish and vegetables; such as yams, sweet potatoes, taro, plantains, sugar-cane, and bread fruit. To these the people of the higher rank add the flesh of hogs and dogs, dressed in the same manner as at the Society Islands. They also eat fowls of the same domestic kind with ours, but they are neither plentiful nor much esteemed by them. Their fish they salt and preserve in gourd shells, not as we at first imagined for the purpose of providing against any temporary scarcity but for the preference they give to salted meats—for we also found that the Aliis used to pickle pieces of pork in the same manner and esteemed it a great delicacy."

"Of animal food they appeared to be in no great want, as they have great numbers of hogs which run without restraint about the houses, 'and if they eat dogs, which is not altogether improbable, their stock of these deemed very considerable.' The quantities of fishing hooks found among them indicated that they procure a tolerable supply of animal food from the sea."

"They bake their vegetables with heated stones; '...and from the quantity which we saw dressed at one time we imagined that all the inhabitants of the village, or at least a considerable number of people, joined in the use of a common oven.'... 'The only artificial dish we saw was a taro pudding which, though very sour, was devoured with avidity by the natives.'"

"They eat off a sort of wooden trencher, and, as far as we are enabled to judge from one instance, the women, if restrained from feeding at the same dish with the men, as is the custom at Tahiti, are at least allowed to eat in the same place near them.

"They are exceedingly cleanly at their meals, and their mode of dressing both their animal and vegetable foods was universally allowed to be greatly superior to ours. The chiefs constantly began their meals with a dose of the extract of pepper root. The women eat apart from the men and are tabooed or forbidden, as has already been mentioned, the use of pork, turtle, and particular kinds of plantains."

Awa

Bad effect amongst the Aliis was noticed from the use of awa.[144]

"...by many of them still more dreadful effects from the immoderate use of the awa. Those who were the most affected by it had their bodies covered with a white scurf, their eyes red and inflamed, their limbs emaciated, the whole frame trembling and paralytic, accompanied with a disability to raise the head. Though this drug does not appear universally to shorten life, as was evident from the cases of Terreeaboo, Kaoo, and some other chiefs, who were very old men, yet it invariably brings on an early and decrepit old age. It is fortunate that the use of it is one of the peculiar privileges of the chiefs. The young son of Terreeaboo, who was about 12 years old, used to boast of his being admitted to drink awa, and showed us in great triumph a small spot on his side that was growing scaly."

"There is something very singular in the history of this pernicious drug. When Captain Cook first visited the Society Islands it was very little known among them. On his second voyage he found the use of it very prevalent at Ulietea; ...At Kauai also it is used with great moderation and the chiefs are in consequence a much finer set of men there than in any of the neighbouring islands. Our good friends, Kaireekeea and old Kaoo, were persuaded by us to refrain from it; and they recovered amazingly during the short time we afterwards remained in the islands."

Arts

"In the different manufactures of these people there appears to be an extraordinary degree of ingenuity and neatness. The texture of Kapa is inferior to that of Tongatabu or Tahiti, but in colouring or staining it the inhabitants of Kauai displayed a superiority of taste..."

"Their colours, indeed, are not very bright, except the red; but the regularity of the figures and stripes is amazing; ... pieces are generally

---

144 Australians are likely to know this root as Kava – *Editor.*

2 by 4 or 5 yards in length, some of them are sewed together. Mats are fabricated with designs. Mats … occasionally make a part of their dress; for, when they offered them to sell, they put them on their backs."

Dishes are made of the Kou trees, extremely neat and well polished. Their fans are made of wicker work. Fishing hooks are ingeniously made, some of bone, many of pearl shell, and others of wood, pointed with bone. "The elegant form and polish of which (fishhooks) could not be exceeded by any European artist."

"They polish their stones by constant friction with pumice stone in water; …"Their adzes were like those of the Society Islands. They have also small instruments composed of a single shark's tooth fixed to the forepart of a dog's jawbone or to a wooden handle.

The business of painting tapa belongs entirely to the women.

Their mats, whether we regard the strength, fineness, or beauty, they certainly excel the world.

Their fishing hooks … we found them, upon trial, much superior to our own.

"The gourds which grow to so enormous a size that some of them are capable of containing from 10 to 12 gallons are applied to all manner of domestic purposes; and in order to fit them the better to their respective uses, they have the ingenuity to give them different forms by tying bandages around them during their growth. Thus some of them are of a long cylindrical form as best adapted to contain their fishing tackle; provisions, their puddings, vegetables, etc., which two sorts have neat, close covers, made likewise of the gourd; others again are exactly the shape of a bottle with a long neck, and in these they keep their water. They have likewise a method of scoring them in a heated instrument so as to give them the appearance of being painted in a variety of neat and elegant forms."

Dress

"The dress of the men consists only of a piece of thick cloth called the malo, about 10 or 12 inches broad, which they pass between the legs and tie around the waist. This is the common dress of all ranks of people. Their mats, some of which are beautifully manufactured, are of various sizes, but mostly about 5 feet long and 4 feet broad. These they throw over their shoulders and bring forward before; but they are seldom used except in time of war, for which purpose they seem better adapted than for ordinary use, being of a thick and cumbersome texture and capable of breaking the blow of a stone or any blunt weapon. Their feet are generally bare, except when they have occasion to travel over the burnt stones, when they secure them with a sort of sandal made of cords twisted from the fibres of the coconut. Such is the ordinary dress of these islanders; but they have another appropriate for their chiefs and used on ceremonious occasions, consisting of a feather cloak and helmet, which, in point of beauty and magnificence, is perhaps equal to that of any nation in the world. Their cloaks are made of different lengths in proportion to the rank of the wearer, some of them reaching no lower than the middle, others trailing on the ground. The inferior chiefs wear also a short cloak resembling the former, made of the long tail feathers of the cock, the tropic and man-of-war birds, with a broad border of the small red and yellow feathers and a collar of the same."

"These feathered dresses seemed to be exceedingly scarce, being appropriated to persons of the highest rank, and worn by the men only."

"The common dress of the women bears a close resemblance of that of the men. They wrap round the waist a piece of cloth that reaches halfway down the thigh, and sometimes in the course of the evening they appeared with loose pieces of fine cloth thrown over their shoulders like the women of Otaheiti. The Pa'u is another dress frequently worn by the younger part of the sex. It is made of the thinnest and finest sort of cloth wrapped several times round the waist and descending to the legs so as to have the appearance of a full short petticoat." Speaking of the feather capes, they say, "...even in countries where dress is more particular, might be recognised elegant." They are compared with the thickest and richest velvet. The natives would not at first part with them for anything we offered, asking no less a price than a musket. However, some were afterwards purchased for very large nails.

Ornaments

"Both sexes wear necklaces made of strings of small variegated shells; and an ornament in the form of a handle of a cup, about two inches long and one-half inch broad, made of wood, stone, or ivory, finely polished, which is hung about the hair with fine threads of twisted hair, doubled sometimes a hundred fold. Instead of this ornament some of them wear on their breast a small human figure made of bone suspended in the same manner."

"Their necklaces are made of shells, or of a hard, shining red berry. Besides which they wear wreaths of dried flowers of the India Mallows, another beautiful ornament called the lei, which is generally put about the neck, but is sometimes tied like a garland around the hair, and sometimes worn in both these ways at once. It is a ruff of the thickness of the finger, made in a curious manner of exceedingly small feathers, woven so close together as to form a surface as smooth as that of the richest velvet. The ground was generally of a red colour with alternate circles of green, yellow, and black."

"At Kauai some of the women wore little figures of the turtle, neatly formed of wood or ivory, tied on their fingers in the manner we wear rings."

Music

"Their music is of a rude kind, having neither figures nor reeds nor instruments of any other sort that we saw, except drums of various sizes. But their songs, which they sung in parts, and accompanied with a gentle motion of the arms in the same manner as the Friendly Islander, had a very pleasing effect."

Games

"They have a game much like our draughts…it is much more intricate.

"Besides these games, they frequently amuse themselves with racing matches between the boys and girls; and here again they wager with great spirit."

"Swimming is not only a necessary art, in which both the men and women are more expert than any people we had hitherto seen, but a favourite diversion amongst them… The surf, which breaks on the coast along the bay, extends to the distance of about 150 yards from the shore, within which space the surges of the sea, accumulating from the shallowness of the water, are dashed against the beach with prodigious violence. Whenever … the surf is increased into its utmost height, they choose that time for this amusement, which is performed in the following manner: 20 or 30 of the natives, taking each a narrow board rounded at the ends, set out together from the shore… As soon as they have gained by these repeated efforts the smooth water beyond the surf they lay themselves at length on their board and prepare for their return. As the surf consists of a number of waves, of which every third is remarked to be always much larger than the others and to flow higher on shore, the rest breaking in the intermediate space, their object is to place themselves on the summit of the largest surf, by which they are driven along with amazing rapidity toward the shore … Those who succeed in their object of reaching the shore have still the greatest danger to encounter. The coast being guarded by a chain of rocks, with here and there a small opening between them, they are obliged to steer their boards through one of these, or, in case of failure, to quit it before they reach the rocks, and, plunging under the waves, make the best of it back again … The boldness and address with which we saw them perform these difficult and dangerous manoeuvres was altogether astonishing and is scarcely to be credited."

Tattooing

"The custom of tattooing the body they have in common with the rest of the natives of the South Sea Islands; but it is only at New Zealand and the Sandwich Islands that they tattoo the face. They have a peculiar custom amongst them, the meaning of which we could never learn, that of tattooing the tip of the tongues of the females."

Canoes

All canoes were about 24 feet long, the bottom of a single piece, hollowed out to the thickness of an inch or more, pointed at each end. They seldom exceed a foot and a half in breadth. Those that go single have outriggers which are shaped and fitted with more judgment than any we had before seen. Some are double. Some use a triangular sail, extended to a mast and boom. The ropes are strong and neatly made.

Some Questions with Respect to Cannibalism

"We first tried by many indirect questions, put to each of them apart, to learn in what manner the rest of the bodies had been disposed of, and finding them very constant in one story—that after the flesh had been cut off it was all burned—we at last put the direct question whether they had not eaten some of it. They immediately showed as much horror at the idea as any European would have done, and asked, very naturally, if that was the custom amongst us?"

"These two circumstances considered, it was extremely difficult to draw any certain conclusion from the actions of a people with whose language and customs we were so imperfectly acquainted."

Note. – This *Congressional Record* was kindly sent to me by the Hon. Victor K. Houston, with permission to fully use it if I so desired. No one man has been more helpful to me in obtaining the valuable material for this work than Mr. Houston. I desire to place on record my deep obligation to him as well as my sincere thanks. Mr. Houston is a son of the late Rear-Admiral Houston, U.S.N., and his mother was a part Hawaiian of Chiefly decent. He is an authority on Hawaiian history and language, as well as a highly cultured man.

The Unveiling of a Memorial to Captain James Cook at Waimea,
Island of Kauai, Territory of Hawaii, 150 years after the discovery
of the Hawaiian Islands by the Great Navigator
(The Hon. D. F. Davis on the left, Carruthers on the right)

26
In conclusion

I have now practically completed the task I set out to perform. I have endeavoured to clear away those calumnies and erroneous stories which for over 150 years have blurred the name and memory of Captain Cook in the minds of many people who have only read one side of the case, and that, partial and prejudiced against him.

I hope that I have succeeded in my purpose without any offensive or harsh criticism of those responsible for starting the unfounded stories which have done such grave wrong to a dead man and his life's work.

Captain Cook was suddenly cut off in the height of his great career, and without any opportunity to defend himself from accusations which he never could have anticipated as likely to be made against his honour and reputation. He died in the conscientious performance of his duty, just as he lived – without a stain on his character.

His traducers lacked both charity and chivalry, when they went out of their way, without any good motive, to vilify a great and noble man immeasurably their superior in all the qualities that go to make a real man. One might have been satisfied to rebuke them mildly as men lacking a balanced judgement, if it were not for the mischief they have done, not only to Captain Cook's reputation, but also to generation after generation of youthful students whose minds have been warped into an unhealthy spirit of derision, where the real facts, if honestly told to them, would have created a wholesome veneration for a great leader of men and the forerunner of an age to come in the great Southern Ocean, which he of all men opened up to civilisation.[145]

The world is all the poorer when men are misled into wrong sentiments and lose the prize of some ennobling passion or influence through noble example.

I Recall Ben Bracken's lines in his fine poem *Not Understood*, in which he says:

"Poor souls with stunted vision

Oft measure giants by their narrow gauge,

The poisoned shafts of falsehood and derision

Are oft impelled 'gainst those who mould the age.

Not understood."

It is said of Lord Macauley that every morning he uttered the prayer:

"From envy, hatred, malice, and all uncharitableness Good Lord deliver us."[146]

It is bad enough when one meets the meaner motives in life: but that is not comparable with what happens when they are used against the dead to destroy remembrance of their good deeds, replacing it with unmerited obloquy. One may be well excused if one deals scathingly

---

[145] Note that it is the students that ultimately matter to Carruthers. The centricity of Cook was about ensuring a positive and healthy future, not simply dwelling on the past. Carruthers' papers reveal that he was even lobbying David Drummond, who was occupying the author's old position as NSW Education Minister for the Bavin Government, to make this book a textbook – *Editor.*

[146] A notable feature of the history and culture wars is the pathology of focusing almost exclusively on tearing things down. It seems psychologically unhealthy, both on an individual level and as a nation. We should have a nuanced and informed view of the past that deals with the blemishes in our history, but becoming as blindly-negative as we were once blindly-positive is worse than hypocritical. Real historical myths should be busted, but it is clear that the main debates around Cook involve differences of perspective rather than fact, and these would never have blown up into mainstream incidents of monument vandalism and comparing Cook to a pandemic were it not for those who wish to use Cook to criticise contemporary society. If politicising Cook were a crime then Carruthers would also be guilty, but at the very least his aims were constructive and hopeful rather than destructive and negative. Role models have their place in a healthy society – *Editor.*

with men who act thus cowardly to the dead, and in so doing pervert the minds of the living.

I can imagine some of my readers saying: "Oh! But all this is out of date. All these lies about Cook are over 100 years old and are dead and forgotten."

That is not so. The lies are repeated time after time, right down to now, and they lose nothing in the telling. As recently as July, 1929, I travelled in a Union Company liner (R.M.S. *Niagara*) from Australia to Honolulu, with 1,000 on board, including crew. A wireless newspaper was printed and circulated on board daily. Twice within ten days there was a reprint of a page from a recent book by a professor of high standing in a University within our Empire. It was headed: "Worship of Captain Cook in Hawaii." It out-Heroded Herod and went one better or rather worse than Ledyard and company in its libels on Captain Cook. These are samples. Speaking of Cook at Kauai it said:

"...The two rulers sent out ambassadors to report on the strange phenomenon, and they were delighted to hear that the strange machines were full of iron. At once one of their warriors, Kapupua, exclaimed: 'I will go and take it, as it is my business to plunder.' He was shot in the adventure, though Cook says nothing about the incident."

(*Note.*- Cook did record it in his Journal on 20th January, 1778.)

"The big guns were fired at night, and the natives said: 'It is the god *Lono*; let us fight him.' But a chiefess dissuaded them, and in order to propitiate the deity sent her daughter with other women on board, who brought off the fatal disease that ultimately decimated the group..."

(*Note.*- Cook never met this woman on or off his ship. See chapter 15.)

"*Before Captain Cook made his first landing in Hawaii his reputation had preceded him.* He was accepted as the god *Lono*, who in departing from his old realm promised to return 'on an island bearing coco-nut trees, swine, and dogs.' *More than* fifteen thousand people and three thousand canoes crowded into the bay. When he landed heralds announced him and cleared the way; all who were near him threw themselves on the ground and covered their faces, whilst others fled before him so that the prostrate were often trampled. At last all who followed or fled got down on their hands and feet and moved like quadrupeds."

(*Note.-* A gross distortion of the facts.)

"He was led to the chief *heiau*, a truncated pyramid of stone, and presented to the chief idols; one of them he kissed in imitation of the two priests who moved before him chanting his deity. Hogs were sacrificed to him whilst a priest wrapped him round with his sacred red *tappa*. They anointed him with the masticated coco-nut and gave him *kava*, or chewed and salivated pepper-root, to drink, and got the pork that he was to eat chewed for him by an old man. He was received by priests at their sacred residence, and as he moved prayers were offered to him and hymns chanted. The king came from Maui and laid a *tapu* on the bay; and the sailors could not get their usual supplies, but by threats and musket firing forced the people to break through the prohibition."

(*Note.-* Another gross distortion of the facts.)

"The king and Kamehameha came in state to the ships and then to Cook's tent on the shore and exchanged names with him, whilst the people lay prostrate and silent all round the bay. But the act of removing the rickety wooden structures and the idols to the ships for firewood stirred the people to anger as sacrilege."[147]

I think this is the worst story in its method and in its words that I have ever read against Cook's name. A complete answer to this story is to be found in the pages of this book (chapters seven to fifteen.)

And that is how men of our own race keep perpetuating these slanders against the man to whom Australia and New Zealand owe their very existence as British Dominions.

When this Professor's book was published two or three years ago, two leading residents of Hawaii – one a Bishop and the other a high official, both Americans – wrote to me and called my attention to the repetition of these old stories by the writer, and asked me to take action to refute them. The writers were indignant. This little incident adds one more argument as to the necessity for some such work as I am now presenting to the public.

When one considers the great benefits that have resulted from Cook's discoveries it seems unthinkable that any Englishman or Australian can lightly tolerate a further silence on matters that should have been fully

---

[147] I have just received and read the most recent of all publications on Captain Cook's Life and Voyages, namely that written by Maurice Thierey, Paris, 1929.

I like M. Thierey's book very much, as it is a judiciously abbreviated account of Cook's Life and Voyages, skilfully presented by a fine writer.

I notice, however, that M. Thierey unfortunately repeats some of the erroneous stories which I have endeavoured to refute in these pages. For instance, on page 233 of his book, he repeats Dr. Kippis's misstatement about the U.S. Congress revoking Benjamin Franklin's letter of safe conduct for Cook and his ships. In Chapter Twenty of this book I think I have proved that Congress did not in any way interfere with the operating of Dr. Franklin's letter, although its arrival in the United States was delayed nearly twelve months.

Again on page 224 M. Thierey refers to the removal of the temple fence by Captain King as an act of sacrilege.

M. Thierey is evidently not aware that, according to the native historians, the old fence and outer effigies of a temple were generally used as firewood when their period of usefulness had ended with their age, and there was no sacrilege in King's act.

On page 212 he repeats the objectionable statement that the inhabitants of the Sandwich Island were cannibals. I think that I have adduced ample proof that this is not so and that Captain Cook was misled into a wrong belief on this matter through the proneness of the natives to answer "Yes" to all questions which they did not fully understand – *Author.*

and authoritatively answered long ago.

There are in Australia, New Zealand, and in the South Pacific Isles, nine million white people, mostly of our race, living comfortably where before Cook's time there was not one white man. In the Hawaiian isles there is a rich and prosperous community of 350,000 people of mixed races – the East and West meeting and blending harmoniously. In Canada there is a population of ten million whites. Captain Cook played a prominent part in regard to all these lands and their earliest settlement. Magnificent cities have replaced the primitive villages of the natives and an undreamt-of progress and prosperity has marked the course of the last 150 years in these new lands. Sydney, Melbourne, Auckland, Wellington, and Honolulu – to name only a few of these cities – are to-day finer perhaps than any city of our Empire (save London) of 150 years ago. We are grateful for this progress and the prosperity that it indicates.

In our gratitude we should more and more cultivate a veneration for the one man to whom, above all others, is due the praise, the honour, and the glory.[148]

I hope nothing in these pages will give a wrong impression of the Hawaiian race either of Cook's time or now. His death was the act of a few, led, if there was any leadership, by a minor chief Pareea, a man not true to the Hawaiian type. He bore a grudge to the Captain and to the members of his expedition, and he was responsible for the theft of the

---

[148] Admiral Sir Wm. Goodenough, speaking at the Royal Geographical Society's meeting in London, December, 1928, said:

"…When the statue at Sydney to Captain Cook was unveiled in 1873 the man who unveiled it – he happened to be my father – spoke of the intense pleasure it would have given Captain Cook, a man of great humanity, to see cottages where all those who were industrious could live in comfort as a result of their labour. If that was true fifty-five years ago, how much more true is it now! Great farmsteads in the country; noble buildings in the cities! He might well look with modest pride on what has been made possible by his explorations and surveys. What an inspiration – I was going to say to the youth of this country but it is not only to them – is Captain Cook's motto, *Nil intentatum reliquit!* We don't know who composed it, for Captain Cook was of those who earn mottoes, do not inherit them; but if words can be indicative of a man's life and character, 'He left nothing untried' is indicative of the character and life of Captain James Cook…" – *Author.*

boat – the thing that led up to the tragic end of Captain Cook.

I have spent long periods in the islands and have met great numbers of the native race. They are a fine people and of good behaviour and manners. Some are wealthy, most are poor, but each class is generous to a fault. Many are poor, simply because they will give away anything they have to one in need. They do not covet riches, nor ape their so-called "betters" as people of civilised races do. They are deeply religious, most of them, and the strain of superstition is strong in them. Hence the creed of the Latter Day Saints has many native adherents. A visit to Kaiwaihao native church in Honolulu opens one's eyes to their religious fervour and devotion. That is an inherited trait of character which, if seen and understood, helps to realise their behaviour towards Cook 150 years ago.

I count amongst my best friends many of the Hawaiians of to-day – lovable men and women to whom kindness and affection to a friend is an innate quality.

I would not, for the life of me, cause pain to one of these, and nothing I have written is intended to do so. My regard for them is deep and sincere because I know that they come of a fine race of ancestors entitled to rank with the best of our civilised peoples in high qualities and a culture of its own class.

I have referred to Governor Wallace R. Farrington in previous chapters. He is a high-class American citizen and one of the finest men I have ever been privileged to meet either in my public or private life. To him is mainly owing the official initiative of all that has been done in the Territory of Hawaii to honour the memory of Captain Cook, and to rescue the historic places at Kaawaloa and Waimea from passing out of the control of the people and the national governments. For his fine action he is deserving of enduring gratitude.

Aerial Photograph of Waimea, Island of Kauai

Appendices

Appendix A

The Cook Monument at Waimea, Kauai (*See* Chapter Twenty-Three)

I had suggested at a meeting of the Pan-Pacific Union and the Lion's Club at Honolulu, two years previously (1926), that a commemorative tablet or monument should be erected at Waimea, in Kauai, so that visitors who were without a guide might easily find the place where Cook first landed on Hawaiian shores. I proposed a resolution, which was adopted at that meeting, that a subscription list should be opened, and I headed it with a subscription of 250 dollars, two other Australians (Messrs. Robert and James Warden) adding substantial sums to this amount at the meeting. The movement was taken up by residents of the Island of Kauai and sufficient money was raised to erect a very fine monument.

My reason for making the above suggestion was because during a previous visit to Kauai I had been driven round that island by a guide-chauffer whom I told that I specially wished to see the place where Captain Cook landed. Repeatedly I reminded him of this. But he never showed me the place. We had stopped at Waimea to fill our petrol tank without any incident. Later in the day, as we neared our original starting-point, I scolded the driver and asked him why he had neglected to take me to the place I desired. He apologised and said: "But we went there and I forgot to tell you!" I said: "Where was it?" "Oh!" he replied, "it was where we got more gas (petrol)." So I told this story to the Honolulu gathering and said that it reminded me of the story of the lady tourist who, after listening to a fine description of Athens and its glories told by a professor, a fellow tourist, turned to her daughter and said :"Mary, were we ever in Athens?" "Yes, Mama," the daughter replied, "don't you remember the place where we couldn't match our red wool? That was Athens, Mama." So I said I only knew the landing place of Cook at Kauai as "the place where we got more gas." I therefore suggested that some memorial in stone should be erected there with an inscription, that visitors might read and so be independent of stupid guides and chauffers.

That is the origin of the movement which resulted in the fine monument at Waimea being erected there and unveiled at the Celebrations in August, 1928.

Appendix B

(See Chapter Twenty-Three)

It was at a meeting of the Pan-Pacific Union at Honolulu in 1924 (at which Governor Farrington presided) that I first suggested that an appropriate celebration should be held somewhere about the date of the 150th anniversary of the death of Cook on the very spot where he died. Mr. A.H. Ford, a director of the Union, and the Rev. W.D. Westervelt commended the movement, and the gathering heartily endorsed my suggestion. Later on Mr. Taylor and Bishop Restarick took up the matter independently, and carried it to a successful conclusion, as an official matter under the auspices of the Federal and Territorial Governments.

Appendix C

The movement for a public reserve to include the place where Cook died and the adjacent land at Kaawaloa, Hawaii (*See* Chapter Twenty-Four)

My first letter to the Governor of the Territory is dated 26th August, 1924, in which I suggested the reservation of land at Kaawaloa, where Captain Cook died. A copy of my communication, together with Governor Farrington's reply is annexed. (*See* Appendix D.)

I also wrote on the 21st September, 1924, to Lord Chelmsford, who was Secretary for the Navy in the Ramsay MacDonald British Government, following up my action in writing to the Governor of the Territory. (*See* Appendix E.)

I had a most cordial reply from Lord Chelmsford, heartily approving my suggestion and stating that he had asked the British Ambassador at Washington to communicate with the Secretary of State of the Federal Government at Washington. (*See* Appendix F.)

I wrote, also, to the Prime Minister of Australia, suggesting he should get in touch with the authorities in Washington. He agreed to the proposals which I had made and directed a letter to be forwarded to Washington through the British Government supporting my suggestions. He intimated to me that the Australian Government would be glad to have the privilege of subscribing towards any cost incurred in the matter of the proposed reservation or park and of access thereto by water.

Correspondence was also opened by me with the Government of New Zealand and, through my friend (the late Honourable Mark Cohen, M.L.C. of New Zealand), I learned that the Wellington Government and Parliament had appropriated the sum of £200 as a contribution towards the work.

Finally I wrote, in 1926, a letter to President Coolidge, suggesting the carrying out of the proposed work and also the holding of the celebration in Hawaii. My friend Professor Duval, of the Bureau of Agriculture at Washington, was arranging for me to visit the President and have an interview with him, but the state of my health at the time prevented my making the long journey, and so I committed a memorandum to the Professor to be presented to the President, showing the reasons why the matter should be carried through.

The Japanese Consul-General at Honolulu heard of my proposals and called upon me and announced that his Government would join in. He said that, as much of the land about the site was owned by the Japanese, his Government would acquire that from the owners and gladly hand it over for the purpose of the monument.

I made this offer public both in Honolulu and in Australia. It was regarded very properly as a graceful gesture of friendship by the Japanese Consul on behalf of his country.

I am not aware of what eventuated in regard to this, as the carrying out of the project remained in the hands of the Territorial Government. I do, however, know that the land required has now been legally appropriated under the laws of the Territory.

Appendix D

Copy of a letter forwarded by Sir Joseph Carruthers to the Hon. W.R. Farrington, Governor of the Territory of Hawaii, dated 26th August, 1924

"His Excellency the Hon. Wallace R. Farrington. Governor of the Territory of Hawaii.

"Dear Sir,

"I beg to submit to you the following suggestions which are the outcome of a visit just paid by me to the monument erected to the memory of Captain James Cook of the British Royal Navy at the bay of Kaawaloa on the Island of Hawaii.

"I wish, however, to make it clear that at present I have, naturally, not had the opportunity of obtaining the assent of either the British Government or the Government of the Australian Commonwealth and States to my suggestions, and therefore will have to submit them to those Governments for their consideration and approval.

"The suggestions are:

"1. That a decent boat-landing jetty be constructed close by the monument in Kaawaloa Bay in order that visitors proceeding to the place via Napoopoo may not have to incur the risk of accidents or serious discomfort by landing from small boats on the rocky foreshore, where there is generally a surge from the ocean which renders a landing rather precarious.

"I feel confident that if this suggestion be carried into practical effect, there will be hundreds of visitors to the scene of Captain Cook's death where now only a few proceed. The cost should not be great as the material for construction lies close to hand and a small stone structure will suffice.

"2. I also beg to suggest that the Government of the Territory of Hawaii take the necessary steps to acquire land which constitutes the small peninsula on which were enacted the events associated with Captain Cook' last days in Hawaii. I judge the area to be about 20 or 30 acres plus the land for a trail to be constructed from the hill-top which surmounts it. The area is (so I am informed) privately owned, thereby putting visitors to a liability as trespassers if they traverse the land without permission from the private owner.

"There should not be such a liability associated with a historic spot famous from the events of the past and held sacred by many millions of people who cherish the memory of the great world navigator Captain Cook, founder of the Australian Dominion and discoverer of the Hawaiian Islands.

"3. I suggest also that when the land is secured as a public reservation, it should be placed in good order, planted with suitable trees, paths made for easy access to points of interest, and a rest and refreshment house constructed to house a caretaker and to provide suitable accommodation to visitors in their brief stay during a day's visit.

"4. I suggest also that negotiations be opened with the Governments of Great Britain and of Australia and the Australian States to ascertain whether they will co-operate with the Territorial Government of Hawaii, in providing funds for the purposes set out in the foregoing suggestions and for suitable up-keep of the land and improvements.

"Although not definitely authorised to pledge any of these Governments mentioned, I feel confident that they will favourably consider the matter and join heartily in carrying out a scheme which will commend itself to the people of Great Britain and Australia, as commemorative of one of the most famous men of history.

"I will pledge myself to doing all that lies in my power and influence to secure the approval of the Governments mentioned. I wish, however, to be fortified in the first place with your favourable expression on the expediency of the matter. Once I am in possession of such, if you care to express your views, I will take action which will prepare these governments for discussion on the subject with your Government.

"I add further that I have taken great pains to ascertain the historical facts associated with Captain Cook's death, and as a result I am convinced that his death occurred through misunderstandings which do not reflect on either the Hawaiian race or on Captain Cook and his officers.

"Unfortunately there are some who do not trouble to study carefully the history as gathered from reliable sources, and who are none too just in their views of the part played in the events of 1779, by either the Hawaiians or Captain Cook and his command. The neglected state of the scenes of those events contributes to some extent to the spread of misconceptions which would be largely dispelled if the governing authorities of the Territory of Hawaii and of Great Britain and Australia gave a lead in honourably commemorating the better view which accords with the real facts. A valuable influence will at once follow on such action, and as well there will be forged another link in the friendship of Australia and Great Britain with these islands and their Government.

"Yours faithfully,

(Sgd.) "J.H. Carruthers."

"Sir Joseph Carruthers, K.C.M.G.,

Member of Parliament, New South Wales,

c/o Alexander Young Hotel,

Honolulu, Hawaii.

"My dear Sir,

"I have received yours of August 26th, in which you outline suggestions for the care of the grounds in the vicinity of Captain Cook's monument at Kaawaloa Bay, Island of Hawaii.

"My first reaction to your suggestion is very favourable, although it does not now occur to me in just what way the plan may be properly worked out.

"I have taken steps to ascertain the ownership of the land and also to review the situation to learn what may properly be done by the Territorial Government.

"I will also communicate with appropriate officers of the Federal Government in Washington to determine what we may properly do. If you have any additional suggestions, I shall be very glad indeed to receive them. I am pleased at this time to express my appreciation of the very interesting and instructive address on Captain Cook and his work that you gave at the Pan-Pacific luncheon this week.

"Yours very truly,

(Sgd.) "W.R. Farrington,

"Governor of Hawaii."

Appendix E

"Honolulu,

"Sept. 21, 1924.

"The Right Honourable

"Lord Chelmsford,

"House of Lords,

"London, Westminster.

"Dear Lord Chelmsford,

"I have been attending a Pan-Pacific Conference at Honolulu for the past few weeks, but am leaving for Sydney to-morrow. During my stay I visited the Island of Hawaii and motored round to the place where Captain Cook was killed in 1779.

"There is a neat monument at Kaawaloa Bay, erected by Englishmen in 1874 on a very small piece of land ceded to Great Britain prior to the American annexation. This monument is on the exact spot where Cook was killed. It is kept in good order in every respect and is in charge of a caretaker appointed by the British Consul.

"To reach this place one has to go by boat from Napoopoo, about one or two miles by water. The transit is effected first in a crazy little flat-bottomed canoe which will carry about three persons, then by motor launch which lies off the Napoopoo jetty awaiting the canoe. The launch proceeds across the Bay, but cannot go right to the shore on account of the swell of the Ocean and the shallow water. So therefore one has to disembark in the canoe; and then the landing on the rocks is precarious as the surge of the sea is very strong with a strong undertow.

"Once a landing is effected the walking is rough, over lava blocks and coral. To walk about the place as one desires means very tiring work. The surroundings are depressing as there is an air of neglect and decay on every side and in a Briton a sense of shame is felt.

"There is a small peninsula of about twenty acres which includes everything of interest in the events of 1779. Of this area only about 50 ft x 50 ft. is public property, viz. the British-owned area of the space for a monument. The surrounding area is held by a Japanese Land Company which does nothing with it.

"I visited the monument and placed thereon a wreath of English roses intertwined with Australian gum leaves, tied with the Australian Blue ribbon and a card fastened thereto with an inscription showing that the wreath was placed there 'in Memory of Captain Cook on behalf of Australia and the grateful people of that country.'

"I may say that I represented the New South Wales Government and the Federal Prime Minister in this matter.

"On my return to Honolulu I saw the Governor of the Territory (Honourable Wallace R. Farrington) and represented the necessity for a small jetty to assist in providing a safe landing-place for passengers, also that the surrounding area should be acquired by his Government and reserved for all time in memory of Captain Cook, and improved in a manner worthy of the public sentiments.

"The Governor expressed himself in hearty accord with my suggestions and asked me to put them in writing so that he might take official action. I, therefore, wrote the enclosed letter to the Governor and received the enclosed reply. (Copies herewith.) Later on the Governor informed me that he had initiated the formal action necessary and had advised the United States Government at Washington of the matter so as to facilitate Federal action.

"He said also that his Government could hardly suggest a contribution to the cost by other Governments; that it would come with more grace, if these Governments offered voluntarily to be associated with the United States and the Territory of Hawaii in the carrying out of the proposals as finally adopted.

"I may add that the leading people here are heartily in accord with the movement and already some of them have provided funds for an Annual Celebration to be held on the same day, 18th or 28th April, when Australia hold its celebration at Cook's Landing Place at Kurnell, Botany Bay. The English and Australian Colony here (Honolulu) are very keen on the matter and so also is the Hawaiian Historical Society which held a special meeting for me to address them on 'Captain Cook.' The Society is publishing my address in pamphlet form.

"I feel sure that Australia will join in the proposals, and on my return to Sydney I will see Mr. Bruce and get him to act.

"I am now, and have been for the past two years, a member of the New South Wales Government (Vice-President of the Executive Council), and I feel quite sure that my colleagues will heartily approve of participation in whatever is necessary to be done, so as to associate Australia with a movement to honour the founder of Australia as a British Dominion. I therefore submit these facts to Your Lordship and ask that you will be good enough to give favourable consideration to the proposals, and if you approve of them, then secure the official approval of the Government of which you are a member...

"Yours faithfully,

(Sgd.) "J.H. Carruthers."

Appendix F

Extracts from a Communication forwarded by Lord Chelmsford (First Lord of the Admiralty) in acknowledgement of Sir Joseph Carruthers's Letter of 21st September, 1924

"So far as one can judge who has not visited the spot, I think your proposals for improving access to the monument to Captain Cook in Hawaii are fully deserving of support, and I am glad that you found the United States Territorial Governor so sympathetic.

"The Admiralty, of course, have a prime interest in this matter, but we can only act through the Foreign Office, and I am asking the Secretary of State to have the matter represented by our Ambassador at Washington, as one in which His Majesty's Government would be highly appreciative of any action that the United States authorities might be able to take."

Appendix G

Copy of Communication received by Sir Joseph Carruthers from Wallace R. Farrington, Governor of Hawaii, dated, Honolulu, 27th April, 1928, inviting the Author to attend the Sesqui-centennial Cook Celebrations.

"My dear Sir Joseph,

"As you are aware, there is to be a celebration of the One hundred and fiftieth Anniversary of the Discovery of the Hawaiian Islands by Captain James Cook, to be held during the week of August 15th to the 20th.

"The Commission appointed under an Act of the Legislature of Hawaii, 1927, to prepare for and carry out the celebrations, has requested the Governor of Hawaii invite you to be present. This I am especially pleased to do, having personal knowledge of your active and practical interest in preserving the monuments to the memory of this Great Explorer. I cordially invite you to be with us during the celebration.

"If you should be appointed by the Prime Minister of Australia as one of the representatives of that Government, this invitation will not be necessary, but in case you are not so appointed, this invitation is sent to impress upon you the sincere wishes of your friends in Hawaii.

"We recall that you initiated the idea of a Cook monument at Waimea, Kauai. This is to be dedicated during the celebration. Largely through your suggestion, I have taken official steps to secure public control of the land area in the vicinity of the Captain Cook monument at Kealakekua Bay, Hawaii. This has been a long legal task, not yet wholly completed, but we hope to secure a definite result before the celebration.

"I can hardly imagine any part of the world that could have a stronger claim on you next August, than the Territory of Hawaii.

"Yours very truly,

(Sgd.) "W.R. Farrington,

"Governor of Hawaii."

Appendix H

Copy of Telegram received by Sir Joseph Carruthers from the Rt. Hon. S.M. Bruce, Prime Minister of Australia, dated 24th May, 1928, asking the Author to act as the official Representative of Australia at the Sesqui-centennial Cook Celebrations

"The Commonwealth Government would be most appreciative if you would act as the Official Representative of Australia at the Anniversary Celebrations of the Discovery of the Hawaiian Islands by Captain Cook, which are to be held in Honolulu.

"The distinguished services which you have rendered in bringing about an appreciation of Captain Cook and his great work renders it singularly appropriate that you should be Australia's Representative, and I sincerely trust you will see your way to accept the Government's invitation.

"S.M. Bruce,

"Commonwealth Offices,

"Melbourne."

(The above invitation was accepted and thereupon a letter of Appointment under the Seal of the Commonwealth, and signed by the Prime Minister, was issued.)

www.ingramcontent.com/pod-product-compliance
Lightning Source LLC
Chambersburg PA
CBHW070340100426
42812CB00005B/1375